C000166054

LETHAL
SHOT

Robert Driscoll was born in Roehampton, south-west London, in May 1976 to Tina, a dental nurse, and Clive Driscoll, an aspiring constable with the Metropolitan Police (he was to retire as a detective chief inspector). He spent a short time at school in West Ewell before the family relocated to leafy Westcott in Surrey, and thereafter he was schooled in and around Dorking. After leaving school, Robert studied engineering at East Surrey College before joining the Royal Marines in February 1998.

Having completed Commando training, jungle training and Arctic training, Robert went on to serve on operations in Kosovo (1999), Afghanistan (2002) and Iraq (2003), before leaving the Marines and following his father into the Metropolitan Police. After his initial police training (2004), he was posted to Southwark Borough South and cut his teeth as a police officer on the streets of Peckham, south-east London.

In 2005, with the war in Afghanistan intensifying, it wasn't long before the lure of active service pulled Robert back to his beloved Royal Marines. On his return to the Corps, he quickly found himself deployed around the world, serving within the Royal Marines and UK Special Forces Group; he was to finish his military career as a sergeant with Juliet Company, 42 Commando RM, on Operation Herrick 14 in Afghanistan (2011), for which he received a Mention in Despatches.

Robert has three beautiful children and now lives with his partner in Devon.

A Royal Marine
Commando in Action

LETHAL SHOT

SERGEANT
ROB DRISCOLL

JOHN BLAKE

Published by John Blake Publishing,
The Plaza,
535 Kings Road,
Chelsea Harbour,
London SW10 0SZ

www.johnblakebooks.com

www.facebook.com/johnblakebooks
twitter.com/jblakebooks

First published in hardback in 2019

ISBN: 978-1-78606-254-3

British Library Cataloguing-in-Publication Data:

A catalogue record for this book is available from the British Library.

Design by www.envydesign.co.uk

Printed and bound in Great Britain by Clays Ltd, Elcograf S.p.A

1 3 5 7 9 10 8 6 4 2

John Blake Publishing is an imprint of Bonnier Books UK
www.bonnierbooks.co.uk

Dedicated to all those who have served or will serve, and to those who support us. Thank you Sam, Will, Ollie, Ellis and Kate for helping me realise true happiness.

ACKNOWLEDGEMENTS

Special acknowledgements to:

Robert Smith: without my chance meeting with him there would be no book.

Jeff Hudson, whose attention to detail, and extraordinary ability to capture the nuance of the moment, have been the keystone in the writing of this account.

Thank you:

Mum, Harry, Dad, Gran and Bang Bang for an amazing childhood, and for providing the foundations for the man I would grow to be.

Thank you:

All the servicemen and women I have had the privilege of working with and for. Thanks for an incredible career and, most importantly, for keeping me alive!

Last but by no means least:

Toby Buchan, and the editing, design, production and sales and marketing teams at John Blake Publishing and Bonnier Books UK, for allowing me the opportunity to tell my story; a process that has had immense therapeutic value. Thank you.

CONTENTS

MAPS

GLOSSARY

2ic	second in command
66	light anti-tank weapon firing a 66mm unguided rocket
ANA	Afghan National Army
AO	area of operation
AOR	area of responsibility
ARG	Amphibious Ready Group
BDA	battle damage assessment
BRF	Brigade Reconnaissance Force
CAS	close air support
Casevac	casualty evacuation
Cdo	Commando
CP	checkpoint
CTC	Commando Training Centre
ECM	electronic countermeasures
EOD	explosive ordnance disposal
EOT	explosive ordnance team

FAC	forward air controller
FET	female engagement team
FOB	forward operating base
GPMG	general-purpose machine gun, 7.62mm calibre
HIIDE	Handheld Interagency Identity Detection Equipment
HLS	helicopter landing site
HVT	high-value targets
ICOM	brand name of a type of hand-held radio or walkie-talkie, used to designate radio chatter among local Afghans, especially insurgents
IED	improvised explosive device
ISAF	International Security Assistance Force
LRRP	(commonly called LuRP) Long-Range Reconnaissance Patrol
LZ	landing zone
Medevac	medical evacuation
Minimi	5.56mm squad automatic weapon in service with British forces
MSR	major supply route
NVGs	night-vision goggles
OC	officer commanding
OEF	Operation Enduring Freedom
OIC	officer in charge
OMLT	Operational Mentoring and Liaison Team
PDT	Pre-Deployment Training
PRC	potential recruit course

PTI	physical-training instructor
QRF	quick reaction force
R1	code term for a reaction force
RMR	Royal Marine Reserve.
ROE	Rules of Engagement
RPG	rocket-propelled grenade
SA80	British standard-issue 5.56mm assault rifle
SF	Special Forces
SFSG	Special Forces Support Group
TAC(P)	Tactical Air Control (Party)
UGL	underslung grenade launcher
WMIK	Weapons Mounted Installation Kit (for Land Rovers)

FIRE A LETHAL SHOT

'We're moving along the coast. All eyes are on the starboard flank. Enemy soldiers could be anywhere. The ship's already been attacked several times. We've done plenty of attacking too, don't you worry. We're looking, we're looking, we're looking. Most of the country has been taken back but you only need one insurgent to cause damage. That's when I saw it.'

'Saw what, Granddad?'

Ten-year-old me was on tenterhooks. Like I always was when Granddad shared his war stories.

'Movement, Robert. Up there in the hills. We thought the buildings were empty but here and there were definite signs of life. One of the buildings had a chimney roaring. In Greece, in September. What are the odds on that?'

I didn't know anything about the Greek climate in 1944, not at that age, but if Granddad thought it was suspicious, then so did I.

'What happened next?'

'So,' he said, 'we raise the alarm. Every gun on that battleship points into the hills. Then the order comes.'

He paused. Smiling at me. Waiting.

'Fire!' I shout.

'That's right. And that's what we do. All of us. We rain hell on those offices and houses. We can see them disintegrate before our eyes. Suddenly one of the doors opens. The one with the chimney. Dozens of German soldiers come running out, but they're not carrying guns. They've got towels wrapped around their waists, some of them not even that. It was a bath house we'd been firing at, you see. The men had been there for a wash.'

'Did you kill them?'

He went silent. The sparkle in his eyes dulled.

'Did I kill them?' he repeated. 'Not intentionally, Robert, no.'

'Why not?'

'I couldn't bring myself to fire on a naked man,' Granddad said. 'It's not the way we do things in this country.'

'So what did you do?'

'I strafed them all the way up the hill. Everywhere they ran there were bullet holes a few inches behind them. A few of them would have got ricochet wounds on their backsides. I couldn't get any closer.'

Couldn't or wouldn't? I had to ask.

'You can only do what your conscience allows,' Granddad said. 'It takes a hell of a lot to fire a lethal shot.'

I laughed. I was ten. I couldn't help it. I was raised on the cowboy films of John Wayne and Clint Eastwood and the wartime escapades of Richard Burton and that man Clint again. Those guys shot anything that moved. Didn't they?

'Someone needs to watch a bit more closely,' Granddad laughed. 'Duke never shot a man who didn't deserve it. Clint neither. None of them did. I hope you never learn for yourself what it means to take a life.'

He could never have known that one day I would take that shot for myself. That I'd look into a man's eyes and make the decision to end his life. The first time is the hardest, but it never gets easy. Each kill is as horrific as the last. But it's what I'm trained to do. I'm a Royal Marine. We train longer and harder than any other section of the

British military with one purpose: to be able to defend our country or attack our enemies more effectively.

Do I question the times I've taken a lethal shot? Sometimes. Do I doubt I made the right call? Never. The decisions I made, the shots I took, saved lives. Lives of men and women under my command, as well as the lives of countless people I'd never met and probably never would. I removed murderers from the field of play during a time of war. Men who were hell-bent on killing me and mine and didn't care about innocents standing in the middle. Even if those innocents were their own people. Those are the reasons you do it. Those are the reasons you make a kill. The *only* reasons.

There's one question you ask before you fire a lethal shot.

"'Will my action save lives?'"

In every instance my answer would be 'yes'. Just like it would be for every other Green Beret I served with on tour. When you're on the battleground, when you're in theatre, when you're dealing with unknown adversaries who would kill you and display your mutilated remains in a tree as soon as blink, that's all that matters. You just hope your bosses, the men who put you in that position, who guide your every decision, will back your play. Only military men know the horrors of what truly goes on. Only they can be your judge. For me and my men, when it came to taking a life, our bosses always had our back. Just as they should.

But not everyone was so lucky. . .

CHAPTER ONE

ARE YOU SURE YOU WERE ON THE RIGHT STAND?

'Can you see him?'

'Over there.'

'Where?'

'Ten metres in front of me.'

'You need to get closer.'

'Roger that.'

I've got the target in my sights. He has no idea I'm here. He's alone. At least for now. I've no idea how long I've been following him. My hands and knees are black with dirt. I'm sweating.

I move forward, slowly, through the undergrowth. I'm nine metres away. Then eight. Seven. Six. I have to time this right. One false move and I'll lose him.

The target's in a heavily overgrown area. Tall trees all around. Cornered.

Four metres away. Close enough. Time to act. I'm out of ammunition. This is going to be bloody.

Go!

I spring from the bush. Sprint forward. My heart's racing. I launch myself at the target and we both hit the ground.

A few seconds later I look up and see a friendly face. He's more than friendly: he's laughing. Laughing at me.

'You made a right meal of that, Rob,' he says. 'It's only a bloody pheasant.'

* * *

I was born in the Queen Mary Hospital, Roehampton, in south-west London, on 9 May 1976 to Clive and Tina Driscoll. According to Dad we came from a long line of Irish O'Driscolls, but the 'O' got lost on the trip over to England. Dad is as English as they come, a proper South London geezer if you hear him speak. Mum's background is also Irish, particularly the Catholic part of it.

Home was a flat in Putney, for a while anyway. When I was two we moved out to Cheam in Surrey where I was joined by a sister, Bonita, and a brother, David. I don't remember much about those early days except Dad not being around much. He was working on the ambulances when I was born, which meant he was out all sorts of hours. Then shortly after our move he signed up for a police training course. The college was only up in Hendon in north-west London, but it might have been on the other side of the world for the amount of time I saw him. He'd go up to Hendon on the Sunday night and not come back till the following Saturday. I remember watching him leave the house one day. I was holding his leg and crying, begging him not to go.

'Come on,' Mum said, 'he'll be back soon.'

And then one day she stopped saying it.

As a kid you never really know what's going on in the adult world. What I can say is that when I was about eight my parents split up. Dad had passed his course and was a fully fledged bobby and somewhere along the line he and Mum had fallen out of love, I suppose. As was usual in those days, Dad moved out and we stayed with Mum. I missed him every day but kids are surprisingly adaptable. I saw him most weekends and never felt I was missing out. I loved hearing stories of him fighting crime and chasing criminals. Even when he admitted how scared he'd been policing the Brixton riots, I just wanted to hear more.

If Dad wasn't around for the weekend I'd often spend time with my granddad, Alfred Jones. Granddad was Mum's dad. He'd served in the Royal Navy and fought in the Second World War like his brothers, not all of whom had returned as physically unscarred as he did.

In Granddad's stories the Navy always came top. Except when they ran up against one particular branch of the UK forces:

The Royal Marines.

'Those damn Green Berets,' he said, 'they were just that bit better than us at everything. That little bit fitter, that little bit bigger, that little bit more prepared for everything. If we got a draw against them it felt like a win. Not that we ever admitted it.'

He didn't need to. The facts spoke for themselves. The Marines, I quickly learned, beat the matelots, as they called the sailors, every single time. At everything. Football, rugby, drinking, chess. You name it. The Marines excelled.

But there was one opponent even the Marines couldn't beat. Once in a blue moon Granddad would move on to an anecdote that would lead to a story that would end up with memories of the D-Day Landings. And that's when he would shut down. Grandma or Mum would normally shepherd me away at that point. But often they wouldn't be in earshot. That's when I'd hear him talk about the fellas he knew who took part in D-Day, the Allied landings in Normandy in June 1944, who risked their own lives and – despite their superior training and their habit of winning every challenge they ever met – never came back.

Never. Came. Back.

It was usually at that point that Grandma came in with a tea for Granddad and a reason for me to head out to the garden to play with my brother and sister.

Then, I remember, when I was eleven, we were all together to watch the Remembrance Day parade on television, after which Granddad went out to meet some friends down the pub. When he came back for dinner there was the usual chat from me and my siblings while Grandma served the roast. But at some point, my granddad just started to cry. Boom, out of nowhere, the tears just started to roll. He didn't get upset or angry with us but it was enough for my gran to usher us out of the room.

'What's wrong with Granddad?'

'Nothing. Nothing at all. Now why don't you watch some television and I'll bring you some ice cream?'

Years later she told me that offering dessert was easier than offering the truth: namely that Granddad had lost so many friends in the war, from the army, the air force, the navy and particularly from the Marines. Every 11 November was hard. Whichever Sunday that Remembrance Day fell on was even worse. For Granddad, when the whole nation stopped for two minutes it felt like a lifetime. He told me once, 'It's not that I don't like the military, but I lost a lot of friends during the war. I'm not sure I would do it again.'

Granddad's wasn't the only military voice in the family. After the separation, Mum met a new fella, Harry. He was ex-army, and proud of it. He'd done National Service in the East Surrey Regiment and been deployed to Cyprus when all the trouble was happening over there. That was his war. Sometimes I got a glimpse of it. Harry was a big old unit and he'd boxed his way through his military service, winning regional championships even. He loved to tell me of this bout or that, the bruisers he put on the canvas and the odd time he was on the ropes. What with all the sport Granddad did and now Harry boxing every day, the military sounded a right laugh. I think that's the side of things Harry in particular wanted to share. But every so often, like Granddad, he'd start a story and then go quiet and sombre, and close his eyes. You knew he was picturing the bloodshed he'd witnessed outside the ring, recalling the friends he'd lost to injury or worse.

'War's not a game,' Granddad used to say. 'It's not like football or boxing. Sometimes everybody loses.'

* * *

From time to time Granddad would say he never wanted any of his grandchildren going into the forces. He especially wanted us to steer clear of those nutjobs the Marines. What he didn't know is that my military training had already begun. But then, I didn't know either.

Because of his army background Harry saw the value in routine and order. Especially where teenagers were concerned. Every day he would make us lay out our school uniforms, as well as keep our rooms spick and span, be punctual, things like that. If we did it well we'd get pocket money at the end of the week. That seemed a fair trade to me. The fact we were being groomed in the art of soldiery went straight over our heads.

There were a lot of things that passed us by. I don't think Harry's divorce from his earlier marriage had been pretty and I know Mum and Dad's wasn't, but somehow I only saw the positive side. Instead of two parents, I had four, once Dad had remarried to Anne. Did I wish I could have seen the old man a bit more often? Of course I did. But policing isn't a nine-to-five job. You don't rise up through the ranks to become Detective Chief Inspector, or bring the killers of Stephen Lawrence to justice, by watching the clock. Even when we were together, I remember watching Dad a couple of times and you could see he wasn't there. He always had a problem at the back of his mind he was trying to work out.

In any case, there weren't enough hours in the day to do everything I wanted to do. For much of my childhood I lived in Westcott, a small town near Dorking in Surrey to which we moved when I was eight. It's a pretty small place, home to barely 2,000 people, and it's green and it's safe. I would finish school and go out and come back five hours later covered in mud and nettle stings. I would love my own children to have that. At weekends I'd only be home for meals, that's if we weren't camping and terrorising the local pheasant population.

I would think, *This is heaven. I never want to leave.*

But then I turned fifteen.

Everything that I loved about Westcott as a young kid I absolutely loathed as a young adult. The countryside, the open spaces, the woods, the freedom – it was all just so *dull*. There wasn't a day that went by without my wishing we'd never moved from Putney. I didn't remember it at all. I just knew it was in London and that's where the action was. London was where it was at.

I didn't just wake up one day and think that playing Robin Hood in the forest wasn't for me any more. It came on slowly. I began to mix with other people and those people had interests a bit different from hunting and shooting. It was nothing hardcore, just marijuana and mushrooms, but any of these substances can make you do crazy things. One day we tried to steal my mum's car to try to get into town. Typical potheads. We were barely two hundred metres down the road when we realised none of us could drive. Somehow we got it back to the house but I don't think it had ever been parked so badly.

Sadly, the car wasn't the only thing I stole from Mum. All drugs, however soft, cost money and I didn't have any. Mum never said a word so I thought I'd got away with it – and, of course, I decided to do it again. This time I wasn't so lucky.

'I knew it was you.'

Harry. Standing in the doorway. Where the hell had he come from?

'What are you talking about?' I said, despite still holding the purse.

'Your mum told me she'd lost the money. That was the only explanation, she said. But that woman never loses anything. How do you think she's going to feel when I tell her we've got a tealeaf on our hands?'

I could picture Mum's disappointed face.

'Please don't tell her,' I begged. 'Please.'

Harry left the door and walked right over to me. He was huge. He towered above me. He was that close I could see the spittle fly from his mouth when he spoke.

'The thing is, Rob, I'm not going to tell her because it would break her heart. But what I will do is make you this promise: if you ever, *ever* do this again I will knock you out.'

I knew there and then that he wasn't joking. Trust me, being punched by an army boxing champion was not something I wanted to experience.

What Harry didn't know was why I needed the money. Or so I thought. Parents always understand more than you think, as I was to find out before too long. Anyway, he was more of an influence on me than I realised at the time. Aged sixteen, with my GCSEs on the horizon, I suddenly announced to Mum, 'There's no point in me doing these – I want to join the army.'

I don't know where that came from. I think I just wanted to get out of studying. And obviously Harry had always painted it up like a laugh-a-minute. Perfect for a pothead like me. To her credit, Mum took me at face value. But it was a very short conversation.

'You can do what you like at eighteen. But until then you'll be getting an education and qualifications.'

And that was that.

I passed my exams, then enrolled on an aeronautical engineering course at East Surrey College in Redhill. That surprised me as well, but obviously it was Mum's idea. Not one of her better ones, as it turned out. I thought I was pretty good at maths but this was hardcore so I very quickly made the decision to get out.

'Okay, you can do mechanical engineering instead,' Mum said.

'But I've got no interest in cars. What do I want to do that for?'

'It'll be useful.'

The truth is, I had little interest in much at all outside of scoring my next bag of weed. Luckily for me, college only improved that side of things. Shortly after I started my HNC (Higher National Certificate) a young lad, a dealer I suppose you'd have to call him, persuaded me to ferry batches of grass from the college over to Dorking. It wasn't far and the amounts were minimal but at the end of the day I was still no more than a common drugs mule. And why not? I'd pick up here, then go there; it was easy money. And obviously I gave my earnings all straight back to the dealer, so we were both happy.

I really thought I was the bee's knees but the Napoleon of crime

I was not. One day Mum said she was going to run me down to the shops to buy some new trainers.

'Great,' I said. I didn't have any money to buy them.

We drove through town and I was my usual teenage self, probably staring out the window, taking nothing in. We pulled up outside this red-brick building on Reigate Road and we got out. I was in my own little world. I don't think it even registered that there were places nearer the shops where we could have parked.

But, then, Mum wasn't going to the shops. She walked round the car and held open the door of the building. That's when I noticed the sign: 'Dorking Police Station'.

'Mum? What's going on?'

'Get in here. Now.'

As soon as I was through the door Mum went up to the counter and said, 'I want to report my son for selling drugs.'

I couldn't believe what I was hearing. I thought my heart was going to stop. My own mum was grassing me up.

I wanted a hole in the ground to open up and swallow me. What I got instead was a chair in an empty office in the station. A sergeant came in – a big, burly fella who made Harry look tiny – and he read me the riot act. He told me what he did to drug dealers, he told me how long they spent in prison and he told me how not all of them made it out again with all their bits and bobs intact. I was terrified. Literally quaking in my seat. I honestly thought this was it for me.

Then the copper asked if I thought I deserved a second chance.

I managed to stammer out, 'Yes, sir.'

'All right. But if you make me regret it, young man, I will lock you up and throw away the key.'

'I won't, I promise.'

So that was that. He led my quivering wreck of a body back out to where Mum was waiting and said, 'I think he's learned his lesson.'

And do you know what? I really had. I ended with the drugs and I got as far away from the people using them as I could. I'd still see them around town, of course, but I stopped socialising with them. The alternative was just too frightening.

It was years and years later when the truth came out. Because marijuana leaves an odour on you, Mum and Harry had put two and two together and come up with an answer they didn't like. They'd discussed it with Dad and between them hatched this plan where they'd 'shop' me to the Old Bill. Of course, there'd been a phone call to the sergeant in advance. The whole thing had been a set-up from start to finish designed to shake some sense into me. I hate to think what they'd have done if it hadn't worked.

* * *

There were repercussions, obviously. For what felt like a year but was probably only a month or two, I was not allowed to do anything on my own. Mum and Harry and Dad told me exactly what I was doing, when I was doing it and where. They'd drive me places just to ensure I got there, they brought all their network of friends up to speed and everywhere I went it was like a dozen eyes were following me. Worst of all, they got me a job washing dishes in a Harvester restaurant. That was not the life I had mapped out for myself.

But things were all right, if I'm honest, and I sort of bobbed from one opportunity to another. Through my course I was offered a day-release apprenticeship as a mechanic with the William Jacks Group over in Dorking. They were basically a local franchise of the Rover car company and were after some young blood to help them keep up with the modern move towards computer diagnostics and software. This was 1994, it was all quite new at the time. I still had no great love for cars – in fact I cycled the five miles from Westcott there and back every day – but when William Jacks offered me a full-time job after I qualified, I snatched their arm off. Just because I wasn't interested in the product didn't mean I didn't like the money. And girls like cars, right?

For a while there it felt like I had my future mapped out. Actually, deep down, I knew that I was only working in engineering as a stop-gap. I'd been told to learn a trade and I'd done that. Now, aged eighteen, nineteen, I knew it was time to start following my own dream. And I knew exactly what that was.

I was going to join the military.

* * *

The decision had nothing to do with Harry or my Granddad. It began with my mate Darren. We'd done our apprenticeships at William Jacks together but instead of working full time he wanted to join the Fire Brigade. He was starting to work on his physique so he suggested I try. I had actually begun to really relish the cycle rides to work so adding a few weights into my day was a natural progression. To make sure we did it right we started looking up fitness programmes in the local library – this was pre-Google, don't forget – and before you knew it we'd started looking into other things. While Darren read up everything he could find on the Fire Brigade I found myself asking the librarian where to find books on military history. I had never marked myself down as a natural student but I loved it. There were plenty of books written by men long dead but there were others that revealed what had gone on around the world more recently. I was hooked. I discovered I had a voracious appetite for learning when I really wanted to.

I also discovered what I wanted to do with the rest of my life.

'Darren,' I said, 'I've got it. I know what I want to be.'

'Well?'

'I'm going to join the air force.'

* * *

Darren took it better than Mum. She just laughed. 'What do you know about planes?' she said. 'You dropped out of aeronautics.'

'I can learn,' I said. 'You watch.'

There was a careers fair around the corner where all branches from the Ministry of Defence and the emergency services would be represented, so Darren and I made up our minds to go along. I think Mum was pleased but she couldn't help reminding me of our conversation from a couple of years earlier.

'What are you joining today?' she laughed. 'Is it still the RAF or are you going back to the army? Your granddad swears by the navy.'

'No,' I said. 'It's the RAF. I'm going to join the air force and that's that.'

And I meant it.

We got to the fair and Darren went straight off to find the Fire Brigade stand. I wandered around until I came across the people from the RAF. They had amazing posters of planes, and pictures of the blue sky and loads and loads of glossy literature covered in photos of young men and women having the time of their lives in planes. I knew right there, right then, that I was going to be signing up for a life of luxury and excitement.

There must have been two dozen young lads and lasses crowded around the advisers' desks. Clearly I wasn't the only one sold on the idea of signing up.

Still, I thought, I'm in no rush. I can wait. What's a few minutes in a queue compared to a lifetime of thrills?

Five minutes went by and the line didn't budge. Another minute and finally someone left the queue and we shuffled up a bit. Ten minutes in, I'd memorised every detail on those posters.

That's when I heard a voice behind me.

'While you're waiting, why don't you have a look over here?'

I turned round and recognised the speaker as wearing the uniform of a Royal Marine. He was only a young lad, a year or two my senior, if that, but he looked dead smart and he was really friendly.

'You look like you're a fit lad,' he said. 'Maybe you should try out for us.'

I looked over at his stand. The Marines' promotional material was not as big on selling the dream as the RAF's – there were no images of laughing pilots and clear skies. What they did have, though, were these very bold messages in large letters: 'Are you good enough to join?' 'Do you think you've got what it takes to join the one per cent?'

I took one look and knew I was in the right queue, thank you very much.

'I'm all right,' I said. 'I'm waiting for the RAF guy.'

'Fair enough,' the marine said. 'I'll leave you to it.'

He began to walk away.

'Unless you fancy doing a few pull-ups while you wait?'

At the back of his stand there was a metal contraption where a lad bigger than I was struggling to lift his own weight for the second time. I'd done my share of press-ups with Darren but that wasn't my strength. I had lung power to burst but I wasn't exactly Arnold Schwarzenegger. Even so, I knew I could beat two.

'Go on, then. I'll have a go.'

And that's the moment I turned my back on the RAF. All thanks to that salesman in a uniform.

We got over to the apparatus and once the previous occupant had crawled away I jumped up. I knocked two off instantly, then three, four, five. All the while the marine is cheering me along like my biggest fan. I was going to stop at six but just his enthusiasm drove me on to seven. Then I dropped down, arms shaking.

'That was awesome,' he said, beaming. 'You should definitely consider signing up with us. You have the potential, no shadow of a doubt.'

'You really think so?'

'No question.'

'Okay, where do I sign?'

When I got home and told them, Mum couldn't stop laughing: she'd predicted I wouldn't join the RAF or the army . . . Harry was mystified. 'Are you sure you were on the right stand?'

* * *

The Marines love their hurdles. You do this, then you do this, then you do this. After signing my life away I got an invitation to go to a test at Guildford. I did my research as best I could and when I turned up wasn't surprised to be given tests in maths, English, a bit of mechanical reasoning – which obviously was a doddle. Then there was an interview and at the end of that I was told it was worth my taking the medical exam at my local GPs. When that was over I got another letter giving me ten weeks to get myself shipshape for the next phase.

The only thing the Marines love more than hurdles are initials. I was told to attend my four-day PRC (potential recruit course) at the CTC (Commando Training Centre) in Lympstone, Devon. Once I worked out what it meant I started training in earnest, reading every book I could find on the Royal Marines and asking anyone for tips. It was actually my dad who came through. A couple of fellas on the Met had done the commando training, and they said, 'Run, run and run some more. Then do it again with heavy boots and a load of weights attached.'

When PRC day came, I polished my boots, put on my suit, packed my case and left the house for the station.

'I'll see you in four days.'

'Nah, you'll be back tomorrow,' Harry said.

God, I wanted desperately to prove him wrong. And I did. But not how I wanted. Harry said I'd be back the next day. In fact, I didn't last that long. When I next walked into the house it was the very same day.

The dream was over.

CHAPTER TWO

AND THERE'S THE MARINE WAY

It had all been going so well.

PRC runs Tuesday to Friday. The Monday night before I was due to go down to Lympstone I cycled down to Dorking station to buy my ticket and double-check the departure times. I was leaving nothing to chance. Or so I thought.

Then on the way back I got knocked off my bike.

I was taken to East Surrey Hospital and diagnosed with a damaged shoulder and mild concussion. The medical advice was not to do anything strenuous for a week or two. They even gave me a letter excusing me from strenuous work on health grounds. I nodded as I left the ward, already certain not to heed a word of it.

The trip from Dorking was okay. I sat reading one of my military books surrounded by dozens of commuters off to work. When we changed trains at Exeter I noticed the commuters had more or less dried up. In their place were a lot of nervous young men in suits probably belonging to their fathers.

At least I know I'm on the right train.

But any air of wonder was extinguished the second we stepped onto the platform at Lympstone Commando station and this gorilla of a man in uniform just started shouting. He basically got us together and marching up to the training centre in silence.

What the hell was I doing thinking that I could hide my injury? We hadn't even arrived and I was already sure I'd cocked up big time. I plucked up the courage and when the gorilla stopped bossing us for a moment I handed over my doctor's note. He read it and sent me off with the others to do the first test.

Sixty minutes later I was summoned to the sick bay. They did a couple of tests and took my blood pressure, then a medic said, 'I'm sorry, you're not fit enough to continue.'

I was crushed. I really thought that was the end. But the main doc said he expected my body to heal so they'd have no problem letting me try again later.

This was spring 1996. It was ten dreary weeks later when I finally made that journey west again. I was annoyed at how long it had taken to reschedule but the moment I got on the train I realised I was in a better position than everyone else. This time I knew exactly where I was going, exactly who I was going to be met by. I could picture the centre. That so-called wasted journey I'd had three months earlier was basically just a reconnaissance mission. I was arriving better prepared than anybody.

There were forty or so lads on the first Tuesday. Each night that went by, though, there'd be one or two new empty beds. I felt for them but of course I'd had two 'gos'. I saw no reason why they couldn't come back stronger – or at least better at running.

Seeing the numbers dwindle, however, was a chilling reminder that any of us were only a bike accident or a twisted ankle away from being evicted. It was only going to get worse. If we managed to pass this test and get on to the Commando Course then that was nine months to get through without injury or mishap.

On the final day, the Friday, we had our last interviews. Then we were all sent outside while the adjudicators made their choices. When I was called back in I was awarded a 'superior pass', informed that I had come top of the thirty lads remaining – and I'd be hearing from them very, very soon about starting proper training.

It's not the done thing in the military to jump for joy – I worked that out on day 1 – but I felt like doing a cartwheel. As I made my way back down to the station I looked at the sign. Suddenly the word 'Commando' didn't look quite so out of reach.

Little did I know.

* * *

The Royal Marines are the light infantry brigade of the Royal Navy. They're the rapid-response unit, able to be dropped into any hotspot in the world in the knowledge that there are none better trained. The majority of personnel come under the umbrella of 3 Commando (Cdo) Brigade.

While the roles and locations are varied, these days just about every one of the 8,000-plus regular and reserve marines has to complete the Commando Course. They all have to become Green Berets. It's as elite as you get.

That's the target for everyone, but, as summer 1996 dragged on I couldn't work out why I wasn't getting the chance. They'd said I'd hear 'very, very' soon – not just 'soon'. By the turn of the year I was going absolutely crazy. Obviously I rang the CTC to chase my application, just to check there wasn't a problem. At first they just told me to wait. When I called back a couple of months later, still with no news, they were more upfront. My predecessors may have lost the 'O' from our surname but we were definitely Irish. And that, coming off the back of the Troubles in Northern Ireland, was not something the military took lightly, it seems.

I had a great girlfriend – a nurse – at the time, a well-paid job and some good mates, but the not knowing was overshadowing everything. I was working out and running every day, my fitness was going up, but not having a goal just made it all feel pointless. Whatever I put myself through would be nothing compared with the physical drills I could expect at Lympstone. As a result, although I'd never been fitter I actually felt fat.

And then I got the letter. Late 1997 the note came through the door. It said, very simply, that I was to become part of 738 Troop and my start date was February 1998.

Everyone on the Lympstone train, I realised when we arrived, was a freshman like myself. We, sixty-two of us, hovered on the platform until we were rounded up by a corporal – Taff, I'll call him – who led us to the centre and to an enormous dormitory: one bed, one locker and one chair each; down one end there was a shower block, toilets and an area full of ironing boards, buckets and the like. Obviously, the cleaners needed to store their gear somewhere.

First we, all sixty-two of us, were sent to stores, where we were issued with all the clothing and footwear we'd need, and to the barber. I asked for a little trim. 'Right you are, sir,' he said, and shaved the whole lot off.

As Taff left us that evening, it was with a promise: 'Those of you who think you're here for thirty-two weeks, think again. If you don't perform every day, you will be out. If you don't perform every minute of every day, you will be out. You might last two weeks, twenty weeks, or thirty-one weeks. I don't care. It's all the same to me. There's no room for part-timers here.'

We were all up and ready by six the following morning, speculating about our first task.

'We're not going to like it,' one lad said.

'Definitely. They like to throw you in at the deep end.'

Taff led us down to the end of the dormitory, dragged out an ironing board and took a shirt from one of the lockers. 'This morning's lesson: ironing,' he announced.

No one dared speak. We watched him – ironing, folding, ironing … Mum made it look easy, but he made it look like some kind of origami. 'There's the marine way of doing things,' he said, 'and there's the wrong way.' He looked us up and down, 'This is the marine way.'

Then it was the boots – yes, they were ironed, too, just a little – and how to shave properly (the marine way).

There was barely five minutes for lunch before Taff put us through our paces in the gym. Any dissent was rewarded with an extra fifty or one hundred press-ups or squats or whatever else came to mind. Everything was hard; every muscle in our bodies hurt.

Induction training lasted a fortnight; every day there was drill practice, two-hour slots of strength and fitness ... there was ironing, polishing and tidying, shaving and freezing nights spent outdoors. Sadly, not all the recruits lasted, but it was a time when we all made good mates – Paul A., Andy Probert, Luke Harmsworth, and later Paul Moynan were among my new friends. Another plus was being issued with weapons – although we were taught only how to strip and polish them; how to use them would come later.

The following weeks we had new, more specialised trainers: in physical training, radio work, surveillance, survival, mortars, heavy weapons, orienteering ... and they were all hard on us, and they were brilliant. But as our sergeant kept reminding us: 'The Marines is for the elite. If you're not up to it, you know where the door is.'

And some did walk out through that door. I could not see how, after all that effort, anyone could do that.

Then it was the Easter holidays. Back to all the comforts and freedoms of home and family, and to my girlfriend. It was hard to ignore the contrasts with the training camp. Paul A. lived near by and we started to meet up in the pub. We talked about the hardships of training, and two days before we were due to return we agreed that we did not want to go on with it. So, on our arrival back at Lympstone we went together to the sergeant and handed in our resignation letters. He just said, 'I'm going to sit on these letters until Friday. If you still feel the same then, then we will begin the process of getting you out of here.'

On Friday we went to him and asked him to forget the letters, and he tore them up. We continued training, which was not without its ups and downs, mostly downs, for any of us. By week 25, there were only sixteen of us left, and we were to dwindle to eleven. We were moved to Sennybridge in Wales for the next steps in commando training. For two weeks we were drilled and drilled and drilled in live firing with no limitations by marines who were nothing if not tough. Things have since changed, but in those days the watchwords were extreme violence, speed and aggression. Everything centred on locating the enemy and destroying them at no matter what cost. The bursts of gunfire and explosions going off around us to simulate the terror and confusion of actual conflict were real. They trained us for everything they could imagine might happen. It was hard work and stressful, but totally exhilarating. This was the marine way.

The final test I knew would be evil. It followed ten days crossing Dartmoor, practising all we'd learned, which was fun but ensured we were totally knackered for the ordeal that was to come, the Commando Test. To make this test a bit more challenging, the tasks were against the clock, and if one failed a task, all failed.

The first task was a 9-mile speed march carrying full battle order (about 21 pounds/9.5 kilos) to be completed in 90 minutes.

Followed by a 6-mile endurance course.

Then came the advanced weapons trials.

Then the killer assault course.

The last was a 30-mile hike carrying about 40 pounds (18 kilos) of kit to be completed in under eight hours.

We made it, and in good time, even though Paul A. did the last fifteen miles on painkillers so powerful he meandered about like one of the Living Dead and the rest of us had to herd him as if he was a wayward sheep.

Considering how much pomp and circumstance there is in the military, what happened next was fairly low key, but that suited all of us. We gathered in a square and a succession of high-ranking officers came out to meet us. Then the brigadier from the CTC arrived and personally shook our hands as he handed over to each of us our very own Green Beret.

The following week was the passing-out ceremony. Everyone had a good presentation but, as well as the standard pass, I was awarded prizes for marksmanship and coming top in other tasks, as well as a 'Diamond' award in recognition of being a section commander throughout my time there. As I walked away with Mum and Dad and the others I could see the look on their faces – you can't buy happiness like that. I was sad though, sad because I didn't want to leave Lympstone, this complex that had given me more pain and trouble than anything in my life.

I was soon back at Lympstone, but just for a nineteen-week signals course, after which I joined 45 Commando in Arbroath, Scotland, where we trained and waited. It was cold. We went to Norway, where we trained. It was even colder. But then we went to Belize for jungle training – and I hoped I would be sent somewhere cold. That is not quite what happened.

* * *

Just because you don't see action doesn't mean you don't prepare for it. At any given moment in the UK there will be a battalion or a commando unit – usually between 16 Air Assault Paras or 3 Commando Brigade – that is code 'R1', which means they are the reaction force. Should anything happen to British interests anywhere in the world, their equipment is packed, they are ready to go instantly. When I joined 45 Commando, we were R1. I read enough news to realise that things in the Balkans might require our involvement.

In 1999 we started to get whispers that the situation in Kosovo was going bad. It was only a matter of time before the UK got involved.

'You know what that means? We're R1. We'll be going.'

There was no official word but the buzz around the base was deafening. When the call came to deploy we'd be ready. We already were.

This is it, boys. We're finally going to be marines . . .

All we were waiting for was the government to give the go-ahead for strike force action. Then, in May, it did.

But we weren't the strike force.

With no explanation – at least to us – the top brass selected 1 Para (1st Battalion, the Parachute Regiment) instead of 45 Commando to move into Kosovo. The mood around the camp sank into gloom. You've never seen so many long faces. That was the trigger that sent so many of the older lads heading for the exit door. Imagine being a footballer and spending your whole career on the bench. The decision definitely cost us a lot of good men.

I followed the news as closely as I could. When the Paras moved up from Macedonia, from where they'd launched their operations, they were met with Serbian resistance. From the reports we got it was pretty obvious the Paras were getting a substantial number of rounds down which only made our mood back home worse.

It stopped almost as quickly as it started, though. I don't think there were any British casualties in the advance from Macedonia up to Pristina. When they arrived in Pristina it was a case of switching from combat operations into peacekeeping support. And that's when the call came to Arbroath.

A full year after the Paras had gone in we were told to ready ourselves for deployment. The news provoked mixed emotions. On the plus side, I'd finally be going over to be a marine in a live situation. On the downside, the Paras had already scooped the best gig. Another downside was knowing how all those lads who'd left the Marines in the last twelve months, largely because of the lack of action, would be kicking themselves. Finally, there was the voice of reason back home. Mum was convinced I would be walking to my death. It didn't help that I'd recently met a new girlfriend in Kent over Christmas. She too was convinced I shouldn't go.

I loved them both, but was I going to listen? This may not have been the Guns N' Roses warfare I'd been hoping for but it could get tasty, we kept being told that. The fact we were being deployed at all was recognition of how dangerous the region was.

But there was another drawback and it was a big one – for me personally.

Most of the 45 Commando lads would be going over as militarised policemen. They'd be out and about in Pristina, identifying threats and dealing with them. I was part of Z Company – a signaller. The only threats I'd be identifying would be interference on the radio signal while listening to my mates do the fun stuff.

From May 2000 until we were actually scheduled to leave in the autumn I began trying to get myself transferred to a more hands-on role. When I'd taken signals as my specialisation the sergeant assured me I could change after eighteen months. I was just about to reach that point, so I put in for a switch to go on general duty. In other words, become a basic foot soldier.

And was rejected.

That was the first lie I was told in the Marines: that I could move around the divisions. It was all personnel-dependent, I was told. If they had the manpower to cover me, they would. They didn't, so they couldn't. Or wouldn't – it's all the same.

Net result: I was gutted. I couldn't believe 45 Commando was going to a war zone and I'd be taking messages.

And then suddenly my luck changed.

'Marine Driscoll, we need you to work security for the advance party. Get ready to leave for Greece.'

'Security', 'advance party', 'Greece'? Whatever it meant, I was up for it.

I was going to get my hands dirty.

CHAPTER THREE

YOU'RE WHERE YOU NEED TO BE

Who said signals was dull?

As soon as we got word in April that we would be going out to Kosovo as part of Operation Agricola, 45 Commando went into immediate prep mode. For the officers, that meant devising a strategy. After a big meeting it was announced that Z Company – my lot – would take responsibility for an area north-east of Pristina. That was great. Now we had something to work with, a focus. For the majority of the company that meant checking equipment, checking vehicles, checking personnel, before departure. Over on the signals desk we were doing something else. We were planning the thing.

Most of our intel in Kosovo was coming from live feeds sent by the men currently on the ground, the ones we'd be replacing. My job was to take their messages and condense them into a format ready for the NCOs and subsequently the officers and decision-makers to ingest. Military messages are all about brevity and format. There's a system for reporting every single topic you can imagine and I'd learned them all on the nineteen-week signals course I'd attended. While we had time in Arbroath to read everything in full, in a theatre of war, time is usually a luxury.

Even being in the Highlands of Scotland during those months leading up to our deployment, there was a palpable feeling of excitement. Of relief, as well. On the face of it, what we were doing was identical to some of the training exercises we'd done over and over. That was the point of training – every exercise had to feel identical to the real thing so you knew how to respond. But just when you think you've always given 100 per cent in practice, you realise there's another level you naturally step up to when it matters. Knowing that every check the boys made on a vehicle could save a marine's life, knowing that every grain of intel I passed down the channels could highlight some tactical advantage, altered everything. In training it's just your career depending on the outcome. On a mobilisation footing it's your life – and those of your colleagues.

That's not to say there wasn't training, of course. This is the Marines, after all. Training, some might say, is what we do best.

Before you go anywhere you are immersed in Pre-Deployment Training (PDT). Lecture halls were packed for weeks with experts telling us all the info we needed to operate on foreign soil. Practical stuff like basic language lessons, geography, cultural differences, anything that could give you an advantage, we had. Usually we took this stuff on board without enthusiasm, but we learned it just the same. It's amazing how even stuffy history lessons come alive when they're part of a mission package.

There was a physical aspect as well. For our final exercise we went down to Salisbury Plain, where some old villages, long abandoned since the military took over the area, had been repurposed as Yugoslavian. The attention to detail in all these things is staggering. We did drill after drill, covering all aspects from peacekeeping, civilian liaison and, if we were lucky, firefights.

Deep down – in fact, not that well hidden at all – this is what we all hoped to get involved in. In a war zone even peacekeeping could turn very violent.

The 3 Brigade command were well aware of this. They knew exactly what they had trained to do. As a result, the longest lessons we got were on 'Rules of Engagement' (ROE). Namely, at what point can you use lethal force? Just because you have a weapon and you identify a person as an 'enemy', you can't just shoot them. Real war is not the movies. The rules of international law and human rights are very clear. If you are representing Her Majesty's Corps of Royal Marines and her country, there are stages you must go through before you take the decision to fire a lethal shot. The aim must always be for a peaceful resolution.

The ROE at any given time are known as 'Card Alpha'. Throughout a campaign the restrictions placed by Card Alpha can be changed either to allow greater flexibility for the men in theatre, or to clamp down further on potential opportunities for discharging your weapon. Nothing is straightforward. It's up to the individual marine himself to know exactly what the state of play is.

None of this was new to us. Every time I stepped out on guard duty at the RM Condor base at Arbroath I was operating under the current Card Alpha restrictions, which had been explained many, many times. Before they let me out with a rifle I had to sit through a stream of videos featuring simulations of enemy attacks before answering one question: at which point do you introduce lethal force? Obviously, patrolling a military base on home soil in peacetime is never going to throw up too many problems. To my knowledge, Arbroath had never come under attack. Being told that Card Alpha still applied in a war zone seemed less intuitive.

I felt then – and I still do – that keeping up with the restrictions of Card Alpha was a lot of responsibility to put on young shoulders.

* * *

Considering we had once been R1 – the rapid-response unit – I was frustrated at how long it took actually to get everything ready. We weren't this all-singing, all-moving, all-dancing dealer of death that you might imagine. There was this methodically slow and very frustrating process that had to be worked through. From the tip-off in April it took nearly five months to get all the ducks in a row. Even then we still had a lot of practical jobs to do. Luckily for me, mine happened to be amazing.

One of the reasons for the slow response was that a lot of the equipment from Arbroath was going to Kosovo by sea. When it reached mainland Greece it would be transported by train up through Macedonia and on to Pristina. This system had been in use for a while but recently one of the trains had been raided. Nothing to do with the war, just bandits seeing an opportunity to acquire some very expensive hardware. Because the next shipment to be loaded onto a train was coming direct from Company HQ – which, as a signaller, is where I worked – it was decided that the cargo needed protecting. There were 600 people in Arbroath who would have killed to have gone. Being one of the signals team I already had a foot in the door.

A planeload of men from HQ were flying out to Pristina to set up. En route, thirty of us were dropped off at Thessaloniki in Greece with our weapons and kit. I didn't know what to expect. It wasn't a trip back to the 1940s.

Immediately, what first caught our eye was this vast supply train, about half a mile long, which had clearly been in service since the Second World War. There was a steam engine at the front and behind that there was one normal passenger carriage followed by six or seven flatbed trucks, each one loaded with things like Land Rovers, sea containers and, identifiable under their covers, radar dishes and even missiles. Then came another passenger carriage followed by half a dozen more flatbeds, and so on, almost literally as far as the eye could see. And thirty of us were there to guard it.

I assume there'll be others.

Beyond the train was a giant hangar, similar to constructions at the Arbroath base, where we were greeted by other marines. We were issued with ammunition and, crucially, our brief.

'Basically,' we were told, 'you're going to ride on the train, and every time it stops get out and look menacing.' Followed by, 'Good. Here's your Card Alpha.' Almost immediately I felt we were under pressure to abide by it.

Because the port had been commandeered by us, it was largely empty. The only other people there, apart from marines and the Greek train driver, were protesters. I was a bit taken aback that they were allowed to wander through the port and yell in our faces. I was surprised that they were brave enough to do so, as well. It turned out that anti-NATO feelings had been running high in the region for some time. It wasn't directed towards us personally. Even so, I saw each one of the protesters as a potential threat. You only need one to take it further than verbal assault.

Finally we were put on the train.

'Where's everyone else?' I asked.

'This is it. Just you.'

We'd all been issued with radios and two hours into our journey mine crackled. It was the sergeant. We were making our first stop. Get ready.

Before the train had fully slowed we were leaping out of the carriage and spreading ourselves out alongside the train.

With the various border checks and drop-offs and driver switches, we were called into action every few hours. I say 'action'. As the journey wore on I found myself studying the people around us when we stopped, almost willing one of them to have a go. I just wanted to get involved. When we got into the mountains of Macedonia, there was a distinct sense that this was bandit country. On board, the sarge told us to be extra vigilant. At the next stop I prayed they'd have another go at stealing our cargo.

They didn't.

There were enough people milling around mysteriously to convince me that if the train weren't guarded then they'd be all over it. But no one was prepared to fight for it. They were strictly opportunists. For three days we repeated the same high-alert procedures. For three days we encountered nothing but locals staring at us like we were a travelling circus.

In the end most of our stops were conducted at night with no civilian interaction.

On arrival, our contact met us at the station and I and my two signals colleagues, Scott and Smudge, were driven into Pristina in a Land Rover. That might sound like a smooth, well-run operation but for me it jarred. We'd just gone three nights without sleep. We were trained to the point of breaking in how to wipe out enemy targets. And we'd been on high-alert for eighty hours. All of us in the back were twitchy as hell, looking for possible antagonists.

The driver picked up on it.

'Guys, you can relax. We're okay here, trust me.'

I wasn't sure whether to believe him. I didn't want to, either. Where was the threat I'd been promised?

The further we drove into Pristina the more I realised he was right. It didn't look or feel like hundreds of opposing troops had torn through the city a year earlier. It actually felt like another Greek holiday destination, one of the ones a bit more inland so with fewer Brits. It was certainly as hot as down south. I wondered whether the rebels had put their fighting on hold until the weather got cooler. I couldn't wait for them to start up again.

Our destination was a military camp near the airport. We were met and told to wait. Four hours later someone came to show us around. Obviously a big emergency situation had called them away.

When we were dumped again somewhere else I quickly learned the truth. There had been no emergency. We were just another logistical problem, no more pressing than getting a load of cardboard boxes shifted.

Finally, we were picked up and ferried to a building where we found the various bunks that would be home for the next seven months. There were more empty beds than not. That was to change over the next few weeks, however, as the personnel from Arbroath began to arrive. It was weird, seeing familiar faces coming into this unfamiliar setting. Then it was time to get to work.

Once again, I was singled out.

* * *

Every unit to arrive brings its own equipment. Since our task was to maintain and operate the signals, that's a lot of equipment. There were three of us signallers in Z Company so actually we had a lot of responsibility compared with the majority of marines over there.

On day 1 we were instructed to install radio equipment at a location in Pristina. It was five miles away. The kit was just about portable with three people. Two of us were told to get on with it. On foot.

It was eerie leaving the base. We had learned the route off by heart although I had my maps at hand. The fact that we were allowed out in a pair was alien to all my training – everyone's training. After about a mile we moved into a more urbanised area. By coincidence another patrol was passing. There were sixteen men, all armed to the teeth, all ready to react to any threat. They looked at us, we looked at them.

'Do you need cover?' one of the lads asked.

'I don't think so. Do we?'

They had a chat. 'No, you'll be all right.'

Bizarre, really. We were patrolling – not even that, more 'walking' – through a war zone in smaller numbers than we used to guard RM Condor. Over five miles in enemy territory you could be attacked a hundred times. Especially if you were carrying hundreds of thousands of pounds' worth of specialist equipment. But, since nobody had been attacked, the planners had decided it was okay for us. I grew to be happy with the decision but that first day was nerve-racking, I admit.

By the time we got further into the city it was apparent that the Kosovans were getting on with their lives as best they could. Shops were open, offices were busy, there were even schoolkids here and there. And what they all had in common was that they took no notice of me. If a bloke kitted out for full-scale warfare walked past me with a cocked rifle I'd bloody well take notice. They were obviously conditioned for a lot worse.

I was installing kit at various sites but the main place was Z Company command, in an old police station. It was single-storey, comprising seven small rooms, individually built from steel faced with concrete and breeze-blocks. Design-wise it reminded me of some of the Greek homes I'd seen on the journey up. There was a roof of terracotta tiles but otherwise it could have been built in Thessaloniki.

It wasn't oversupplied with windows, but two of them we kitted out with black blinds. That was our ops room. There was a board on the wall filled with maps covered in Day-Glo sticky labels and Post-it notes containing the highest sensitivity intelligence. It was pretty low-tech, I suppose, but it did the job.

The walls in the radio room were covered with info as well. Photos of persons of interest, sites of activity, basic intelligence. In the middle of the room was a wooden desk – like everything else, shipped over from the UK – where one of the three signallers would sit.

Once all of 45 Commando had arrived we settled into a rhythm. Working eight hours on, sixteen off, I rotated with my two Z Company colleagues in the radio HQ building listening to and recording all the transmissions coming in from the various patrols out on the streets. Having had ten days or so of setting up and familiarising myself with our surroundings, I could picture where most of the reports were coming from, which helped syphon the critical information from the distractions.

My role was purely functional. I would sit, headphones on, listening and transcribing. Everything was recorded but it was my job to sift through and extract the essential stuff as it went live. Not all messages would be important. Much of the radio traffic was mundane. It was my role to prioritise messages, then pass the ones I'd selected to the person sitting next to me, the duty officer. It was he who would take my reports and make a decision whether to push them further up the chain of command. If that was the case I'd be tasked with constructing a message in 'marine speak', something as clear as mud to any casual observer but absolutely to the point for anyone at Company HQ.

In training the duty officer had usually been a corporal. For most of my early shifts *in situ*, however, I found myself working with the building's officer in charge (OIC), Captain Steve McCulley.

Given that there were only three of us in the room at a time, plus the intensity of the work, you get fairly close to your colleagues. Despite his superior rank Steve was more approachable than most. It turned out he was really into his fitness as well, particularly cycling, so we started training together with the other signallers, Smudge and Scott, as well as a few corporals.

Hobnobbing with the bosses seemed perfectly natural, considering the cramped working conditions and the small number of us doing that crucial work. In fact, such fraternisation between the ranks was widely frowned upon.

Obviously we never got the memo about commissioned officers and marines not mixing because the group of us made a good team outside and inside the cramped offices. Steve had a knack for discerning the important kernels of information buried in quite long reports, and I became expert at condensing them into digestible communiqués for HQ. Yet, as the weeks turned into months, I realised I was suffering a bit of cabin fever. My role was important, I knew that, but the excitement – the hands-on stuff – was happening outside our breeze-block walls.

If it was just me going stir crazy I'd have had to suck it up. Luckily, Scott and Smudge felt the same, so we worked out a new rota so that each week two of us would do twelve hours on and twelve off. That left the third limb spare. This is where sweet-talking and calling in favours came in. All three of us just wanted to go out on patrol, which meant speaking directly to the corporals in charge. I'm not sure how by-the-book it was, but since each corporal had good working relations with us, they bought into it. We were all familiar voices, if not faces. They knew we could be trusted. And they could always use an extra body.

And so each week one of us would go out with a patrol, then another the second week, then the third of us the week after that. Then we'd repeat the process. It was purely a timetable cooked up between the three of us signallers, with Steve's blessing. We all just wanted to play to our strengths – and to be able to say that we had got our hands dirty.

The work was varied. On patrol we carried out a lot of vehicle checkpoints, searching cars, as well as lots of patrolling around the various areas.

On one of my first patrols we were called to a village where shooting had been reported. We arrived mob-handed, and found the owners of two farms shooting at each other. It was like watching a bad cowboy film. They were literally hiding behind their own little walls then popping up every so often to take a shot.

My first instinct was, *Identify the victim – suppress the aggressor.* This was quickly followed by, *I have no fucking clue who is who.*

All this goes through your mind extremely quickly. Luckily, as soon as they saw us all the farmers threw down their weapons. We didn't even have to raise our voices. Once the locations were secured we brought the interpreter in. What, we wanted to know, could possibly have led to this fight to the death?

'One farmer says a cow from the other farm strayed on to his field.'

'Is that all?'

'Yes.'

To a certain extent the people of Kosovo humoured us, or even toyed with us. One of our jobs was confiscating unlicensed weapons. Sometimes our doing so would be the result of a stop-and-search in the street, but more usually it was based on some intel passed via Steve. The first raid I did proved quite fruitful. We came away from one row of houses with boxes of pistols and rifles. Outside I said to the translator attached to the patrol, 'These look so old I'm amazed they even work.'

The translator shrugged.

'You don't think they give you their sexy weapons, do you?'

After the *Reservoir Dogs* approach to settling neighbourly disputes, and now this, I thought I'd seen it all. Virtually the next patrol I had to revisit that opinion.

Wherever you go around the world you will find traditions that seem at odds with your own upbringing. Part of our Pre-Deployment Training had focused on this. However much I read about 'blood feuds', though, nothing prepares you for seeing the reality.

Dating from the fifteenth century, Kosovo's blood feud law or *krvna osveta* gives a victim legal authority to right a wrong with equal fury. For example, if a truck driver mows down and kills a little girl, that girl's father is entitled to take the life of one of the driver's children. Depending on whether you arrived in Kosovo by birth canal or international flight, it's either logical or barbaric.

I saw a few nasty retaliations which both parties accepted were 'fair', although in the main, these were few and far between. What I didn't know is that they were saving their grievances for something called 'Blood Sunday'.

It was madness itself. For one day the whole country exploded. If you've seen the film *The Purge* – a horror story in which for one day there are no laws – it might give you some idea of what we were up against. From the crack of dawn we started receiving reports of people being gunned down in the street in broad daylight. We arrived at the scene of the first incident and questioned some witnesses, who all casually gave us the name of the murderer. One asked us why we were interfering in justice.

My next call was to intervene again between two neighbours. In this instance the so-called justice system was struggling. One of the neighbours had posted a grenade through the other's letterbox. No one was killed or injured. Rather than accept this 'justice', the victim then went after his neighbour with all guns blazing. Apparently it all got very tasty. When we arrived, though, the area was quiet. Foolishly, I thought our presence had quelled them into stopping. Not true. They'd just run out of ammo.

The best we could do was hand the lot over to a group of British police who had been brought to Kosovo to mentor the local force. This hardly improved matters, for their hands were tied as much as ours. What can you do when the whole country thinks that summary justice – a.k.a. violent revenge – is okay? When even the Kosovo police had taken the day off just to settle vendettas of their own

Not everything was so alien to us, however. There was a genuine Mafia presence in Pristina, which is more or less the same as a Mafia presence anywhere in the world. We did a lot of work with other governmental departments, simply supplying information that we had collected about vehicles and their whereabouts. Everything we learned was passed up the line via our colleagues stuck back at HQ. Every so often an order for action would be passed back as a result.

One of the worst Mafia crimes was human trafficking. There's an argument that Card Alpha should have been rescinded for these particular perpetrators. It seemed that every week I was out on patrol we would shut down another pimp or 'body dealer'. The most spectacular of these events occurred in the spring of 2000. I was with a Z Company patrol on a joint operation with the local police, targeting a building on the outskirts of the city. It was another Greek-looking construction although taller, two storeys high, and it had a high wall around its perimeter that in itself was enough to raise our suspicions. In conjunction with the Kosovan National Police we stormed the gate, then the front door. The latter was easier said than done. The door was of reinforced steel, so we had to call up the boys with the big toys. Inside we found a room full of naked, scared girls. They were all hooked on drugs, and all behaved in a strangely over-familiar manner with the lads rescuing them. To this day I wonder whether they remember anything about that raid. And whether they managed to stay away from that lifestyle once we had left.

On days like that I really felt we were a force for good. Other times we looked like amateurs. Embarrassingly, on one occasion our own forces played a role. Somehow we got wind of information that there was going to be a significant attack on one of our helicopters. It was just a whisper at that stage, but it was enough to make everyone's ears prick up. Given the shortage of any real activity there was a sense of excitement around Z Company, because we were going to be the ones to shut this potential attack down.

Everyone jumped at the chance to get involved. The surveillance team were as bored by the lack of activity as anyone. Thanks to them we tracked down a farmhouse in a particular village where, according to the snippets of intel coming in via our boys, the Germans and the Americans, we would find a missile stash, a gang of cut-throat bombers and leaders of the rebel militia. A trail of crumbs it may have been, but there was no doubt where it led.

If we had been rushed off our feet in the region then maybe we would have gone in immediately, all guns blazing. Since we had the time, though, we planned the shit out of what we were going to do. We even carried out a mock raid on another farmhouse just so everyone knew their jobs when the real deal happened.

You can only rehearse so much. On the day of the operation we mobilised before dawn. Stealth was the watchword. We wanted to catch the ringleaders red-handed. We'd done the drills. Everyone knew their tasks and their positions. I admit, I was bubbling with excitement. We all were. This was the most meticulously planned operation any of us had been involved in. It was also potentially the most dangerous.

Bring it on.

The various entry teams were in place. The commander on the ground checked with his leaders, then gave the signal. The farmhouse went from a normal quiet country scene to a mass of bodies charging at the doors and windows.

As I sprinted towards the building I expected shots to rain down from the building at any second. They didn't come. We entered through the rear and still I waited for the welcoming committee that didn't materialise. Each corner I turned held, in my mind, the threat of an assailant just around it. There were none.

The upstairs team had more luck. Even as we swept downstairs I could hear suspects being cuffed and dragged outside. After ten minutes of screaming, shouting, stamping, crashing and searching we all rendezvoused in the yard to assess our victory.

There, surrounded by a circle of armed men, stood an old man and woman, in their pyjamas. Next to them were two grandchildren.

I'm looking at my mates; they're looking at me.

'Are these the bombers?'

'Don't think so.'

'Did we find the missiles?'

'Not yet.'

While we stood there the other teams reported back. They all had the same story. 'Nothing to see here.' It was disappointing, but that quickly turned to confusion. Then downright embarrassment.

'We've been played.'

It was the only conclusion. Someone, somewhere had a beef with this particular farmer, and had set the whole thing up. Maybe they thought the damned NATO forces would be more heavy-handed than we were. Maybe they predicted we'd do exactly as we did. The only thing I can say for sure is that this outwardly sleepy war-torn village had managed to con the world's leading military powerhouse – for the United States led the NATO coalition – with little more than a few well-placed whispers.

For the majority of us on the ground the exhilaration of the raid was genuine, even if the mission was not. For those of us working in signals, it was harder to bear. Steve himself was phlegmatic.

'It's war. It happens. We do the best we can with the intel we have.'

'But, mate, it went tits-up today.'

'But what if it hadn't?'

His positivity was legendary and, I have to say, contagious. Three more morose signallers you could not have found, but he turned us all around.

* * *

Because of my time at HQ seeing the threads of intel come in and then going out on patrol to act on them, I received a bigger picture of what we were doing in Kosovo than maybe a lot of others. The Card Alpha rules seemed unworkable in the field, but since, in seven months in the territory, no one in Z Company had discharged a single round, it was a moot point. I also saw that you can't always trust the people on the same side. It was one thing being played by rival crime lords, but occasionally we were stitched up by people within NATO.

It's common knowledge that Germany's GCG9 and America and France's equivalent special forces were operating in Kosovo at the same time as we were. We didn't really come into contact, but occasionally one of those would feed us a titbit of intel. They might do it upfront or, more likely, in a more clandestine fashion, so that we wouldn't know it had come from them. Why? Because their operational boundaries were even tighter than ours. If they felt there was any shadow of doubt about one of their missions they'd encourage us to 'discover' the intel and carry out the raid ourselves.

A couple of times we jumped in feet first and it paid off. Other times we blundered in, totally in the dark, and it showed.

I didn't actually mind. I was just grateful for the chance of action. After seven long months, that's all Pristina had boiled down to for me: a chance. I'd come to Kosovo to scratch an itch and I really hadn't. It was still there, arguably worse than ever. For half a year I'd been dressed like a commando but done little that warranted the title. I'd learned new skills in policing and diplomacy, as well as in waiting. Other than that, I couldn't say my first tour had been the success I had wished for.

At the end of those seven months, as we were packing to leave Kosovo, Steve McCulley asked me what my plans were.

'I think you're perfect officer material,' he added

'I'm not sure, Steve. I don't know how you stick it.'

He loved being a captain. He loved leading men, both in the field and in the office.

I told him I wanted to be a marine.

'You are a marine.'

'A *marine* marine. I want to get my hands dirty. I want to get on the front line. I want to make a difference.'

Steve assured me we had all made a difference. It just wasn't through action in the field, as I had hoped.

'I'll tell you what I really want, Steve, and that is try to get into the SBS. But they won't let me out of signals.'

'Don't be so sure about that,' he said.

With Steve's help I drafted a new letter to the assignments board. If there's one person who knows his way around military procedure, it's Captain McCulley. We pointed out exactly why the board had no choice but to release me from signals. Under his guidance, I also put in for the SBS aptitude test. By the time we were ready to leave Pristina I had my answers.

Yes, and yes.

Thanks, Kosovo, you've been great. But now it's time for some real work.

CHAPTER FOUR

ARE YOUR FEET DRY?

We flew into Glasgow, and the glamour didn't stop there. Everyone involved in Kosovo was awarded a campaign medal during a big old ceremony at Arbroath. Watching Remembrance Day parades with Granddad, we'd see all these old boys and young lads with their various colours pinned to their lapels. Now *I* had one. The colour of the ribbon denotes the tour, and for Kosovo the colours were blue and white. I have to admit, wearing it on my blues – my parade uniform – gave me more of a boost than I had expected it to. I was proud, actually.

I just wished I could have done more to earn it.

I still couldn't get over that sense of a missed opportunity in Pristina. My desire to serve on the front line was getting greater, not less. Wherever I went after 45 Commando I just wanted to be in the thick of it – although getting away from Scotland had its appeal as well. The SBS seemed the best of all worlds. While we were being global policemen in Kosovo they were running around actually fighting. They were storming buildings, creeping up on targets and slitting throats. And they were based down south, at Poole, in Dorset.

It's fair to say that of the UK Special Forces, the SAS – the Special Air Service Regiment – is the most famous. The boys from Hereford, as they're known, are the ones that get the public talking. They've been involved in some high-profile operations over the years, and been the subject of plenty of films.

The roots of both services go back to the Second World War. For a long time the SBS – which for a time was known as the Special Boat Squadron – existed in the shadows. Their motto used to be 'Not by strength but by guile', and they prided themselves on remaining unknown. Apart from James Bond and Paddy (later Lord) Ashdown, not many people are known to have served in it.

Traditionally, Hereford tends to attract the army boys whereas the SBS has proved more popular with marines, so to me it seemed logical to go with the flow. Operationally, both forces are very similar. If anything, the SBS has the greater range because while it is trained in all the land-based fighting that the SAS covers, including parachute jumps and helicopter assaults, it also has submarine and water-based utility. As specialists go, they are more all-rounders.

Like everything else in the military, you don't just apply to get into the SBS. You have to attend an aptitude course to see if you are a strong enough candidate for the actual selection process. And so, in April 2001, I found myself in Poole, preparing for the worst week of my life.

Again.

It's impressive, really, how you think you can't be pushed any further, can't be made to feel any smaller, and then the military finds an extra gear. Of course, it was punishing physically. There were upper-body tests, mobility assessments and a hell of a lot of running around. There was also an emphasis on the mental side. You need to be able to digest information and produce results quickly, so they were throwing stuff at us.

Learning curves don't get much steeper. It wouldn't be a boat service without a load of water work. We were given rudimentary instructions and diving gear, then literally thrown in at the deep end with diving gear. No allowance was made for those of us who had never done it before; indeed, the instructors actually preferred it if you hadn't. That way they could chart how quickly you could adapt to a new challenge. For days afterwards I had blisters on my hands from canoeing, an infection from diving in dirty, muddy water, and dizziness from swimming a length and a half of an Olympic-size pool underwater. Did I mention the instructors were bastards?

Psychologically, nothing I've ever done in training prepared me for the final exercise. It's called a combat fitness test and at its core was an 8-mile (13-kilometre) run carrying 55 pounds (25 kilos) of kit plus a weapon. It's a standard Marines test with a couple of twists. Number one, the time you're given to accomplish it is reduced. Number two, not everyone is allowed to finish.

We were about to set off when the instructor said, 'You have to run full speed until one person drops out. If no one drops out you are all disqualified.'

It's evil. There is no other word.

We set off, and obviously there was more pressure because no one wants to be the one dropping back. You also don't want to set off at a stupid pace that you can't maintain. Somewhere in the middle there's a speed that you can manage that others can't. It only needs one person to be having a bad day.

The problem, however, is that everyone else is thinking the same thing. You've got twenty other men, all equally skilled, equally fit and equally motivated. The speed of the pack got faster and faster, and even though running was my speciality I felt the old legs beginning to wobble. If someone didn't give up soon I had a genuine fear it could be me.

For nearly two kilometres we kept the pace up, and then finally it happened. A lad who had actually been quite strong all week and had been pacing in the centre of the group suddenly just swore and disappeared behind us as though he'd been sucked out of the back of a plane. I can only imagine how gutting it felt for him, but to be honest I didn't care. The second he vanished the rest of us virtually ground to a halt. We all needed a breather whether we cared to admit it or not.

It was horrible willing someone else to fail. It went against all the camaraderie that we'd built up over our careers in the forces. Still, rather him than me. Of the thirty people who started the week, I was one of twenty who passed.

'Congratulations, Marine,' the trainer said. 'You'll get a letter but we would like to invite you to start selection with us in summer.'

Plainly I should have snatched his hand off. The sooner I started selection the sooner I'd qualify for the SBS. But here was the thing. The course was about nine months long. That meant another nine months without front-line action. I don't know why it was so important to me to get out there but the longer I went without doing it the more obsessed I became. I don't know if it came from growing up with male family who were all operational: Dad, doing his bit in the Met, Granddad in the Second World War, Harry. At some level, did I want to take my place alongside them in the family annals? Whatever the reason, I knew my chances of seeing action would be greatly increased if I joined the SBS. But after three years in the Marines without achieving what I'd wanted to do, I was in too much of a hurry to wait any longer. Imagine training to be a lion tamer and in three years you never got to see a lion. No more delays. I decided to defer my selection and go back to the ranks.

I just hope I don't regret it . . .

* * *

No one has a crystal ball. Deferring my selection for the SBS was a huge call, and I hoped it was the right one. I thought of those lads who'd served eight or nine years in Arbroath without seeing action – then quit before we moved into Kosovo. You have to get the big decisions right. Time would tell whether I had.

When I'd put in my request to leave 45 Commando I'd asked for a posting on general duties in the south. For about two minutes I got what I wanted.

40 Commando is based near Taunton, Somerset. Like RM Condor, the base was split into two, one half accommodation, the other working areas. There the similarities ended. The camp itself is much smaller, but Taunton is a metropolis compared with Arbroath. Coming from another market town, Guildford, I felt more comfortable there than I had up in the Highland wilderness.

I joined Charlie Company as a basic marine, but found there was a basic respect for me from the lads of equal rank and even above because this was my second draft and they knew I'd been operational with 45 Commando. I didn't tell them how empty it had left me. Or that the experience was the reason why I had decided to leave HQ and go on general duties. Maybe I should have done. On my first day the company sergeant-major said, 'We're going to promote you to corporal.'

I couldn't believe it. They didn't even know me. It would mean more responsibility and more money, but it also meant going on another bloody course first. How on earth was I going to tell them I wasn't interested? Who turns down a promotion on their first day?

'I'm sorry, Sergeant-Major, I've just turned down SBS selection because I wanted to work, so I have to turn this down as well.'

Actually, he was relieved, impressed even. He was old school, and believed you should put in six or seven years before you got rewarded. How can you tell others what to do if you haven't done it yourself?

It was my second big decision in as many weeks. I regretted it almost instantly. We'd just got our orders for the next few months: mountain training.

So I was going on a course after all, with less pay, less responsibility and in the country that warm weather forgot. Scotland (again).

Nice one, Rob.

It got worse. When we reached the Isle of Skye I realised we weren't even the main event. The Brigade Reconnaissance Force was up there training and they needed something to hunt. We were the 'something'. In fact, it was a lot of fun. Towards the end the sergeant-major told five of us – me, Pete Howe and three others – that there were three lance-corporal positions coming up. We'd all shown leadership qualities up on the mountain, would we like to undertake an extra task for one of the posts?

God, another decision.

I've always loved being tested. The five of us did an extra afternoon's work and I was one of those selected, on merit this time. It would be a £10-a-day pay rise, which I thought was a fortune, and best of all it was a local promotion. I wouldn't have to go on any courses and it was only in effect while I served with 40 Commando. Perfect, then.

* * *

Because it is an arm of the Royal Navy, a lot of people assume that the Marines are sea-based. In three years of being qualified I'd done Arctic training, mountain training, even jungle training, but I hadn't been on water once. Now, in the summer of 2001, that was about to change.

Part of the country's military readiness is its Amphibious Ready Group (ARG). At any time there is a Royal Navy warship touring the seas, packed to the gills with artillery and a strike force-capable unit. In August 2001 the ship was the flagship of the Royal Navy, the amphibious assault ship HMS *Ocean*, and the unit was 40 Commando. We were the R1 of the water.

There's plenty of repetition in the military. I had not expected how much. My first role as a lance corporal was to join the advance party for the company's roll-out. So, just as I had been in the signals, I was sent out to prepare the ground.

HMS *Ocean* was massive: 203 metres long, 35 metres wide, with a top speed of 18 knots (21 kph). She carried 18 helicopters, 40 vehicles, and had a crew of 285 plus 180 Fleet Air Arm or RAF personnel. Crucially for us, however, she had capacity for an armed force of 830 Royal Marines. It was my job, along with other corporals, to get on board early to work out where the hell everyone was going to go.

The permanent Royal Navy crew is in charge of the actual running of the ship. We're not responsible for piloting the thing or manning the guns, loading the missiles or protecting the ship. The Navy has all that covered. We're there purely to be ferried from A to B and to be the meanest bastards we can be on arrival. That's not to say we didn't have a role to play if the ship came under attack. Before the unit arrived I had to be on top of all security protocols and all safety procedures.

The group's first destination was Portugal. For departure the entire company lined the deck, in uniform, standing to. Once we were at sea the training started. To a large extent it was as though we were on land. The PT drills, the artillery training, the strategy meetings, they could all have taken place anywhere. The only difference was having to familiarise yourself with your station if the ship came under attack.

The cabins were as small as you may imagine. Everyone had a bunk and a locker and that was about it. I shared with a bunch of great lads. Marines mingle effortlessly and it didn't take long for me, Sibsy, Briggsy and another lad called Rob to hit it off. (Rob was fairly studious, and in fact later became a teacher.)

I could feel the change in the temperature the further south we sailed. When we arrived in Lisbon at the end of August it was like mid-July back home. For the ship's arrival in port we once again took our stations around the deck. The display is as much a show of strength as an impressive sight. It also let the locals know exactly what they were in for.

As it turned out, there was no strategic purpose to our stopover in Lisbon. We were there purely for rest and recreation (R&R), and when that had ended we sailed down to Gibraltar, then eastwards to Cyprus.

Training of British forces in Cyprus has been going on for years, for the island is perfectly equipped for what we needed to do. Exercise 1 was pure ARG. We were split into sections and, under emergency conditions, ordered to board helicopters and storm the target beach in a full-on aerial assault. We were only firing blanks, but it was exhilarating. Not just for me: C Company was alive. The amount of kinetic energy, the sheer volume of bodies and the display of hardware took me straight back to books I had read about military history. It didn't matter who we went up against. You could not imagine our being bested by any force on earth.

After the pure amphibious work we relocated from the ship to Camp Bloodhound in the south of the island. We weren't the only ones there. An American contingent had been attached to the ARG for the duration of the exercises. Before we did anything we had to erect our own tents, and after that the training didn't let up, with much of it focused on team versus team. Again, the hardware, the energy, the aggression and firepower, they were all up there. It was as much fun as you can have with blanks. Only the ridiculous heat put any negatives on the day. At a time when half the island was still in swimwear, we were bogged down in armour and kit weighing 30 pounds (13.5 kilos).

The temperatures didn't drop just because it was now September. A few days after our arrival at Bloodhound we were in the middle of an exercise when suddenly it was stopped. No explanation, no clue, just one simple order: 'Back to camp.' It was the middle of the day, we were roasting, and any break in work is happily received. Still, there was something odd about the way it happened. Marine training is relentless. It stops for nothing. Something was definitely up. I just didn't know what.

We made our way back to our tents sharpish. No one knew what was happening. There were no mobile phones or television. Crucially, no intel from above, either, although we were put on standby. It was clear we were responding to some unknown event.

After what seemed an age one of the American sergeants came into the camp. He summoned all the US contingent and led them into one of the makeshift buildings. The rumours flying around ranged from the bizarre to the ridiculous. None of them, though, was as unimaginable as the truth. The Americans were shell-shocked afterwards as they told us what had happened. Two passenger jets had been flown into New York's Twin Towers. It was Tuesday, 11 September 2001.

* * *

When British troops were sent into Kosovo, the mood in Arbroath had been one of eager anticipation. If there was going to be a rumble, we wanted to be the ones bringing the noise. But as details about what would come to be called 9/11 gradually seeped down to us, we couldn't afford to be so gung-ho. Thousands of people had died. We couldn't forget that. It wasn't right to get excited so quickly. Especially with some of our American colleagues having relatives and friends in the Big Apple. At that stage no one knew who was dead and who was alive.

More importantly, what opponent could we fight? In Kosovo the enemy was clear. This time there wasn't a foreign agency claiming responsibility. When it did emerge that the terrorist attack had been the work of al-Qaeda, we were none the wiser. Osama bin Laden, the group's leader, was apparently a native of Saudi Arabia. We couldn't go to war against the Saudis, could we? – given Britain's long alliance with the country.

There followed a stagnant pause during which everything kind of stopped. For forty-eight hours we didn't train, we didn't march, we just sat on our beds and surmised. What, we wondered, were the officers doing inside those buildings all day? What were the options they were discussing? I hated being kept in the dark. For the first time since April I found myself missing the signals branch. If I was still on comms I'd be in that room with the officers, and would know exactly what was being said, what plans were in the pipeline. On paper I had more responsibility and rank than ever before, yet I was getting all my gen. on a need-to-know basis, just like everyone else. And I fucking hated it. Had I cocked up by leaving that branch? Was it another decision I'd got wrong?

The only thing that kept me sane was knowing that if we were mobilised I was better served as a general-duties player. But 'if' can be a big word.

After two or three days word began to circulate that Afghanistan might be a potential target. Why, it wasn't clear. Suddenly everything I'd read about that hellish country came flooding back.

'Anybody that goes into Afghanistan is going to have a fight on his hands.'

'Yeah,' Other Rob said. 'These are not people to be underestimated.'

'But you know what?' Briggsy said, 'I still hope it's us.'

No one disagreed.

You could have cut the atmosphere in the camp with a bayonet. We were desperate to be called upon. Surely it was only a matter of time. We were on HMS *Ocean*, the R1 of the Navy, we were just a ride through the Suez Canal away from the perceived enemy and we were primed to the *n*th degree to go. We had helicopters, weapons, ammunition, we were fresh, we were keen and we were near by. What more could the politicians and strategists back home need?

As the list of New York's civilian casualties piled up the talk in the newspapers grew more aggressive. There was definitely going to be a response. Our news supply was second-hand at best – actual papers took a week to reach us – but as reports filtered through of ships heading out to the Arabian Sea I started to feel just a little nervous. *Oh my God, this is actually real. We're going to get the call.* I couldn't help smiling.

This is going to be our war.

Finally, the metaphorical white smoke emerged from the officers' building. They had a plan. It was time to move out.

This is it, I thought. Adrenalin levels were already sky high. There was a chance they were about to tip over the edge.

Then we got the order. We were returning to HMS *Ocean*. But we weren't heading to Afghanistan. We were going to Oman.

To train.

* * *

It was Kosovo all over again. What part of R1 was someone out there not understanding? Were they telling me there was a better-equipped, more highly trained force on the doorstep than ours? It didn't matter that I was in a unit of more than 600 people. When you keep getting overlooked for what's rightfully yours it's hard not to take it personally.

We were soon shocked out of our disappointment. The route to Oman was via the Suez Canal. Generally this was a safe passage. However messy Britain's relationship with Egypt had been historically, fully armed helicopter carriers weren't generally considered targets. But, a few weeks earlier, nor had Manhattan skyscrapers.

As we approached Port Said the command was for full-alert battle-readiness. The ship's crew all had their stations. Each part of the ship was split between sailors and their fixed-gun positions augmented by us with general-purpose machine guns (GPMG). There was a weapon primed every ten yards, the full 360 degrees. Orders were clear: fire on anything that comes near this damn ship.

The fact we were on red alert tells you that the officers had concerns. If there was a specific threat it was kept from us. Most the lads were okay with that. I was doing my nut wishing I could be party to the intel. We were about to steer slowly through Egyptian waters and I didn't honestly know whether they'd played any role in the terrorist attacks. We were completely in the dark.

The Suez Canal is 120 miles (193 kilometres) long from top to bottom. Some of it runs through vast swaths of desert where you're lucky to see an animal, let alone a human. Elsewhere it's like rowing up the Seine: a narrow waterway through thriving urban areas. You can almost smell the people on the banks, they're that close.

The not knowing was the worst aspect. In the really narrow parts of the canal a kid could have lobbed a bottle and it might have hit us. The ship's that big. Imagine what an aggressor with a gun could do. For eight hours we didn't dare blink as we cut our way through.

The wider sections had their own difficulties. With nothing to see but orange land and blue sky it's harder to keep your energy up. I was begging for just a farmer to go by on his tractor simply to break up the monotony. I'm proud that no one let their guard down. Marines sleep when they're allowed to, not before. Only when we hit the deeper waters of the Red Sea were we were allowed to take a step back. As the coastline disappeared our machine guns became less useful. Anything that occurred now could be handled by the ship's own defences.

We arrived at Muscat, the capital of Oman, without incident and disembarked. Again we stayed in tents we erected ourselves, this time in a fairly ad-hoc camp. Bloodhound it was not. We were miles from anywhere, cut off from everything. Whatever was happening post-9/11 it was happening with us still in the dark. The mood, as a result, was a mixture of sombre reflection and agitation. We were a strike force without anything to strike. Whatever the brass had lined up for us would have to be exceptional to make up for the disappointment of missing out on front-line service.

We were in Oman for a planned six-week programme. The first part was not dissimilar to the jungle training in Belize. We were working with tanks, and on desert navigation, tactics and warfare. Throw in the heat and new equipment and it was pretty intense. The second part was more role-play, teams versus teams. It was a big deal. The scale of the exercise was mind-blowing, which only made you more conscious of how it could be better deployed on the other side of the Gulf. But would that have been as profitable?

Midway through we were joined by a division of army boys. Now the war games kicked up a gear. They had their Challenger 2 tanks and all manner of state-of-the-art vehicles and artillery. We had our trenches in the ground, our rifles and GPMGs, our bergans and our wits.

Oh, and superior training, skill and expertise. The only problem was, we weren't allowed to use them. The point of exercise was to prove the unsurpassed capabilities of the hardware – for the simple reason that potential buyers from all over the Arab world were present as observers. If you're going to be cynical about it, we were one giant advert for an arms dealer – that dealer being the UK government. The last thing they wanted was the Royal Marines, defending against the army and their high-tech weapons and equipment, showing off their natural superiority.

Week after week we obliged. We played the role of baddies to a T. We conducted raids, we attacked, we tracked, we retreated, we did everything you'd expect from a crack military unit. It was all done at 100 per cent effort, the only way we knew how. Ultimately, though, we were overpowered – we had to be: it was in the script – and the army forces and their shiny toys won the day.

It was hard to stomach. There were so many ways I could see that we could overturn a result, had we been permitted. On more than one occasion I was tempted to say, 'Fuck it all.'

It turned out I was not alone.

On one particular afternoon we were all manning our trenches. The script said that an armoured vehicle – in this case, a Warrior infantry fighting vehicle – would approach our position, open fire and we'd roll on our bellies, feet in the air, like good dead pups. We knew the score, we'd done it so often. It never got any better.

On this occasion the Warrior roamed into sight. It 'opened fire' and we all 'died'. *Almost* all. When the dust settled and the infantrymen in the tank opened their hatch a lone figure leapt from the trenches. He ran screaming at the tank, pelting the emerging soldiers with rocks. They didn't know what hit them – although it was obviously rocks. In the end they started scurrying back inside the Warrior, but not before our man scrambled up the side, ripped open the turret hatch and chucked a large stone inside.

'Grenade!' he yelled. 'You're all fucking dead!'

It was crazy, it was brilliant, and for us 'dead' marines it was a lifesaver. There wasn't a man among us who believed for one minute that a battalion of army regulars could touch a crack marine unit. And this crazy man had proved it. For a week afterwards morale was through the roof. Yes, it may have cost a few billion pounds in lost sales, but what's money?

The man in question I'll call 'the Canadian', for obvious reasons. He's a good friend of mine and mad as a box of frogs. But you'd want him on your side, not against you, no question. In peacetime he's entertainment itself. In wartime he's an animal. Perfect, really. And just what you need to keep your spirits up when you realise you're never, ever, going to see action on the front line.

* * *

When we left the ship and went into the desert we lost connection with everything. The whole of the outside world didn't really apply to us any more, for it would have been a distraction. Mail came every couple of weeks, newspapers were a long time out of date, communications were only for the people giving orders. For us, being so far out of the loop was not getting any easier.

Post from home affected everyone, of course. When you're away for months on end your personal mail is considered a priority, especially if you have a girlfriend who is a bit hacked off because you keep disappearing. It wasn't a daily service by any means but every so often you'd see a corporal with a postbag in the most unlikely of places. In early November he found me.

I was lying with four other guys in a trench that it had taken us most the morning to dig. We were in full battle kit and sweating a pound of weight an hour, I swear. During a slight lull in proceedings before the next staged attack a shadow suddenly loomed over us.

Two of us got letters. Three didn't. Maybe next month it would be their turn. I took off my gloves and ripped open mine. I hoped it was from Deborah, my girlfriend, but unless she'd acquired an MOD franking machine I was out of luck.

The letter read simply: 'You have been chosen for SBS selection on 23 January 2002.'

Shit. Another decision.

* * *

You could be forgiven for thinking that I didn't want to join the Special Boat Service. I did. A lot. Doing so would all but guarantee front-line action. Just not soon enough. I looked at where I was. Geographically, that was obviously Oman, barely a paddle to Afghanistan, comparatively speaking. Situationally, our six-week war games/marketing exercise were drawing to a close. We had to go somewhere next. My money was on north-east – to Afghanistan, only 1,100 miles or so by air. It made sense. On 7 October the United States had launched Operation Enduring Freedom (OEF) in coalition with the UK. The mission was in response to the Taliban government's refusal to hand over to America Osama bin Laden and other al-Qaeda members. Its objective: to remove the Taliban government and destroy the terrorist cell. It was only a matter of time before NATO and world opinion joined them. The clock was ticking. As far as I could tell, 40 Commando was on the cusp of going into theatre.

Or was it? Was I jumping to conclusions? The intel around the camp hadn't changed. We were still being told nothing. The only information passed directly to us was that Christmas – our Christmas, that is – was cancelled.

I needed clarification. I spoke to my sergeant-major.

'Are we going into Afghanistan?'

'Honestly, I don't know.'

'But we're not going home for Christmas?'

'That could mean something or it could not. You know how it is.'

Opinions were divided 50/50. Everyone I spoke to said the opposite to the last guy. We were either skipping Christmas because we were setting sail for Afghanistan. Or we were skipping Christmas to wait and wait and wait, then go in in six months later as a peacekeeping force.

Not for the first time I cursed no longer being inside the inner sanctum of signals branch. What to do? I really wanted to get my hands dirty. If I tried out for the SBS I definitely would. But what if the ARG on board HMS *Ocean* entered the fray first?

With a heavy heart I accepted the invitation to SBS selection and informed my superior, the company sergeant-major. He was annoyed but wheels started turning almost at once, and two days later I was on a flight back to England. I wasn't alone. The Canadian and one other marine were going to selection as well. At least the journey home would be lively.

All three of us had suffered the same anguish. By the time we landed in London, though, we'd convinced ourselves that we'd done the right thing.

'There's no fucking way Charlie Company is going to Afghan,' the Canadian said.

The two of us agreed.

Ten days later I turned on the news. HMS *Ocean* was powering her way through the Arabian Sea.

Her destination? Afghanistan.

* * *

I've suffered a load of lonely Christmases during my time in the Marines, but 2001 was the worst. I was with my family, I was with my girlfriend, I was with my friends. But I wasn't where I wanted to be. C Company, 40 Commando, according to the news, had landed in Afghan and boldly secured Bagram airport for the coalition troops. Whichever way you looked at it, my Decision 4 had been a disaster. Not that anyone else realised.

'C Company?' Mum said. 'Isn't that who you used to work for? You're lucky not to be there.'

Thanks, Mum . . .

Had I just grown homesick? Is that what my decision had boiled down to? I rang the Canadian. He was as pissed off as me, although more phlegmatic.

'It was a shit decision, we all know it, move on. Just knuckle down for selection.'

Christmas was frustrating but the weeks afterwards were worse. Every day I'd run and run and run and then run some more. Up hills, down hills, carrying weights, not carrying weights. All of it on my own. It's not like I had a choice. Everyone I knew had a job. They had somewhere to be during the day. In the Marines you never train on your own. At least in the evenings I could go out and try to obliterate the brain cells that made had such crappy decisions.

* * *

Selection for the SBS is another set of tests. A lot of tests. You have the hills phase which is four weeks, two weeks of advanced weapons training and PT, six weeks in the jungle, then two weeks of counter-terrorism training, so about fourteen weeks before you get the chance to start SBS training proper. Deborah wasn't thrilled that I'd be away that long but at least, she said, 'You're only training.' It's not like I was in the line of fire.

Before my selection I hadn't met anyone who'd passed. As miserable as I was at not being operational, I was confident that I had what it took. If I could just get there.

I'd already got through the week of aptitude tests to get loaded on to selection. Apparently, there was another hurdle – surprise, surprise! – a horrific fortnight's physical beat-up down in Poole. We did so much running with backpacks that just putting a shirt on hurt the blisters on my spine. But only then was I allowed to progress.

Selection, finally. I'd sacrificed so much to get there it was actually an anti-climax to find just another Marines-style horror show at the end of it. We were up in the Brecon Beacons in South Wales, in an environment and climate that fitted the occasion. I'd like to say I that aced everything, but it was bloody hard. And indiscriminate. Crossing a river, men stronger than I were washed downstream because of the terrible conditions and weather. But I got through the first week, the second and the third. And I nearly made the fourth. Test week consists of six marches averaging 30 kilometres a day, with the last being 'Endurance'. This is a beast: a 68-kilometre run with a full 25 kilos of kit. Not for the faint of heart or, it turned out, the unfortunate. On day 1 I was doing okay, on target for time when suddenly I felt my ankle give. I was running so fast I didn't see the rabbit hole. As tough as my boots were, with the extra weight on my back, the ankle joint just gave out. It felt as though my foot had been ripped clean off.

Somehow I made it across the line within the time. That evening, though, my ankle was the size of a melon. Sick bay said you've not broken anything so in theory you could start this march. I went back to my dorm and pulled on my boots and 25-kilo pack. I could not even stand. The next morning I tried again. Even worse. Even if I were able to get to the start line, what were my chances of completing a run of something over forty miles miles?

Regretfully, I had to withdraw. Most of the other hopefuls were crushed on my behalf. Mike Jones, another marine and a great lad, was one of those who said, 'You have to try out for this again. Promise me, as soon as you're healed, you'll apply again. Don't give up on this.' Even so, one bastard, an army man, took a different view. 'They don't make marines like they used to,' he said. Luckily for him he said it out of my crutch's range.

I was put on a bus back to SBS HQ in Poole, reflecting en route on yet another disastrous decision. When I arrived at Poole the officer in charge admitted that he didn't know what to do with me.

'Can't I rejoin C Company?'

'They're over in Afghan.'

'I know.'

'Well, obviously not then.'

'Please?'

It didn't matter how I phrased it, linking up again with 40 Commando was not an option. I was left to stew for a couple of days, and then a junior officer handed me a letter with my new posting: HQ & Sigs.

Oh fuck . . .

* * *

Number 1, I was sick of signals. Number 2: UK Amphibious Group HQ is not even a Commando unit.

I really thought my decisions couldn't get any worse. HQ & Sigs is a support group for the big boys. Not only does it not do strikeforce operations, it mostly doesn't even want to. Most of their work is specialist and, although crucial, oh so dull. It includes specialist vehicle mechanics, specialist drivers, specialist logistics experts and, obviously, specialist signallers. There was one section, however, that didn't smack of suburbia, as it were.

Almost hidden beneath the HQ & Sigs umbrella is the Brigade Patrol Troop. Now this definitely is not dull. These guys are the surveillance and reconnaissance unit for the whole of 3 Commando Brigade. They sit somewhere between conventional forces and the SF guys, and they are never short of action. If I wasn't going to go mad at HQ & Sigs, I had to get on board.

When I turned up at Plymouth's Stonehouse Barracks, which, if I'm honest, is a fine place to turn up to (known as 'the spiritual home of the Royal Marines', the main buildings date from the eighteenth century), I came straight out with my request. The provost scratched his head. 'The next aptitude test for Patrol Troop is full. Ask me again later.'

That sounded positive.

'What shall I do in the meantime? Have you got anything similar?'

He smiled. Never a good sign.

'Just wait over there a minute, would you?'

Which turned out to be one of those special military minutes. Forty-eight hours later I found myself out on car park duty. *Specialist* car park duty, no doubt. From potential Special Forces recruit to running a car park, all in a matter of days. I'd say I was gutted, but it was worse than that. I found myself with a lot of spare time to think on guard duty, and I realised a truth that I had been ignoring for too long.

I'm in the wrong job.

And I didn't just mean that car park. The Marines had led to nothing but disappointment. I was conning myself if I thought that would ever change.

It did change, though – for the worse. A few weeks later they finally worked out what to do with me: stores, or 'logistics', as it was euphemistically termed. If you needed a pair of green combat trousers, I was the guy to come to. If you wanted fresh bedding, you would come and see me. I wanted Brigade Patrol Troop and I got blankets. It was so far from what I should have been doing over at Bagram Airbase in Afghanistan that it was funny.

A lot of people would have been offended by my attitude. Luckily for me, the guys running stores were diamonds. The 'Two Georges', as they were known. One of them, George, was the commando quartermaster –

in charge of issuing all stores. He had served in the Falklands campaign of 1982, and having done his time in the front line was perfectly happy to have it out of his system. The other, George, was in charge of the air defence troop. He had a similar story. Along with another guy, Mark Wicks – curiously, not 'George' – they ran my life.

They could have made it very difficult for me, but all three recognised my frustration. Yes, they all knew that it was my own stupid decisions that had got me there. They also knew that the Marines would treat you like a pawns on a chessboard if you let them. So they were out to buck that. If there was a single opportunity for me to get outside stores and go on a visit, drive a vehicle, fire some weapons, one of the Georges would always put me up for it. They could not have been more helpful to me. I think they recognised a kindred spirit, albeit one quite a few years behind them in the system.

Yet however great my bosses were, I couldn't escape the truth: I was a marine not being a marine. A fully trained potential killing machine doing the work of a sales assistant in Topshop. How had it all gone so wrong? Knowing that the answer was because of my own bloody decisions didn't help.

I was in such a fug that when George 1 came in one day with news I barely listened.

'Well,' he said, 'you got your wish.'

'What's that?'

'HQ & Sigs – we're going to Afghan.'

I think he expected a few cartwheels, or the like. Honestly, though, I didn't have it in me. By rights I should have been in Afghanistan already. I should have been fighting my way through Bagram. I should have been getting my hands dirty. Not going over to work in a glorified clothes shop.

'That's great, George,' I said. 'I can't wait.'

'I thought you'd be pleased.'

I was. So pleased that later that night I posted my application to join the Metropolitan Police.

Decision No. 5.

CHAPTER FIVE

BE CAREFUL WHAT YOU WISH FOR

Y ou can blame my dad.

I wasn't fulfilled in the Marines and he knew it. The only part of being at Stonehouse I couldn't fault was the social life. Plymouth is an amazing place for young people to let their hair down, even when it's cut to within an inch of its life. I had some great friends there like Mike Jones, good marines, solid people. Away from the nightlife they all seemed to be having more fun than me. All my life Dad's been the one who's stopped me walking away from a challenge. So when he said, 'Maybe you need a change of career,' I knew it wasn't me being weak.

'Doing what though? I don't want to go back to motor engineering.'

'What about the Met? I think you'll find it's a lot more hands-on than what you're doing.'

And so I started the process, which is almost as laborious as trying to get into the Marines. It would take time. This was the start of 2002. I'd have eighteen months' notice to work out first, so nothing was going to happen immediately. It was just a relief to set the wheels in motion.

Some of my mates questioned my decision, obviously, and not only the ones down in Plymouth.

I sound a right miserable sod sometimes. I don't think I am. That's how run down the lack of opportunities had made me feel. I just wanted to do what I'd trained for. And if the Marines wouldn't let me, then I needed to make things happen for myself.

* * *

The problem with contemporary books about Afghanistan is that they're instantly out of date. Everything I read about the country aboard HMS *Ocean* seemed like old Pathé newsreels by the time it was announced that HQ & Sigs were heading out there. Things were changing daily. Everything had escalated. Whatever we were going over to do had the potential to be incredibly noisy, as they say in the military.

The Taliban, their rule over the country ended by the US invasion, were hiding in the southern mountains. The plan was to send a brigade of mountain troops as a show of force, not only to prove that we had the numbers, but to demonstrate how quickly they could be deployed in-country.

When 45 Commando had mobilised for Kosovo in 2000, we'd had four months to prepare. This time we had two weeks. Telling Deborah was awkward.

'How long are you going for?'

'I don't know.'

'And I'm just supposed to sit here and wait?'

She was mad as hell, but she said, 'At least you'll only be in the stores. You won't be in danger.'

And that was the problem.

A brigade's deployment is a big deal. But being busy can't hide being bored. Even in the maelstrom of activity George 1 recognised I was going out of my mind.

'I've got a little job for you,' he said.

Vehicles are an essential part of modern warfare. We had dozens of Land Rovers in Plymouth ready to go. They were all what's known as WMIKs (Weapons Mounted Installation Kit) – in other words, they carried enough weaponry to take on a small army. Which is why we needed to get them up to the RAF's Brize Norton airbase in Oxfordshire asap.

A bunch of us from stores left Plymouth at six o'clock in the morning. It was a cold February morning in 2002, and there we were, wearing goggles, driving roofless vehicles designed for desert operation. I can't say we looked anything other than ridiculous. At Brize Norton we were told to prep the WMIKs for travel. That means dropping tyre pressures, disconnecting radio and batteries, basically hours of work.

Then a guy said, 'Have you got your gear?'

'Yes.'

'Okay, then, get on the plane.'

That was it. I was going to Afghanistan.

Everything happened so quickly it was insane. There were a dozen of us on the plane, us drivers and others from elsewhere in the unit. We didn't know each other or our mission. Or even our route. We must have changed planes five times, all the same rigmarole. Get the vehicles, move the vehicles, get yourself on board. And we are not talking British Airways business class. Twenty-six hours later, on our third stop – which we worked out was Pakistan; we weren't told – we were separated from the Land Rovers and put on a Russian plane. At the time, Aeroflot's safety record for civilian transport was among the worst in the world. This wasn't civilian transport.

All of the crew were smoking. Everything was tied together with rope. And I swear where you peed, this hole in the main fuselage, went straight out into the ether. What did it matter, though? I and my eleven colleagues were just equipment being moved from A to B, no different from the Land Rovers. Comfort was never a consideration.

Nor was information. We weren't told anything. When we landed again I asked where we were. I got one word.

'Kabul.'

'Is this our final destination?'

'Wait over there.'

That was it. No explanation. It was pitch dark. Apart from a few runway lights and the glow of a building I assumed to be air traffic control, the only other thing I could see was the Russian plane. Ten minutes after dropping us off it left again. Almost immediately another aircraft landed and taxied to a stop. Its back doors opened and we were told to board.

Now this was a proper warplane and, judging by the amount of Brylcreem and the number of moustaches and guns, very obviously an American one. The mood among the US troops already on board was exactly as you see in the movies. Loud, brash, gung-ho. We took off again and when, after about an hour, we landed it was like a scene from *Good Morning, Vietnam*. No creeping into an airport this time. Wheels touched down, the aircraft taxied for a few minutes, braked to a halt, then the party started. The huge tailgates opened, a fierce red light came on and out of speakers that must have been 3 feet tall they started playing Elvis Presley's 'A Little Less Conversation' at full volume. It was surreal. A proper American touchdown. The whole presentation was only ruined by the sight of a dozen totally green Royal Marines, forty hours into serious sleep deprivation, staggering bleary-eyed out into the darkness.

Talk about making an entrance. But no sooner had we disembarked than the tailgates closed, the plane taxied away and the bunch of us from Plymouth were left, once again, alone and scratching our heads.

I sat on my bergan, looked up at the stars and thought, *What the hell has just happened?*

* * *

We sat on the end of the runway for hours. As exhausted as I was I couldn't sleep. No one did. We didn't talk, either. We had become zombies.

I've never seen such darkness. No light pollution at all. I knew we were on a runway because that was where we had landed, but beyond that, nothing. As morning began to break I could make out vast shapes in the distance. Mountains, in every direction I looked. Memories of the Soviet forces chasing their own tails across that landscape came flooding back. How did people even survive up there? It was cold on the runway. It had to be freezing up there.

Eventually we heard engines. From the other end of the runway headlights emerged from the gloom and three Land Rovers, identical to the ones in which we'd started our journey, pulled up. Driving one was George 2 from stores, the man in charge of the air defence troop.

'Welcome to Bagram,' he smiled.

We drove in silence pretty much in a straight line for a couple of miles until we arrived at a dusty field where a couple of olive-green military tents were waiting for us. I was surprised we didn't have to put them up. Using head torches, we claimed our own berths. There was no electricity, no utilities. It didn't matter. We only wanted to sleep.

What seemed like seconds later we were woken for breakfast. Stepping, blinking, out of the tent, I looked over was the runway we'd driven down. It was like an old war museum. The shells of burnt-out Russian planes, military and civilian, lined the runway, which was itself pockmarked with craters made by heavy artillery shells. Clearly the last invaders had come under serious fire as they fled the country. Decades later, nothing had been repaired or replaced.

To the east of the runway some aircraft hangars were still intact, and had been claimed by the forces of the various nationalities *in situ*. The Americans had one, we had one and a few other European countries were in the process of renovating their own. They were in the process of building their own little camps.

The role of an advance party hasn't changed much since Roman times. Back then the vanguard would arrive and start erecting tents for the legionnaires. Two thousand years later that's exactly what we were ordered to do in a large field next to one already claimed by the Yanks. Each tent was large enough to sleep a dozen men and leave them room to live, work and administrate themselves. Behind us came the engineers to wire in generators for electricity. In four days we erected sixty of the bastard things, which in conditions at home would have proved tiring. In Bagram it was torture.

The swing in temperature from middle of the night to middle

of the day was like opening a fridge, then an oven. We all started the fatigues with a warm jacket. By eight there were layers coming off. By nine we were pretty much naked. Of sixty tents I'd say that fifty plus were put up by men wearing little more than pants and a rifle. It was hard, hard work but at least we were only working with canvas and tent pegs. Around our field there was a team of engineers constructing a wall out of 'Hesco bastion' – 3-foot-square wire-mesh and hessian cages built up like a Lego wall, which are then filled with aggregate as protection against explosions and small-arms fire. The Americans had already established a quarry just off site. All day long a convoy of trucks went to and fro, filling the Hesco cubes with earth and rocks. By the time the lads were finished our tents were no longer inside a field. We were in a fortress with bombproof walls 12 foot high and 3 foot thick. In the neighbouring fields the Americans had built the same.

Occupying a foreign country, you really do start from scratch. While we were building our little slice of Britain there were engineers constructing a hospital, offices, shops – anything you would find in an average town. In a few days the masses would descend. Bagram needed to be ready to cope with anything.

Punishing and monotonous as the work was, I enjoyed being in a small group, rather than just one of the hordes gearing up to arrive. I liked seeing the nuts and bolts of the operation. Watching this incredible place being built from the ground up was eye-opening. By contrast, being kept out of the loop in Oman had nearly driven me mad.

The main runway ran along one side of the fortress and on the other side was a road that had been named Disney Drive, which linked everything up. You didn't veer off the road if you could help it, for nother relic of the Russian invasion was the huge number of landmines all around the area. Our field had supposedly been cleared before we'd set up the tents, but that didn't stop me finding something suspicious on day 1.

'Er, guys,' I said, 'I've got a situation here.'

I had been hammering a peg into the ground when it hit something metallic just under the surface. Everyone dropped what they were doing and ran over. They all said the same thing.

'Don't move.'

The good thing about being in the advance party is that there's always a bomb squad around. Two guys came running over, boxes of tools and blast suits with them. They cleared the earth from the device next to my hand, then had a poke around. I'm kneeling there in my Y-fronts thinking, *This is not how I want to go.*

'It's okay,' one of them said. 'It's dormant. It's been there too long.'

We found a good dozen more before we'd finished, all of them equally dud. But, as the bomb squad guy said, 'We've cleared hundreds of live ones. This area's riddled with them. You can't take any chances.'

Every country has its own way of doing things. The Norwegian approach to clearing a minefield was unlike anything I'd ever seen before. I watched one morning as a soldier pulled on a bomb suit and then was helped into what looked like weird clown shoes. They were made of plastic, and huge. That wasn't the weird part. While he stood there another soldier inflated his shoes with an air pump and sent him out with his mine detector into a known minefield. It's ingenious, really. Fully inflated his shoes were so wide and flat, like airbeds, that his weight, and thus the pressure from each steps, was spread over a large area. A landmines is usually detonated by pressure when a person steps on it or a vehicle drives over it, although there are other trigger mechanisms. When the Norwegian team did find something, they would detonate it from a safe distance and move on. As bizarre as this method looked it was incredibly efficient. Compared to the British, who are trained to inch along with metal detectors, the Norwegian soldiers cleared that field in record time.

As I said, all cultures have their own ways of clearing explosives, as I was to find out. When we weren't building at Bagram, my little advance party took our turn on guard duty. I remember one of the first of these stints, when. I was in the tower looking out over the airfield. The Norwegians were clearing a field which no one from the coalition forces had been in before. On the other side of the field there was a farmer ploughing his land with a donkey. Suddenly there's this big explosion. My radio crackles into life. Alarms start going off. The whole camp thinks we're under attack. All around me I can see men and women scrambling to stand to, weapons ready. I'm the only one who can see that not only are we not under attack, but that all the Norwegians are fine – which can't be said for the three-legged donkey over in the farmer's field.

I managed to get the message across to HQ and then I watched, mesmerised, as the farmer, who had been at the plough being drawn by the donkey, brushed himself down then pulled out a pistol and shot the badly injured animal. Then he walked over to another field, got hold of another donkey, hitched it to the plough and continued to work as though nothing had happened. I guess it's what you're used to.

The farmer's laissez-faire approach was understandable, heroic even. He'd lived among landmines for most his life. His kids' behaviour, on the other hand, was a bit harder to swallow.

On my first night-time watch I was back in the same tower. I could see over the same farm plus two or three others further away. Even with the camp's generators we kept electric light to a minimum at night. It didn't matter. My night-vision goggles (NVGs) allowed me to see as far and as clearly in pitch black as I would be able to at midday. It was clear that the locals didn't know this.

I was scanning the area and I noticed activity at the first farm. I saw a teenage boy, aged about sixteen or seventeen, and watched as he walked round to the field where the sheep and goats were kept. He went in, selected a goat, then walked it back the way he had come, towards the farmhouse. Then he tied it to a tree, pulled his trousers down and started having his way with the creature.

Just when you think you've seen everything . . . That is not something they teach you in PDT. It was gross, but I couldn't stop watching. I thought at first the boy might be an exhibitionist, but I could tell that he had no idea we were watching. He couldn't see us, why should we be able to see him? I'd like to report that was a one-off. In truth, every time I stood on night duty I'd see at least one young man and one (arguably) lucky animal.

When I wasn't playing Peeping Tom on the locals there was training to be done. I'd try to get my run out of the way in the early morning, because by midday the heat would begin to takes its toll. We would go for firing practice on the range the Americans had built at the end of Disney Drive, and there was a certain amount of interaction with local Afghans, most of who seemed to be trying to sell us ancient military kit, including weapons, that the Russians had left behind when they pulled out in 1989.

'Fun' was a good word for those early days at Bagram. The real work started when the manpower began to arrive. The air defence troops sent their advance party who made up the majority of the guard force. Then the Brigade Reconnaissance Force (BRF) started to arrive, the troop in charge of surveillance and reconnaissance – the troop I wanted to join. The motor transport people flew in, then many of the signallers. They all had a lot of equipment, but the one thing they all had in common was that they needed more – and that meant returning to my day job with George 1. Instead of handing out blankets, however, we were supplying body armour and weapons, but knowing you won't be using any of it yourself is a bit soul-destroying.

But I had a plan. Half a plan, at least. One of the last groups to arrive was 45 Commando, but it was them I most looked forward to seeing. They had their own camp near to ours, and because I still knew a lot of the Arbroath lads I started hanging out there as much as possible. Part of the reason was socialising. The rest was tactical: if there was any chance of networking my way out of the store room to do anything in the field, anything at all, then I needed to take it.

It had worked in Kosovo. *Why not here?*

As it turned out, it was a few mates I had in the BRF who proved the most helpful. One of their sub-units, the Tactical Air Control Parties, were light on manpower. It's a specialist job, like most from HQ & Sigs, and highly prestigious. The TACPs are the people who go into theatre, establish where an enemy threat is located, then direct an air assault to that precise spot. A TAC Party comprises an officer – the main man, whose job is close air support (CAS) – and two signallers. It's quite a sexy job and, depending on the scenario, can be very dangerous. In this case, given where they were being sent, it was decided the TACPs needed protection, so each three-man team was bolstered by another two bodies. We didn't need to be specialist, we didn't need to know about signals. Our basic requirement was to be able to protect the talent and carry extra supplies and ammunition (although the fact that I did have a signals background didn't hurt).

Each mission was to last for ten to twelve days, so getting George 1 to sign off on me disappearing for nearly a fortnight was my biggest hurdle. But he knew that I was desperate to get out in the field, to see real action, and he wasn't going to be the one to hold me back.

'Cheers, George,' I said, 'I owe you.'

'Yes, you do.'

The irony wasn't lost on me that of all the crap decisions I'd made, the best opportunity looked like being the one decision that I hadn't taken.

* * *

I was genuinely excited at being involved. Even the thought of the journey was getting the adrenalin going. All the helicopter training in the world cannot prepare you for the thrill of actually boarding a CH-47 Chinook for the first time in anger. It's such an iconic military symbol. Its huge size, the twin rotors, the way the tailgate just drops down so you walk up the wide ramp at the back, the fact that it's been around since the 1960s, its incredible top speed of 170 knots (nearly 200 mph/320 kph) – it's the stuff of legend.

I wasn't the only one excited. In the run-up to the mission the ground crew started ripping everything out of the Chinooks. It looked like they were searching for something. In reality, they were cutting out all excess weight. Because Bagram itself was already 1,500 metres above sea level, by the time we got into the mountains we'd be so high and the air so thin that the choppers would have to work harder to maintain lift. Hence stripping out anything that wasn't mission critical. Who needs seats anyway?

I thought I'd be flying with just my group, led by a CAS officer called Phil Guy. The more planning that went into these Long-Range Reconnaissance Patrols (LRRPs, pronounced 'lurps') the more those plans started to change. Our revised mission orders were to fly out, dominate an area, comb it for Taliban and, if successful, take them down. You can't dominate with five people. In fact, given the hostility of the enemy and the terrain, it had been decided to send larger groups – or 'multiples' – into each site. We'd have snipers, surveillance experts, mountain leaders, you name it, the full works. Each Chinook would carry a dozen men. On occasion five multiples would mobilise together. If this mob couldn't locate and destroy a group of enemy fighters, then nobody could.

When the Chinook took off for the first time I was smiling like a kid. One of the usual TACP guys caught me.

'I wouldn't look so happy if I were you.'

'Why?'

He gestured to the cockpit.

'Female pilot.'

Then he pulled a worried face and went back to talking to his mate.

I wasn't the only person who heard him and, men being men, we shared a moment of joking about the pilot's handbag getting caught on the clutch, whether she'd be able to park, that sort of crap. Totally out of order. In one respect, though, it turned out we weren't far wrong. The female pilot *couldn't* park. But then, no one would have been able to.

We'd been flying for a couple of hours when the Chinook slowed and came into the hover, and Phil Guy said, 'It's too steep to land. We're blade-sailing in.'

Everyone else knew what this meant. I got a rough idea when the giant back doors started to winch down. The temperature might have been over 300 degrees on the ground but the wind that came howling in was Arctic. When I caught my breath I could see what the plan was. The tail ramp was lowered until it protruded by about 3.5 metres. Once it was fully extended like a drawbridge the pilot inched us towards the ridgeline until she got a touch. Phil gave the ramp a stamp then waved his arm.

'Move out.'

One by one everyone checked that their equipment was tight on their backs, cocked their weapons in case of a hostile reception the other side, then ran down this temporary airborne ramp onto the waiting mountain edge. No one thought once about the 3000-metre drop on either side of the 3 x 4-metre ramp. In fact, the guy who'd mocked the 'woman driver' was first off. He was a total wind-up merchant. He had absolute confidence in his pilot. And by then, so had everyone else.

Phil's biggest concern was whether Taliban forces were near by. A dozen men scurrying down a ramp, one at a time, would be easy targets, like picking off fish in a barrel. The most irresistible target, though, was the Chinook itself. As soon as the lads hit terra firma they went into full cover mode, scanning everywhere for potential threats. One single shot fired and the helicopter would pull up and away. You had better not be on the ramp when it did.

I admit I had to take a couple of breaths while I waited in the chopper to join them. I could see it in my mind: you're carrying so much weight, one gust of wind and you could be lifted right off. And that's if a sniper doesn't get you. *What the hell am I doing?* Suddenly it was my turn and the time for doubts was gone. 'Come on, Rob,' I said, 'let's do this,' and off I ran into thin air. It was incredible, really. The only thing more impressive was watching it from outside. That Chinook did not budge a millimetre. I've driven on bridges less stable than that ramp. The only mistake came from one of the lads, who shot off so quickly he slipped and his bergan went over the side. That was eerie, watching it plummet for seconds before it struck the mountainside hundreds of feet below. Moments earlier it had been attached to his arm.

When we were clear Phil gave the word and the chopper pulled forwards, the ramp still down. Every second counts when you're a potential target. As the door wound shut the CH-47 gave a little pirouette so the pilot could salute us all. I can assure you now that that is the first and last time I ever doubted the ability of a woman in the Marines. Anywhere, in fact. So I guess some good came out of my time in Afghan.

The area secured, Phil had a word with the guy who'd dropped his bergan and told him to go and fetch it. I was assigned to go with him. To this day I can't believe we did that. Two men walking and scrambling for a couple of hours on their own in hostile territory would be unheard of today.

It's a major principle of the Marines that you never leave a trace of where you've been. They beat it into you at Lympstone. They're normally talking about litter, So the idea of abandoning a whole bergan would make their heads spin. Whenever we leave anywhere we burn everything we're not carrying out. It's a huge element of fieldcraft.

We got down and up the mountain without incident. Whatever intelligence had led us to this particular rockface, it was out of date. We marched every day and found no trace of Taliban. Returning to Bagram without a shot being fired was anticlimactic for everyone. For me, it was worse because I had to pick up my store duties. George 1 was sympathetic, but he did say, 'Be careful what you wish for.'

I knew he'd had a hard time during the Falklands conflict. He'd told me stories of desperately trying to dig a hole in the mountainside to escape the fire from the Argentinian snipers picking off his friends. It had changed him, he knew that. But he also knew you can't tell a testosterone-filled young man not to be excited about getting his first real taste of action.

* * *

I thought my next release with the TACP had more potential. The American forces active in Tora Bora – a Taliban stronghold in a complex of caves to the east, close to the border with Pakistan – had suffered casualties. The men on the ground couldn't get to them. You never leave a man behind, alive, wounded or dead, so choppers were scrambled to collect the bodies. It's frightening how quickly it all came together. One minute I was in the store, the next I was suited up and piling into the back of one of seven idling Chinooks. We were in the air before the rear doors were even up. It was that kind of mission.

Near the target area the Chinooks split up. From what I could see from the window and make out from the radio chatter, we were all surveying different points of the danger zone, scanning for Taliban threats. The noise of seven Chinooks is deafening. Anyone on the ground not intimidated into fleeing is either brave or stupid. Or on a suicide mission – a very real possibility in that region. We all put down at vantage points above the stranded Americans and secured the area. Down below the emergency boys – US Special Forces sent in to rescue or recover the casualties – were in and out in minutes. Job done.

Two missions, no shots fired, lethal or otherwise.

Maybe next time . . .

My enthusiasm levels never dropped. The patrols were all potentially extremely dangerous. I always believed that the next mission would be the one. Five or six sorties in, however, the closest we had come to enemy weapons was by accident.

A patrol had ventured into a village to question the locals through interpreters. The rest of us formed a security cordon around the village.

'No, no, no one bad here,' a village elder was saying. 'The Taliban have never been here.'

While he was talking one of the lads leant against a wall for a breather. There was a crash and the next thing we knew he was on his back in a pile of rubble – surrounded by high-end machine guns. The building was a massive ammunitions cache, and obviously everyone in that village would have known this. Not that the elder was giving anything away.

'I don't know how they got there. The Taliban never come here.'

Yeah, yeah, yeah.

You learn never to take what the locals say at face value. So when in another village an Afghan said, 'You might want to check that cave

in the mountain because the Russians used to use it,' we immediately
thought it would be either a red herring or a trap. Phil led us up, on
full red alert. We took the cave from several directions at once – and
unearthed the largest haul of explosives ever found in the country.
Tons of the stuff. Much of it was Russian, but there was a lot more
that had been stockpiled more recently. We called in the bomb boys
and they detonated the lot, taking down much of the mountain in
the process.

Yet despite one false lead after another, you could never drop your
guard. Just because we weren't being shot at, there were plenty of other
patrols suffering casualties and losses. The threat was definitely there –
just never 'there' there. I lost count of the times we arrived at a scene to
find clear evidence of Taliban activity but no bodies. They were either
very lucky, or very clever.

Two months and half a dozen missions in, my most exciting
contribution had been coordinating a landing site with the supply
helicopter so we could get refills of water. As the highest level of
infantrymen, marines are trained to carry more weight than other
troops, and in a mountain patrol most of that weight will be water.
Even Green Berets can't carry enough for a fortnight, though, so every
four days fresh packs would be despatched. Because I was part of the
Tactical Air Control Party, nine times out of ten I was the guy managing
the resupply. We'd mark out a secure landing area, the chopper would
touch down for however many seconds it took to chuck out the food
and drink, then it would bounce back up and away.

It's important that every man is responsible for his own supplies.
We carried enough meals for five days. Each one is in a silver-foil
packet that you heat in boiling water then rip open and hold as you
eat the contents. It sounds basic, but the food itself was okay.

Not dropping our standards ran through everything. Even up a
mountain thousands of miles from home we were all expected to be as
fastidious as ever, from how we ran our camp to how we administrated
ourselves. That meant proper areas for toilets that could cope with up
to fifty people, proper positions dug into the earth to sleep in – and of

course perfectly smooth faces. Because of the need not to waste water we didn't wash, we cleaned our teeth without toothpaste, but what we never skimped on was shaving. There was a practical application, however. The threat of a chemical attack was very real. We all carried gas masks, and these seal a lot more efficiently if they're not having to be fitted over a beard. So going unshaven was a practical concern, although it was clearly not one shared by the Americans, who proudly wore their moustaches and designer stubble and thought they looked the dogs' bollocks.

Not everyone agreed with them. One day we were working our way around a series of villages to the east of a wadi – a dried-up riverbed. Being lower than ground level the wadi gave us natural cover in which to sleep. This was a big mission, five Chinooks' worth of personnel lined up along the bed. The routine stays the same: sentries through the night and a full company 'stand to' with weapons primed first thing in the morning and last thing at night, the two most likely times to be attacked. Anyone not on radio duties will take up his position, ready to respond to any threat. We must have done this fifty or sixty times in one place or another. Not once did we see a soul – except this time.

A sentry spotted the threat first. Walking towards us was a group of six young Afghan men, all armed. I could see at least two AK-47s and recognised other variants. These boys were not messing around.

So why were they so exposed, and in broad daylight?

My first instinct is that they're a distraction. Is some greater threat creeping up on us from behind? But the sentries on that side shake their heads.

Nothing.

So what are these fuckers doing?

This is it, I'm thinking, *action stations.*

Card Alpha was operational. The ROE were clear. We couldn't fire a lethal shot unless attacked. The decision Phil Guy and the other officers had to make was, at what point did a threat become an attack? For all we knew these Afghans were weighed down with bomb vests.

If they got close enough they could decimate us without firing a shot.

What the hell are they doing?

I can feel the tension in the wadi. Everyone's at 100 per cent readiness. Phil's radioing in for advice – for clarification on Card Alpha. Then someone calls out, 'Captain – look at their guns.'

Anyone near a pair of bins grabbed them.

What the . . . ?

Sticking out of the muzzle of every one of the Afghans' rifles was a flower. Poppies, mainly. I wasn't buying it. It made no sense.

If this isn't a diversion, I don't know what is.

Phil summoned the interpreters. This is where those guys earn their money. They're not infantry-trained but they still have to get out into the front line.

In their own language they called out what I assume was 'What's your intention?'

The men stopped and waved and smiled. Then one called back, 'We've come to visit the brave British men.' And that's when I noticed they were all wearing makeup.

Phil gave the order and we spilled out of the wadi to surround them. They didn't look scared, or threatening. They actually looked happy. The chat among thems was gleeful, if anything. I asked an interpreter what they were saying. He looked almost tongue-tied.

'They're saying how pretty you all are with your lovely shaved faces!'

I've heard it all now, I thought. These men, of an obvious persuasion, had risked their lives to get a look at the famous clean-shaven marines. They were sick, they said, of staring at hairy Afghans and stubbly Yanks.

We're only human, so a bit of flattery earned them a cup of tea and a bite to eat from our foil ration bags. Then they skipped off as menacingly as they'd arrived.

* * *

My tour in Afghanistan was coming to an end. I'd arrived in February. It was now May. In one of the camps near by I'd chat to few of the Special Forces guys I'd met. They were seeing action every time they left camp. It was torturing me that the TACP kept having near misses.

'Maybe you'll get lucky next time,' one of them said. 'And we can come and tidy up for you.'

'Fuck you.'

Little did he know it, but our luck did change. Although not for everyone. A lot of our LRRPs were to the south of Kabul, to Gardez, to places of interest along the Pakistan border. For my final sortie we were in Khost, south-east of Gardez and close to the border. On this occasion the intel was solid. Massive recent Taliban activity, so another operation for fifty of us. But we didn't fly out immediately. There was a gap of several days while support vehicles made the journey by road. I knew what result that would bring: another missed opportunity. Even so, HQ had to get one right eventually. Didn't they?

Where we set up camp was barren desert. We parked the vehicles, dug trenches to sleep in and settled down for the evening. We were almost certainly a tad blasé by now. I was sitting on my bergan talking shit to the guy next to me. Others were sleeping, some were eating, some were playing cards.

And then some were shooting.

Out of nowhere the sound of repeated gunfire tore through the silence. The sentry was unleashing all barrels.

'Fuck, we're under attack!'

We're all dressed for action. Our weapons are within reach. We can be up and aiming the dangerous end of a rifle outwards in seconds. I did and so did everyone else around me.

And we were all too late.

In the distance was the smoking husk of a van. Next to it were the dismembered remains of an Afghan national. All around me were ten men high-fiving each other for a successful defence of the camp. And, more importantly, a successful kill.

That adrenalin spike you get when you think your life's in danger takes an age to subside. The more I heard how the sentry had spotted a van acting mysteriously and radioed the other sentries to stand to, the more I wished I'd been on look-out duty. The driver had stepped out of the van and lined up to shoot at the one sentry he could see. As he did, the sentry fired back. At the same moment ten BRF boys stood up from the trench. One of the guys had a UGL 23 – an underslung grenade launcher fitted beneath the barrel of his rifle – and scored a direct hit on the van. It and its passengers were destroyed on impact. The rest of the lads emptied a magazine each into the hostile.

Bloody typical, I thought. *Why wasn't I on sentry duty?*

And that was it. That was my Afghanistan. Thrilling at times, but ultimately unfulfilling. The government, more interested in the bigger picture, declared our mission a success and the order was given to pull out. If that mission had been to prove how quickly the brigade could deploy, how much intelligence it could gather and how few casualties it would suffer. then it had been a success. But on a personal level, it had offered more than it delivered.

Everyone left. One day 45 Commando were there. The next day they weren't. My camp emptied itself just as fast till the only marines still hanging around were those who'd arrived first. Every single tent we'd erected we now had to take down – and burn. Cheaper, it's said, than carrying them home – and the Marine code said we definitely couldn't leave them behind. And then, suddenly, we were done. I looked at the field. What had been a bustling community for four and a half months was an empty shell. A ghost town.

I didn't have high hopes for the journey home. We were put on a bus with no suspension to Kabul airport, about 60 kilometres due south. I could imagine that the bus's aircraft equivalent was already waiting for us. At the airport we sat in a tent, waiting for our flight. A large white jumbo jet landed, taxied to a halt and completely blocked our view. I couldn't believe it when we were told that it was there for us. It was an Icelandair passenger plane. Civilians would be on board. What the hell were they going to think of us?

I never found out. The stewardesses, on the other hand, could not have been lovelier. The food and the drink and the beautiful flight attendants just kept on coming. It was the happiest I'd been since I'd boarded that Chinook.

Just my luck, I thought, *if we get shot out of the sky before I've tasted everything.*

* * *

When we built the fire at Bagram, it wasn't just the tents that burned. I felt my love of the Marines die as well. It just hadn't lived up to my expectations. As I watched the flames I knew I'd done the right thing in applying for the Met. My girlfriend, Deborah, certainly thought so. No sooner was I back than we decided to take the step of moving in together. We both needed some commitment in our lives.

We all had a break. Back in Plymouth I started on some more courses, this time aimed at transitioning me from the military into civilian life. For the rest of the year my marine 'work' took a back seat. They knew I was leaving, I knew I was leaving. It was just a matter of counting down the days and trying to stay busy, which I managed to do successfully beyond Christmas and into the new year. And then one day I bumped into George 2. I hadn't seen him since Afghan.

'Are you coming with us?' he asked, as bullish as ever.

'Coming with you where?'

He pulled a face.

'Where?' he laughed. 'Iraq of course. We leave in two weeks.'

Ohhhhh shiiiiittt . . .

CHAPTER SIX

KOSOVO, AFGHANISTAN, IRAQ – AND PECKHAM

Towards the end of 2002 there were rumours that the UK was going to become involved in some sort of action in Iraq, a member of President Bush's 'Axis of Evil'. America was rattling its sabre, and we weren't usually far behind. I didn't think much of it. *Nothing to do with me*. And then I was asked to extend my service. It's like that line from *The Godfather III*: 'Just when I try to get out, they pull me back in.' No sooner had George 2 planted the seed than it was all I could think about. I could have said no but I didn't want to. Six months of sitting on my hands since returning from Afghanistan probably contributed. I was bored. The police didn't want me till June the following year. What else was I going to do?

It didn't take me long to land a job with my old logistics mates. None of the work sounded particularly sexy but I'd worry about changing that when I got to Iraq. So far my best results had come when I didn't plan them.

Next stop: telling Deborah.

I'd like to say I handled it well, but I suppose it was the beginning of the end of our relationship. In her eyes I'd pledged my life to her, and here I was sodding off for another six months on my own.

I kept saying, 'This won't stop me joining the police,' but I don't think she was in the mood to listen.

For some reason she didn't believe my interest in the Marines had ended. That this tour meant nothing . . .

* * *

Yet again I was in the advance party. Same story: get this vehicle to Brize Norton and jump on the plane with it. The only difference was that this time there were only three of us. Oh, and on this occasion they actually told me where we were heading: Kuwait City.

Like Bagram, the city was already overrun with American troops. Unlike Bagram, there was no evidence of the war Kuwait had been involved in more than a decade earlier. It was bustling, there were motorways, nice cars, there didn't seem to be any sign of conflict or poverty, just people going out about their business. Kuwait City was urbanised, functional, modern – the exact opposite of anything I had seen in Afghan.

Once again, our arrival saw us dumped on an airfield. This time there was a welcoming committee to chauffeur us to Camp Commando, just north of the city. The fact that I was travelling with an officer and a colour sergeant probably made a difference. The seniors in question were the Quartermaster and George 1, so I couldn't have been in better company. I was even upgraded to acting corporal to ensure I had similar privileges.

We were billeted in an air-conditioned American tent. Not only did I not have to erect it myself, there was electricity, little screened-off areas that served as separate rooms, even televisions. That was nothing, however, compared with the construction job going on west of the city in Camp Doha. The place was like a small town. There was a gym bigger than anything I'd seen back home, and even restaurants like Pizza Hut, McDonald's and KFC were being built for the incoming hordes. There was military hardware everywhere you looked, large armoured vehicles, everything on a massive scale. Even though our camp, Commando, was largely unpopulated, our little band of forty or so marines was still dwarfed by the hundreds of Yanks doing their advanced prep. When the troops did start to arrive, the UK forces would multiply in hundreds while the Americans grew in thousands.

It was very clear that this was going to be, once again, an American war. All the briefings were given by Americans. These were something else. In the UK a major or a lieutenant-colonel will shuffle amiably in front of a group of officers, NCOs and other ranks and run through the order of the day. The US equivalent was rather more showbiz. There was music, there were lights, and there was a general issuing a call to arms so passionate, so evangelical, that it would have had a pacifist reaching for a rifle. And they did this every time.

Despite the activity in the camp, there was actually an attempt at stealth. The Iraqis obviously knew that something was happening, but the intention was that they shouldn't know what. Not until it was too late. A lot of my days were spent travelling in unmarked cars with senior officers. My role was strictly that of security but I got to see everything they saw. There wasn't a possible location we didn't scout. For a while Babiyan Island, two miles from the border with Iraq, was considered as a jumping-off point for the invasion. Then we moved even closer. The plan was to establish hundreds of small camps along the border by pushing up mounds of sand with bulldozers to create a gun line. I saw it grow from conception to reality in a matter of days.

It was great being involved in the advance party. Seeing all the factors that led to the decisions. But knowing that HMS *Ocean* was on her way with 40 Commando, that 42 Commando would be flying in within days and that 45 were already training to support UKSF, I had that sinking feeling that, when the going got tough, I'd be nowhere near the action. Again.

It was time to get networking. My best chance was with the TACP I'd worked with in Bagram. The second those boys arrived I was pestering Phil Guy for a switch.

'Rob, I'm sorry, we're on maximum capacity this time. The whole brigade's here. There are no vacancies.'

'Okay, but I'm going to ask again.'

'I expect nothing else.'

It was the same story everywhere else, but I didn't let up. In the meantime, there was training and preparation. At this stage we all believed that Saddam Hussein, Iraq's oppressive leader, had access to chemical and nuclear weapons, so everyone had to be trained in specialist equipment to detect an attack. We were also put on a course of naps tablets – nerve agent pre-treatment pills designed to protect your nervous system in the event of a chemical attack. But that was only half the story. If you are exposed you still need to inject yourself with a pen that was now part of the kit, as were gas masks.

It was exciting, but it was only a matter of time before my real work in stores started. Shipments were arriving daily and once 3 Commando Brigade began to arrive those had to be distributed. I was assigning beds, weapons, medication, gas masks, boots, you name it, all from my little corner of Camp Commando. It was like a tiny British principality in the middle of the USA.

By the end of the February our guys were *in situ*. Training was slick. There was a real mood in the camp that D-Day was imminent. Then the word came that we were to stow all our personal belongings. This could only mean one thing: the greatest military operation since the Second World War was days away.

We waited and we waited and we waited. The first week of March came and went. By the time the second week had passed without incident I wasn't alone in thinking that, after all, nothing was going to happen. Obviously the powers that be had found some diplomatic solution instead.

And then, on 19 March, the order was given.

'We're going to war.'

* * *

'Shock and awe', they called it. The vast blanket bombing of Iraq's border posts and then Baghdad itself was so spectacular, so relentless, that the Iraqi forces had no time to regroup, recover or counter. The truth is, though, that people at home probably saw more of it on

TV than we did. What we did see and hear made everyone at Camp Commando desperate to get involved. *Everyone*.

The massive aerial bombardment was incredible. The sky lit up with the trails of cruise missiles. We were just on the edge of the desert, about ten miles south of the Iraqi border, and could see on the horizon to the north of us absolute fury raining down from the skies. For four or five hours, all I could hear were helicopters, fast jets, missiles – immense firepower flying overhead. We were sitting and waiting for the final word about when the troops were to get on the helicopters to follow the aerial bombardment in. I remember looking at the guys boarding the helicopter as part of the advance party, some of them my really close friends. I was gutted not to be joining them.

Phil Guy's TACP team were flying out to support 42 Commando .I desperately wanted to get involved. Again, I asked Phil if there was a chance he could squeeze me on to his mission. Again, the captain said, 'Not this time.'

On 21 March I watched as a flight of Sea Knight helicopters set off for their various landing zones – 'LZs'. I was proud of Phil and everyone else but, God, did I wish I was on board. They all disappeared into the distance and I went back to work. A few hours later I heard a commotion outside. I ran out and there in the distance, in the desert, I could just make out a ball of fire. Men were shouting, scrambling transport.

I stopped a junior marine. 'Is it one of ours?'

'We think so, Corporal.'

'Was it shot down?'

'Don't know.'

The base was in turmoil. How had Saddam's troops managed to get that near us? Patrols were despatched, defences engaged. In the meantime, first responders were reaching the crash site. When the news came on the radio my heart sank.

'Sea Knight CH-46 down – no survivors.'

Shit!

'Enemy fire not ruled out but unlikely.'

For the next forty-eight hours I carried on with my duties, delivering munitions to outposts in the desert, completely in the dark about the crash. That's the way of it. Then the intel started to seep out. It was only by checking in with the other Sea Knights that HQ worked out which chopper had gone down, and how. The report said it had been hindered by a sandstorm. There was a mechanical problem and the pilot couldn't land and so had been heading back when the aircraft hit difficulties. When it came down, all eight Royal Marines and four US troops were killed on impact, as were the crew. One of the marines was Captain Philip Guy.

I was gutted for him, for his family, his friends. He wasn't yet thirty, and had his whole life ahead of him. As did everyone else on board. I knew each and every Brit, plus the one South African affiliated to us. I'd worked with some of them at Stonehouse and had issued kit to the rest. We were all brothers. We all thought we'd be going home together. What happened to them seemed so horribly unfair.

And one fact didn't escape me. I had pleaded and cajoled to be active with TACP. I had begged Phil Guy to let me go with him. If he had said 'Yes', my name would be on that list of people whose next of kin were being contacted right then.

George 1's words had never sounded more relevant.

Be careful what you wish for.

* * *

All those US briefings had made me desperate to kick some ass, like the American ground troops already geed up for the big invasion,. Luckily, being in charge of ammunitions, I was at least going to move when my company did.

And we were moving.

The Americans were making a charge for Baghdad, in the centre of Iraq. The British were going for Basra, which is on the Shatt-al-Arab waterway, the confluence of the Tigris and Euprates rivers in the south. The military being the military, there was a race. The Brits were doing their best to get into Basra and secure it before Baghdad fell to the US forces. Which meant all of us – including stores – were going mobile.

Hundreds of troops piled into every vehicle we had and the column pushed out. My team had dozens of trucks loaded with supplies. For once I didn't get the dull job of driving one. Six marines were given quad bikes to scout ahead and provide security with the on-bike rocket launchers. I was one of them. Obviously, one of the thousands of courses I'd taken had covered quad bikes.

We drove up through the border. I'd been close to it many times and seen it every which way through binoculars. Crossing the demilitarised zone – about 500 metres of nothing between the two countries – was eerie. Then we hit Iraq soil and suddenly we were surrounded by friendly faces. Between the giant signs reading 'Welcome to Iraq' Royal Marines Police waved us all through. That's when it got really weird. Everywhere we looked, murals of Saddam Hussein covered the walls of buildings – and they'd all been defaced. The most polite ones had given him a clown's nose. Others showed him with different bits of genitalia added.

The journey through the border towns was eerie, slow and arduous. Eerie, because the towns were deserted. Slow, just in case lone Saddam supporters were lurking in the abandoned buildings. Arduous, because the weather was shit. If all you know about deserts is that they never have any rain, you may want to rethink that. It poured down water in biblical proportions. If you had been at all superstitious you might have thought that it was a sign that what we were doing was wrong. Sandstorms clogged our vision, rain-soaked sand clogged our wheels. Suddenly the quad bike, while highly mobile, was the one vehicle no one wanted to be on.

Luckily, no one was superstitious.

Driving through a desert is everything you'd imagine. That is, if you imagine sand for 360 degrees. The road was a single straight stretch of tarmac that disappeared into the horizon. Either side were deep irrigation ditches made of concrete. For miles at a time there was nothing to see or hear but ourselves.

We were several hours inside the country when the whole convoy stopped. I assumed it was the result of radio traffic that I wasn't privy to. Even above the noise of our idling engines, however, the reason was unmistakable.

Gunfire.

And close.

The men in the WMIKs were all standing to. The threat was real.

We waited for an hour, then the command to advance was given. Two miles further down the road we reached a small factory town. Buildings on all sides were burning. In the road and lying scattered elsewhere were the corpses of fallen Iraqis. Whatever we'd heard had been serious.

And we'd missed it all.

We were that close behind the first wave. Yet time after time, every time we reached the scene of a firefight the party was already over. Everywhere we arrived there were traces of 40 Commando's work. But that was as close as we got.

Our final destination was another factory town about twenty miles inside the border, some thirty miles south of Basra. It had already been cleared by 40 Commando and US forces – as I was to hear later in graphic detail from some of my friends in the company. Once we had secured the site and unloaded the equipment, those of us in logistics (i.e. stores) turned around and hightailed it back to Kuwait to fetch another shipment. That might have been terrifying if we hadn't just made the same journey. I knew the biggest threat to my safety on the way back was the weather. The first three days of my war were basically spent driving up and down that one road. After the seventh time I was willing an enemy to pop up just to keep me awake.

I decided that if the fight wouldn't come to me, then I would hunt the fight. Once we were established in a petro-chemical plant in the township I volunteered myself for absolutely everything outside the camp. If there were any convoys going into Basra then I would get on a convoy. If someone was needed to lead a company of guys into an area behind us, such as the troops providing security for the gun line,

I stuck up my hand. I'd been all over the area on my quad bike. There was no better tour guide.

On one such familiarisation patrol I was with a troop of marines ranging in rank from captain down to marine. The instructions were to patrol on foot and clear a local village. That doesn't mean kill everyone there: just make sure there are no undesirables hiding out among the locals. It's a show of force. Remembering the village elder in Afghanistan who'd lied through his teeth about the Taliban, I wasn't exactly confident of the results.

Because I had driven through the village a couple of times and knew the ground, I was asked to lead the troop up.

'With pleasure, sir.'

This is my time.

It was a night patrol. The invasion had seen the disappearance of the police force and all the security that had originally been in those areas, so naturally a vacuum occurred in which looting and retribution killings and other crimes were rife. Our senior guys in charge wanted to show the civilian population that, invaders or not, we could still protect the region. But the population had already taken matters into their own hands. A vigilante force was reputed to be in operation. They didn't know us and we didn't know them. So we needed to be alert.

We approached the town in traditional single file. From my daytime sorties I knew all the alleys and back routes. Working through these in stealth mode we spotted through our night-vision goggles a lot of people wandering around. People with guns.

Part of me was relieved.

At least it's not goats.

There were fifty of us, and I was confident that we could handle any threat. The pressing question was: did these people constitute a threat? Would Card Alpha be tested? Would we need to fire a lethal shot? Even as invaders in a hostile country, we had to be aware of the law.

Even if our enemy wasn't.

We were all trained for full-on combat. Coming up with a measure less extreme came less naturally. There was a moment when we weren't entirely sure what to do. In the end the patrol leader, a young captain, decided to give away our position to see what this group of people would do. Would they engage us? Would they be curious?

A Schermuly (usually pronounced 'schmooli'), named after its inventor, William Schermuly, is a hand-held flare that fires 1,000 metres up into the air, then comes down slowly on a parachute, lighting up some 300 square metres like a 1,000-watt firework. Firing one is a gamble. They call it 'recce by fire' because in illuminating your enemy you're giving away your own position. Sometimes there is no alternative, however. We launched three Schermulys over the locals. They didn't do anything. They just stood and watched, mouths open like kids on Bonfire Night. The captain was satisfied.

'Move forward.'

As a precaution, the Minimis (5.56mm squad machine guns) were moved to the front of the crocodile file. That aside, we tried to advance as non-threateningly as possible.

We were in a town square, with, to our left and right, two small tower blocks on either side. As we reached the square a drunk suddenly lunged out of nowhere. That was something we had definitely not been expecting in a Muslim country. He fell onto the bloke next to me. If he had done that today we'd assume he was a suicide bomber, but in 2003 that scourge was nothing like as common as it would become. As for the rest of the village, the armed men put their weapons down and came over to us, smiling, as if to say, 'We are not the enemy.' Our patrol was divided into three sections, and I was in the leading one, but we had only one interpreter with us and he was with the captain in the third section. With little or no understanding the locals' language we couldn't let our guard down completely, and so they probably found their country's great liberators stand-offish, at best.

Once the interpreter had joined us, we were directed to the police station, about a two-mile mile hike into town. By the time we arrived word had got round. People were gathered with their sick or injured children for the so-called saviours to heal. I was twenty-six years old and armed to the gills, yet strangers were bringing me their wounded kids. (*When I'm your best bet,* I thought, *you know you're in trouble.*) We were even given a baby that had been abandoned by its parents. It was very emotional, but also worrying. There were a lot of moral dilemmas for the young officer to ponder.

And I mean *a lot.* We were there two days in the end. He called in water and food and medical supplies and we responded like people, not soldiers. We didn't turn anyone away, even when we knew their injuries weren't caused by anything to do with the current fighting. Ultimately, I know there were people alive when we left who never would have made it if we hadn't shown up.

That didn't mean everyone wanted our help. I was brought one child who in my opinion had been stabbed, although the parents said otherwise. As I treated him a gang of older teens who'd been standing near by started to get twitchy. I didn't feel safe. The whole area was a tinderbox. Then one of the youths threw a stone. I don't know if he was expecting twenty-plus loaded rifles to be aimed at his head, but that's what he got. Whatever it may have looked like, we were first and foremost marines, not medics.

Knowing the village was suffering because of sanctions instigated by the West and war damage that had shattered the main water supply, it was impossible not to want to do as much as possible. But we were just tens of men. What they needed were hundreds. We were there as security, not engineers or builders or doctors. There would be other people coming after us. Or at least that's what we told the civilians – and ourselves.

After our two days in the village I took part in several other patrols before we pushed further ahead to Basra. Once there, I was surprised to see people going about their daily business more or less normally. I didn't encounter any hostility, although neither were the locals as friendly as they had been in the village to the south. My most vivid memory is of catching up with my mates from 40 Commando and hearing how they'd stormed the city. Under fire, and everything.

And here I was hoovering up the dregs a few days later.

For me, Iraq was a tour that promised so much, when the American command announced its mission concluded with the capture of Saddam Hussein I was actually glad. To have been so close to the action – such massive action – and yet still not to have taken any active part was the nudge I needed. When I considered that there were men in the Met who had fired their weapons – fired a lethal shot – more recently than I had, I knew once and for all that it was time to go. On my return to the UK I left the Royal Marines and, in 2004, began training with the Metropolitan Police.

* * *

You can knock on the door only so many times without being let in. It was time to stop knocking.

Within weeks on the new job I knew I'd done the right thing. I was still on probation, patrolling my patch in South London, on the famous Old Kent Road. I'm not saying it's one of the cheapest properties on the Monopoly board for a reason, but suddenly there was a radio alert warning of a high-speed chase in our area. Even as I listened I heard – then saw – a white BMW whizz past, closely followed by two black unmarked police cars. The BMW stopped just past us and a passenger jumped out of the back and started shooting at the police cars, which also stopped. The police shot him and then another guy jumped out of the BMW and they shot him as well. It all happened right before my eyes. I don't think I've ever seen anything more exciting.

I only got to roll out the yellow police tape, not deal with the bodies, but that sniff of action confirmed that not only was I on the right track, but that everything I wanted was right on my doorstep. Kosovo, Afghanistan, Iraq – and Peckham. Who is to say where the real war zone is?

Peckham police station should have had a revolving door. You were never more than a few minutes away from a crime. I thought my first arrest as a beat cop would really stay with me but it was so closely followed by my second and third and fourth that they all blur. Fun times, I have to say.

In your probation years you get moved around different divisions for ten weeks at a time. I loved that, as I thrive on variety. I even enjoyed my period as a school liaison officer. Loads of little kids lapping up your stories, what's not to like?

My favourite attachment, however, was to the rapid-response unit. The detective I was under could sniff criminality a mile away. For action, though, Bonfire Night takes some beating. We must have confiscated thousands of pounds' worth of, basically, gunpowder from kids intent on firing them anywhere but into the sky. Case in point: towards the end of the night we were called to the North Peckham Estate, then one of the most deprived areas in Europe, let alone the borough, and since demolished. As soon as we arrived something felt off. I could hear laughing from behind a car. Then suddenly this missile came zooming at us. If I hadn't dived to the ground I'd have lost an eye. By the time I looked up there were more fireworks coming at us, this time from all directions, like a barrage from heavy mortars. I managed to get back into the car but the bombardment continued.

This really was like Iraq.

The only downside with the job that I could see was the pervading attitude within the Met itself. As a commando you expect to be moved around like a pawn to wherever the danger is. As a police officer, it's as though the senior command want to protect you at the expense of the public. There were loads of scenarios where I felt I was in a position to apprehend a villain or put a stop to a situation, but my mentor officer would say, 'Hold back, wait for back-up.' Nine times out of ten the perpetrator would get away. On one occasion we came back from a foot patrol down Peckham High Street and I noticed that the backs of our tunics were layered in spit. How many people must have been gobbing on us I hate to imagine, but I was all up for going back out to find them. My guvnor said, 'No, it's not worth it.'

It bloody well was to me.

The worst occasion was when I was across the road from an

amusement arcade when I heard the radio chatter that a robbery was in progress in one of the slot-machine venues inside. It was broad daylight, and I looked through the window and confirmed it.

Over the radio I said, 'I've got eyes on the perp. Permission to apprehend?'

'That's a negative. We have information that he is armed.'

I looked again.

'No, I repeat no. There is no weapon. Permission to apprehend.'

'Stand down, MD665. That's an order.'

And so I watched as the guy filled a bag with cash then sauntered out into the sun. He walked towards me and actually winked as he went by. It was obviously not his first job. And he obviously knew how the system worked.

I'm not saying that this particular incident was the tipping point but so many little episodes like that began to fill my day that it wasn't long before I realised that I didn't respect the organisation. I respected the individual coppers I met, they all work bloody hard. But our hands were tied by unseen overlords who seemed more interested in PR than public safety.

Suddenly Card Alpha didn't seem quite so restrictive. In fact, it started to look damned appealing. So much so that when my Marines mates down in the West Country started telling me that they were gearing up for a proper go at Afghanistan I felt that tingle of excitement I'd had when Kosovo, Iraq and Bagram had been in the wind. I tried to ignore it but in the end I asked my guvnor if I could join the RMR – the Royal Marine Reserve. This works in the same way as the Army Reserves (formerly the Territorial Army): you keep your job – and your salary – and train in your own time, but can be called to serve when necessary. It's the best of both worlds and plenty of police have served in the reserve forces over the years.

The problem was, I was not yet a policeman. To qualify I needed to finish probation and get five years' service under my belt.

'But the war will be over by then,' I protested.

'I'm sorry, Constable, that's the way it works.'

The truth is, I didn't really want to go to Afghanistan. More than anything I just missed the physicality of my old life. I missed the camaraderie, the daily challenges, the knowledge that I was among the elite of my kind. I just missed being a marine.

Being told I couldn't be one for a few more years, not even as a volunteer, not even at weekends, triggered a response in me that I never expected.

I handed in my resignation from the police and returned to Lympstone.

* * *

I've made some crap decisions in my life, but this was not one of them.

I didn't mind the two-week refresher course at CTC. I didn't mind being busted down to the bottom rung again as a simple marine. I didn't mind being made to feel like a raw recruit with the OCD-level ironing and saluting. I didn't even mind that for my foreseeable future I'd just be doing courses again. My obsession with front-line action had passed. I was just happy being back where I belonged.

For the remainder of 2005 I was back with 40 Commando at Norton Manor, Taunton. I was happy to knuckle down with whatever they threw at me. What they actually threw at me was a promotion. The Marines being the Marines, however, you don't just 'get' a promotion, you have to pass a promotion course. And you can only go on that course if you've already been promoted. So in order to qualify as a corporal I first had to become lance-corporal – the rank I'd held in 40 Commando in Kosovo, seemingly a lifetime ago. Next stop an eleven-week Junior Command Course at CTC.

Even while I was on the course, I already had my eye on the programme after that. I'd tried and failed to get loaded onto the mountain leader course before Afghan. Now I had another chance. By the time it came round it was 2006 and I was in peak physical condition. I needed to be: it was a nine-month course. I could see no reason why I shouldn't pass. Unfortunately, my body had other ideas.

Week 5, and one of the tests was to carry a guy twice my size up Sennen Cove, a stone's throw from Land's End. All the way up I could feel my ankle and my calf – my old SBS tryout injury – screaming at me. I made it and was halfway through the eight-mile run back to our accommodation when my friend Noisy said, 'Rob, I don't know what's wrong but your right leg – it's about twice the size of your left one.'

It felt like it, too. I got hold of some painkillers and made it back to camp. I could barely breathe at the end, let alone run. The course leader took one look and said, 'We'd better get you back to Lympstone because there's something seriously wrong with your leg.' I was in too much pain to really follow what was going on. But I soon snapped awake when the base medic said, 'You've ruptured your calf – I'm afraid we'll have to remove you from the course.'

I was gutted, obviously. For the second time a frailty in my leg – the same frailty – had kept me from taking that next step up. A few years earlier I'd have felt like chucking the TV out the window with frustration. The new mature me found the bright side. Better to be thrown out after only five weeks. Imagine getting to eight months and failing. You'd be suicidal.

There was another positive, as well. Mountain leaders, by definition, are away most of the time. Again, I used to thrive on that. But towards the end of 2006 I met someone in Taunton who I wanted to stay home for. Her name was Carly, she had a lovely son called Sam, and being a local girl she knew all about the Marines and their constant disappearing act. For that reason she was more than a bit wary of getting involved with me. When injury ruled me out of the ML course I think she found me that bit more attractive a proposition.

It was mutual. I spent three months in rehab and most of that time I was plotting how best to stay in the Marines and yet stay local to Carly. Then I hit upon the answer: I'd do a physical-training instructor's course. It's one of the longest in the calendar and arguably the most important. PTIs are the guys who turn raw recruits into killing machines, civilians into commandos. Everything that follows begins with them.

Carly was delighted. We both were, and with extra reason. Our whirlwind romance had resulted in Carly becoming pregnant. Getting that news was a big moment – asking her to marry me a minute later was another one. Now, more than ever, I needed to be local.

We married in March 2007 and seven months later, in October, our son Will was born. Three months after that, in the new year, I finally started my course. I thought I knew what fitness was, but this took it up another level. Throw in middle-of-the-night feeds with Will and the forty-minute commute between CTC and our place in Taunton, and you'd have been pushed to find anyone in the UK at that time more in need of sleep.

The PT course has legendary status in the service just for how shit it treats the students. There are so many rules which, if broken, result in a physical beating from your trainers. It sounds horrific, and it is. It always has been and always will be.

I don't know who was happier when the course ended: I, for getting through it with all my teeth intact, or Carly, for knowing she had at least two years during which I wold be working on our doorstep.

Some of our friends were not so lucky, however. I came home one night to find Carly in tears. I immediately thought there was something wrong with Will or Sam but she said, 'No. It's Steve. Donna thinks he might die.'

Donna was one of her best friends, and Steve was a mountain of a man who'd got me through my recce leader's course. They were both good friends of ours. Steve was over in Afghan on one of the early Herrick operations (Operation Herrick was the codename for all British military operations in Afghanistan from 2002 until the end of military operations by UK forces in 2014). Word had just come back that he'd been caught in an ambush. The marines had gone out on patrol with the Afghan police. The two groups had split up, and then the Afghans had opened fire on the Brits. Steve was shot a number of times, and the rounds made a mess of his abdomen and everything below. Donna was right to be worried. We all were.

Steve survived and was shipped home for specialist care as soon as he was stable. When we went to visit him it was shocking. This giant, this pure physical presence, was barely a skeleton in the bed. His muscle mass had vanished. He looked a broken man.

You can't help thinking, *This is the reality of war.*

As the war in Afghan took hold Carly and I started to see more and more of our friends return from the front with limbs missing. That is if they returned at all. Some of the worst casualties were among the SF guys. When a war is on, the television news becomes a nightly ritual – you just want to keep up with what the boys are doing. I was watching the news one evening in summer 2007 when I suddenly froze. On the screen was a picture of a young man I knew very well, Corporal Mike Jones, one of the great guys I met at SBS training. Since then we'd patrolled together in Afghan and Iraq, and had both been based in Plymouth. Just a few months earlier we'd shared meals during junior-command training. He was, in short, a friend. And now he was on the news. I was too stunned to hear what the broadcaster was saying. I didn't need to. It was obvious.

Mike was the sixty-eighth British serviceman to fall since the country's involvement in the Afghan campaign began in 2001. He would not be the last.

Military towns can be very dark places when the troops are away. Carly had grown up with living in a suddenly much emptier town and the prospect of death or wounding, conditioned to it by friends of the family and neighbours. It's a unique situation. On the one hand, the troops and their families are conditioned to expect the worst. On the other, the worst is something they never get over.

More than ever, she was relieved that my job meant that I was not going anywhere. And, if I'm being honest, so was I.

* * *

As the newbie on the PTI staff I got all the glamour jobs, like making tea. It didn't bother me. I was no longer a potential victim for the trainers to pick on. I was one of those trainers.

Some of the other guys had been there for years. Pete Howe, who'd gone up for corporal with me back in the day, was a good mate (despite my pipping him to that promotion) – now that we were both on the same side of the pupil/teacher divide. Pete was actually the envy of the whole camp. Once in a blue moon – well, every three years, to be precise – the Special Forces Support Group (SFSG) recruits a leader from the PT branch. Pete was the next man up. No one knew exactly what he would be doing, but we all agreed it would involve action of the most violent and secretive kind.

Like all of us, Pete loved his sport. Among his many talents he was a terrific footballer. About a week before he was due to leave us he was playing in a five-a-side match, and managed to break a leg – audibly. I was in a building close to the pitch and actually heard the sickening sound of his leg snapping. A moment later the door behind me flew open and the PT sergeant-major, shot out.

'What the hell was that noise?'

Like me, he'd heard it inside the building.

'Pete Howe, sir,' I said. 'I think he's broken his leg.'

'Shit. He's meant to be going on draft next week.'

'I know,' I said, 'gutting. If you need a replacement I'm available.'

It was a joke. A flippant remark. I thought no more of it.

A couple of hours after the match I got a phone call from the PT sergeant-major, who said, 'Rob, will you come and see the "drafty"?' – the branch officer in charge of drafting. I made my way to his office. As soon as we'd finished saluting he said, 'Are you serious?'

'About what?'

'I need to know if you really think you could do this billet with the SFSG because they are going active very soon and they need a body.'

Christ.

'Well, I'm para-trained, I've served in Kosovo, Iraq, Afghan, I'm a corporal . . . ' I basically blurted out my whole CV.

'But are you interested?' he said. 'Are you up for it?'

I took a moment, and realised that, yes, yes I was.

'More than you will know, sir.'

'Excellent, Driscoll.

It all happened so fast. I was back in the staff room before I thought, *Carly is going to kill me.* And, indeed, she was distraught, claiming we had agreed that it was too dangerous. I couldn't disagree with her. But the second I was offered the chance I knew I'd been lying to myself about being 'over' wanting to see action.

* * *

Within two weeks I was packing my stuff at Lympstone and heading off to Wales and straight onto an advanced firing course. En route I couldn't help smiling.

Another decision I didn't make.

Another great, great result.

* * *

After a circuitous route around various Welsh bases I was delivered to the Brecon Beacons. I met the rest of the troop as they were midway through a firing package. I walked in and, after a couple of introductions, drew a weapon and was given a load of ammunition. We spent four weeks running around the ranges up there working on all the basic skills. I didn't learn anything new, but there was definitely more intensity (and more money). It was also more realistic.

The four weeks in the mountains took us up to Christmas and leave, which I spent at home. It was great to see Carly and the boys, obviously. Come the new year, however, I had to break it to her.

'I'm going away now with the Special Forces. I can't tell you where and I don't know when I'll be back.'

* * *

It had begun with a request from a foreign entity; specifically the government of another country. They wanted help training their troops to cope with insurgents. I suppose at some level they were willing to pay, an echo of the military-catalogue sales pitch to the Omanis all those years ago.

The mission was simple: train as many men as you can to as high a standard as you can. We were there for four months working to a four-week cycle, so that's four groups of men who passed through the system. It was . . . *interesting*.

Without mentioning specifics, I can say, as you can discover online, that both forces went out to Afghan as part of the so-called 'kill or capture' of high-value targets (HVTs). Accompanying them were the SFSG. HVTs rarely sleep without a small army around them.

Above them would be aircraft plus a Spectre – the legendary Lockheed AC-130 gunship, a heavily armed version of the C-130 Hercules developed for ground attack and close air support. Nothing would be left to chance. In fact, SF prefer a deck massively stacked in their favour.

Some of the equipment the SF guys had was out of this world, almost futuristic. And it made a lot of what you were doing seem unreal. For example, each man's weapon was equipped with a laser sight. These weren't what killed the targets – it's not *Star Wars* – but they might as well have done. Meanwhile, the aircraft overhead would be flying too high to be heard. But I imagine they could see everything from up there.

Invisible fire support from above, silencers, laser beams, infra-red goggles – it all sounds like a computer game. And I imagine that's exactly how it felt.

I imagine that, in action, all the SF and SFSGs could hear would be the dull, click-click-click-clicking sound of rounds travelling through the air. I imagine that they saw their targets fall they would never fully feel connected to the process, even when the voice in their headphones said, 'Target down'. They would feel almost detached from the outcome.

I imagine.

I learned more than I can reveal on duty with the SF. We were busy. Very busy. And I wanted to stay busy but mid-assignment I received my mail – even when you're operating undercover the postman finds you. I had been selected for a promotion course. Did I want to go through with it?

Promotion courses come round once a year. Other things come round even less frequently. Carly was pregnant with our second child. If I stayed with the SFSG I'd miss the birth. I admit the temptation to stay was huge. Thanks to one mistimed tackle I was finally enjoying the 'action' I'd trained for. The action I'd dreamed of. But I was a family man now. I had responsibilities. A promotion would bring in more money.

I returned home early in 2010. Ollie was born in April. But that was not the only good news. As soon as I finished my training, as soon as I made sergeant, I was offered the chance to join 42 Commando, which I took. No sooner had I arrived than I heard a familiar voice.

'Well, if it isn't Sergeant Driscoll.'

'Captain – I mean, *Major* McCulley. How are you doing, sir?'

The formalities lasted barely seconds. This was the man who had transformed my Kosovo experience and helped me to get out of 45 Commando. We were mates, it was great to see him. But that didn't mean business didn't come up over a cup of tea.

'Here's the thing, Rob. We're pushing out to Afghanistan as part of Herrick 14. I've got a vacancy for group leader. It's a fighting group. It's front line. It's going to get noisy. The question is: do you fancy it?'

We both knew the answer.

CHAPTER SEVEN

IT'S MY TRAINSET NOW

'I wouldn't get too excited, mate, we've pretty much won this war already.'

The speaker was a Para sergeant I'll call 'Frank'. He ran the Mulladad station in Afghanistan's notorious Helmand Province. Apart from a sun-cooked face he looked like shit. Six months in theatre will do that to a man.

'Yeah,' I laughed, 'like I'm going to trust the word of a para.'

Now it was Frank's turn to smile.

'Don't get me wrong, we've had a hellish tour. But we kicked Afghan ass. You *hats* can just put your feet up for six months.'

Paras call every other branch of the armed services 'hats'. They're fair like that.

The ribbing aside, he could tell I was disappointed. The news back home over the last six months had shown 3 Para having a torrid time all over the region. Now that they were being replaced by commandos it seemed that we'd missed the party again. My heart sank, if I'm honest. Half a year without my family, leading my own group of men in my own compound in Hell, and I was going to see fuck all action yet again. Just my luck.

'On the bright side,' Frank said, 'you'll have plenty of time to work on your tans.'

* * *

Steve McCulley wasn't the only person who asked me to join his company. I had four offers in total, all of them promising me action to some extent or another. There was no question of who I'd go with. Steve and I had history. I admired the way he worked and he'd also shown me great generosity in the past. And he was doing it again: he didn't want me to go out to Afghan as a foot soldier. He wanted me to be a leader of men.

Fighting-wise, 42 Commando consisted of four combat companies and one support company. Major McCulley commanded J(uliet) Company and its 120 men, soon to be bolstered to 170-plus for the forthcoming campaign. Traditionally, a company is divided into three troops, each with a commissioned troop commander in charge, but for operations in Afghanistan a new template was required. Three troops couldn't cover all the bases that needed manning, and so it was decided to create 'multiples' – smaller groups of men still led usually by a commissioned officer.

In 2010–11 OCs (officers commanding) were short on the ground and so 42 Commando HQ was forced to field-promote to fill the gaps. Steve had seven posts to fill and three young OCs, so each troop's sergeant was assigned to lead a multiple. That still left one vacancy, which is where I came in. It was a huge honour and a massive change in protocol because the military love a dense chain of command and here we all were reporting directly to the company commander – in other words, Steve. I was honoured to be one of them. I would get my own multiple of seventeen men and be given a checkpoint (CP) in Helmand to man and patrol from. Everything that happened in that area would become my responsibility. I couldn't wait to get going.

By the time I joined, 42 was already two months into Pre-Deployment Training. I caught the last half. That's when I met the lads. The three OC troop sergeants were Ollie Augustin, Lloyd – whom we called 'M'lord' – and Tom Phillips. The day-to-day sergeants usually reporting to them included a mate from Taunton – and unsung hero of Iraq – Al Blackman. Like me, he was late arriving, due to the death of his father. Then there was a guy I'll call 'H', plus Si Jones. But, together with me, everyone now had the same responsibilities. For the next seven months at least. To be fair to the three original OCs, they took the shakeup in delegation structure well. For two months of PDT we were blood brothers. I hoped it wouldn't become more literal.

I didn't know anyone apart from Steve and Al, but the CTC pumps out similar types of people. Pick anyone from the lads in our various multiples – Corporal Sibsy (formerly of 40 Commando), James Wright, Corporal Bruce, Kaz, Lance Corporal Snake, Matt, Duncs, Adz, Corporal Mac – and they were all but identical. Less chalk and cheese than cheese and cheese, and all on very similar wavelengths. Within an afternoon we found enough similarities to know we were cut from the same cloth.

The PDT was intense, with a huge amount of training on weapons. There were non-lethal combat options to go through, arrest techniques, a substantial improvised explosive device (IED) awareness package, plus guidance on leading men in action. Although, as the trainers said, nothing would prepare us like experience.

In rare moments of downtime we discussed everything. We covered the worst-case scenarios, the potential outcomes, the tedium of peacetime. All of it came under the microscope when I, Al and the others were shooting the breeze. We didn't see danger. We only saw potential – potential excitement, potential fun, potential victory.

We finally flew out to Afghanistan in April as part of Operation Herrick 14. According to military papers, that lasted from May to October 2011. Prior to us, Herricks 1 to 13 had run from 2002 onwards. The early manifestations had been nominal. UK forces in-country were barely in the hundreds at that stage. In 2006 everything escalated. Or, in civilian terms, 'worsened'. Task Force Helmand was deployed in its thousands. The Afghan threat would, at any cost, be neutralised. As big as I felt at being given my own command, I knew how small I was in the larger picture.

Part of our PDT down in Plymouth had been ideological: 42 Commando wasn't going into Afghan to storm the castle. We were despatched to win hearts and minds by helping to restore order to the war-ravaged country. We were going to help build schools, hospitals and roads, and prepare the Afghan police and military to take full responsibility for national security. We were even going to catalogue the citizens. All of it worthy but dull.

Luckily, we also had to prepare for a determined and motivated enemy.

It probably won't surprise anyone by now to learn that I was part of the advance party. I don't think I've ever gone anywhere for the military without the back-up being hundreds of miles behind. The six other multiple leaders travelled with me. We landed at Camp Bastion, a large British Army airbase in the north of Helmand Province, and were shown to a big tent all to ourselves. Me, Al, Si, Ollie, H, M'lord and Phil. At that point it still felt like a holiday with mates.

I had seen Camp Bastion during my first tour in Afghanistan, when it had consisted of just some sea containers with nothing much else around it. Not very substantial at all. By 2011 it had become a small city. It was bustling. The fenced perimeter ran for 20 miles, and all the essentials were within it. The buildings were mainly steel containers, enclosed by high-grade fencing. The canteen was massive, probably the size of two football pitches, and staffed by Americans and British. When we arrived hundreds and hundreds of people were there being fed, and, even though everyone had a time slot during which to eat, none of us was on the sort of time restriction I'd known back at CTC.

We spent a week at Bastion. Part of this was for acclimatisation to the weather – even in March temperatures were in the mid-20s. The rest our time there was focused training. Transported everywhere in buses, we did a whirlwind 'round-robin' sample of almost everything. Two hours of first aid, two hours of counter-IED training, two hours' firing, two hours of cultural studies, two hours of absorbing specific information on the area we were going into.

The rest of the time was our own, and in its own way was probably just as valuable. More often than not when we weren't working we'd catch a few rays. We played football or volleyball, or in quieter times shared stories about our lives and the people close to us. These were small things, personal things, but they brought us all closer.

You might be forgiven for thinking that we were on some weird Club 18–30 holiday. There were daily reminders that we weren't. On day 2 at Bastion we were leaving the canteen when an alarm sounded. A few seconds later there was an explosion at the far end of the camp. The local insurgents – the Taliban, in other words – had launched a primitive IED over the fence, but not from just outside the perimeter. We saw similar attacks a couple of times a day. Insurgents would launch a home-made missile from up to ten miles away. Yes, their margin of error was huge, but so was Camp Bastion. With 15,000 men and women around the camp, the odds of connecting with one or two were high, and we did take casualties during my time there.

According to our daily briefings, IEDs were the insurgency's greatest and most terrifying weapon. I already knew that. We had living proof among us.

Our second day was full of surprises. It was also when I spotted three blokes in rags. Men with long hair, tattered uniforms, almost ghostly in manner. They barely looked human.

I asked one of the Bastion staff who they were.

He laughed.

'They, my friend, are you in six months' time.'

It took a lot of staring for us to realise that he was right. That once upon a time these wraith-like zombies had been fresh-faced arrivals like us. I spotted another lot the following day. They walked with their shoulders proudly back, but otherwise there was little to remind observers that they were from the military. Their uniforms were unrecognisably battered and stained. It was only by asking that I learned they were from

3 Para, escorting a colleague injured by an IED mine to the hospital. We were there to relieve 3 Para. I had to grab a word.

Even as the paras were talking to us they seemed disconnected. They were malnourished, exhausted and, despite their best efforts to hide it, all any of them wanted was to go home. They were sick of the lack of sleep, they were sick of trying to help people who wouldn't help themselves, and they were sick of IEDs claiming their mates.

For anyone in their right minds that meeting should have sounded an alarm. For me and my companions it was just another intriguing feature of the war. The safe option would have been to wangle things so as to stay billeted at Camp Bastion till September. But no one wanted the safe option. We wanted to get out into the field.

When the day came to roll out we were bouncing like dogs at a back door. We collected our weapons from the armoury and drew a day's worth of ammunition and grenades, just enough to protect us and our transport on the journey. It was nice to have someone else give me this rather than my handing it to them. Then, armed to the teeth, we boarded a Chinook and, leaving the comfort and security of Camp Bastion below, flew into the unknown.

* * *

The area of Helmand we were going into was just under 10 miles to the north, and slightly to the west, of the region's capital, Lashkar Gah. In Persian the name means 'army barracks', which was fitting because, since the 2002 overthrow of the Taliban, American and International Security Assistance Force (ISAF) troops – including British forces – had been living there in serious numbers. Now it was our turn.

Our forward operating base (FOB) – Bastion's little brother, if you like – was a camp called Shazaad. Picture a dartboard with Shazaad as the bullseye. As a result it's the safest place in the area. Set around the camp, moving outwards in waves, are a number of checkpoints (CPs), each manned by a multiple of men. Going north along one of three major supply routes (MSR) we named 'Dorset', at about the 'treble 20' mark, was a CP called Mulladad. That, for the next half a

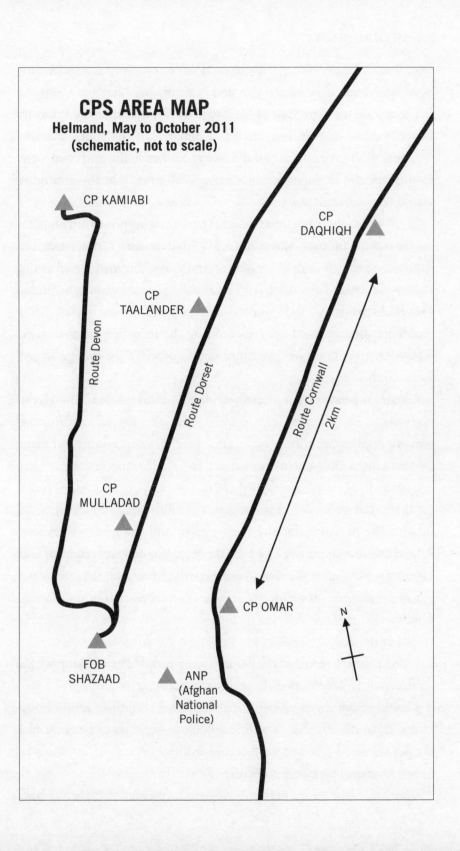

CPS AREA MAP
Helmand, May to October 2011
(schematic, not to scale)

CP KAMIABI

CP DAQHIQH

CP TAALANDER

Route Devon

Route Dorset

Route Cornwall

2km

CP MULLADAD

CP OMAR

N

FOB SHAZAAD

ANP
(Afghan
National
Police)

year, was to be my home. North, at 'double top', was Taalander, run by M'lord, with Si Jones as his second in command (2ic) and Corporal Bruce among his men. East of Mulladad was Al Blackman's CP Omar. North-west of us was Sergeant H's Kamiabi. To the south-west we had Tom Phillips and Corporal Sibsy at Shiran. Ollie and Sam were further afield. On paper it made sense to all of us. On the ground it would be a different story.

We flew at night. Afghanistan doesn't have amazing power distribution so the entire journey was completed in darkness. Only when we approached the grounds of an old factory – now commandeered as the FOB – did we find any light. And what it illuminated was Afghanistan. Proper Afghanistan, the country that you see on the news. Mud buildings, dirt tracks, roads criss-crossing the irrigation-canal system, local Afghans going about their business oblivious to the foreign armed forces in their midst.

Closer to home, what I saw was dozens more ghosts. They were everywhere in Shazaad. The sunken eyes, the ingrained dirt, the remains of once-proudly ironed uniforms, they were a sight, and there we were, bouncing down from the CH-47, all shiny and new. Our bags were in better shape than these men were. A part of me was sad for them, but there were advantages to the filth because they blended in with the brown walls, the brown earth and the dirty vehicles. I, Al and the rest stood out like sore thumbs. We may as well have had targets on our backs. We were staying overnight and so, the second we reached our tents, I took off my uniform and stamped it into the mud. Ollie caught me.

'What the hell?'

'I don't want to look any different to the people I'm working with.'

'Fair point.' Ten minutes later we were all doing it.

I could rough up my desert kit all I liked, I could put mud on my face and hands, but there was one difference between us newbies and the occupants of Shazaad we just couldn't hide.

Just how *hyper* we were to be there.

That only got more extreme when the Shazaad CO, a captain,

ran us through the locale. They had an ops room with TV monitors showing images from cameras around the FOB, allowing them to maintain a twenty-four-hour watch over any part of the base and the area around it.

Two minutes later we'd seen all over various checkpoints. The thing that really stood out was how close some of them were. Mine – Mulladad – was barely 700 metres north-west of where we were standing. Taalander was about the same distance further to the north-west, on the same road. The FOB commander explained.

'Trust me, they're far enough apart when the roads get lined every single day with IEDs,' he said. 'It takes an hour to walk between two CPs – if you do it right.'

The other thing we could see via the balloon's cameras was the canal irrigation system which provided natural borders to each CP's AOR (area of responsibility), as well as water for the fields that stretched as far as the eye could see. Because of the abundant vegetation, the area was known to us as the 'Green Zone', but it had other names. Legend had it that that part of the country could provide food for the whole population, and so for a while it was known as the 'Garden of Afghanistan'. When those food crops were replaced over time by a single plant – the opium poppy – it became the 'Drug Garden of the World'. At the time, approximately 90 per cent of the world's heroin was grown right there.

The irony, however, was that, according to our briefings, the whole region had been created by the Americans in an attempt to strengthen local resolve during the Russian occupation from 1979 to 1989. Fast forward a generation and the opium for which the Americans were indirectly responsible was funding the Taliban and the insurgency against them. And us.

But that wasn't the case any more, was it? Not according to the troops in Shazaad. Nor those I was about to replace. According to them, the dangerous stuff was over. The mission now was policing and data collection.

That night the seven of us from Bastion had a chat. We would all have been gutted if the fighting was over, but none of us believed it was. The IED problem, in particular, hadn't gone away. As a result, we actually came up with a bit of a plan. When we went out on patrols in the first few weeks we'd try to go with whichever CP was nearest. So in my case that would be Al's troop in Omar, due east of us, or M'lord's up in Taalander. If you imagine a clock face, one route, Dorset, ran north-west along the midnight line from Shazaad via Mulladad to Taalander; another route, Devon, ran from the centre to 1 o'clock out to H's Kamiabi; Cornwall, leading to Omar, was the 2 o'clock position.

'We should always try to be within six hundred metres of each other,' I said.

It was agreed. We all shook hands, said goodnight, and the next morning went our separate ways.

* * *

I was driven the 700 metres along the dusty track to Mulladad the next morning and dropped outside a compound protected by 12-foot walls, a sentry tower, barricaded at its base, set just outside the compound, and rolls of barbed wire, while Ollie, Al and the others continued onwards to their CPs.

I was surprised to be greeted by a welcome party. I was less surprised at how they looked. More ghosts. More of these creatures who used to be men once. That's how they appeared. They were standing there in shorts, the uniforms hanging off them, absolutely stinking, their hair long and unkempt – it hadn't been washed for weeks, by the look of it. They were quite muscular but very skinny, and armed to the teeth, with their body armour close at hand.

But welcoming they were not. I went up to shake one guy's hand and he blanked me, proper mugged me off. But he did pick up my luggage and lead me into the CP. Apparently he had only been there to see if the mail had arrived. Oh, and he was a para.

Stepping into the compound was like that moment in the pub in *An American Werewolf in London*: everyone stopped what they were doing and just stared me up and down. There was I, slightly sunburnt, probably looking quite well fed, healthy, shaven, with clean hair and a still-shiny Marine uniform. And there were these people, with their Para rags and their camaraderie as tight as a drum. The last thing they wanted was an interloper.

I don't mind admitting that it was intimidating. I was the only marine among twenty paras, not one of whom would piss in my ear if my brain was on fire. The only person who looked genuinely happy to see me was Sergeant Frank, the CP commander.

Because, with me there, he knew he would soon be going home.

The way the military moves its chess pieces around the board is interesting. My multiple wasn't just going to be dropped into Mulladad en masse. The high command operates an RIP system – relief in place – whereby personnel arrive to shadow their predecessor before taking over their spot. There are no individuals in the military, remember: Replacement B follows Replacement A. It's just a question of logistics. So, for one week I would be shadowing Frank. I ate where he did, I slept where he did, and of course I monitored how he ran the CP.

The most important thing Frank could do was show me the area. Directly outside the compound the terrain was not unlike the English countryside, but completely flat. It was March, so everything was starting to get lush and green. There was maize growing, wheat and other grains, and either side of the canals was a patchwork of meadows. Frank said the locals called them *jerubs*. Each was owned by a different family, as were all the various mud buildings and enclosed compounds in the vicinity. From what I remembered of history, back in the Middle Ages English peasants used to build homes using the 'wattle and daub' technique, yet here we were, a thousand years later and it was still employed. Effectively so. The mud is applied layer after layer and the sun bakes it until suddenly you have a building to survive all weathers. Our own compound, once the home of an Afghan family, was a case in point.

Clearly, our CP was in the middle of a farming community. But not all the crops were maize and wheat. There were meadows not too distant that showed the distinctive stems of poppies. They weren't even hidden. As far as the locals were concerned, growing opium was a money-making venture like growing vegetables or raising goats – part of their daily lives.

Frank explained that part of the job was to find the opium fields, identify the owners and pass the info up food chain of command. The Afghan government had already given the order for opium farming to be discontinued, but it was going to take more than a law made in Kabul to enforce the order.

Day 2, and my first patrol. Six hours of marching, with care, in full battle armour in the unbearable heat. For me, the conditions were not the worst challenge. When we set out the paras were still blanking me. After they saw how comfortably I could load up my kit and carry it without sweat – if not without sweating – they began to thaw. A couple of hours into our patrol and the jokes were flowing. I'd proved I wasn't a dick. That was as much as I could hope for.

In that six hours we barely covered a couple of miles simply because of the way we had to work. Throughout the duration of the war, insurgents had used IEDs to great effect. But it wasn't only the components that were improvised – so was the way the devices were deployed. Frank told me how fresh IEDs would spring up every day, often just around a bend on a track where a patrol was walking. That's how responsive the enemy was. They would monitor a patrol's direction – from where, who only knew – then estimate where they'd be after covering another 200 metres. So each patrol went out in single file with the front guy – the point man – carrying a Vallon mine detector to sweep the ground for potential threats. If the rest of us wanted to stay alive, we literally had to tread in his footsteps.

Yet accidents do happen. To minimise risk, the second man marched 3 metres back and the next man another 3 metres behind him, and so on. Sometimes the gap between men would be 5 metres. That way, if a device did detonate it wouldn't kill or maim more than one man.

Improvised explosive devices were the only things that bothered Frank. At the compound he took me up to a flat roof, the building's highest point, and stood there, fully exposed, pointing out the rough direction of the other camps.

'Are you crazy?'

Every bone in my body – every instinct, every ounce of my training – said you never put your head above the parapet, certainly not your whole body. I refused to get further up than a crouch. It must have looked stupid – one standing tall, the other on his knees.

'Typical marine,' Frank laughed.

It was then he told me that, in terms of fighting, everything was over now, although they'd gone through Hell on the way. And not just from IEDs. The next day, on patrol, I saw the evidence.

'Over there, that ruin of a building, that's where we were attacked,' he said. 'Behind you, those destroyed trees are where we took out a team.' On and on, more and more devastation caused by bullets and bombs. It was eerie. Quiet, as well. Maybe Frank was right. Maybe it was all over.

Each day we visited one or two of the other checkpoints. One of them was riddled with bullet holes and its buildings were rubble, damaged or being rebuilt. Clearly the threat operated at different levels throughout the region. So why was everyone saying it was over?

It certainly looked as though the locals thought so, however. Despite the obvious freshness of some of the devastation there were people in the fields harvesting their non-opium crops. It was a slightly surreal sight.

One of the first camps we went to was Omar, Al Blackman's watch. On his arrival he'd gone through the same initiation by derision as I had at Mulladad, but by now some of his guys were beginning to arrive so the odds were shifting. Corporal Chris Watson, Marine Jack Hammond and the Canadian medic Kaz were among the first. They were all great guys but Kaz stood out. Always upbeat, great for morale and a medic, so worth being nice to. Al also had the added weight of running an OMLT – an Operational Mentoring and Liaison Team – designed to bring a squad of Afghan forces up to Marine standards, so they were arriving as well.

As my guys began to arrive I got to know the ways of the paras a bit more. It turned out that not all of their stink was accidental. On day 2 I asked a corporal about the shower situation.

He said, 'I haven't showered in eight weeks.'

'Is there a problem with water?'

'Nah, after a few weeks your body cleans itself.'

I pinched my nose.

'Are you sure about that?'

It's just one of those differences between us and them. Marines are absolutely the opposite. The Navy – and the Royal Marines is part of the Royal Navy – shower three times a day, so my wanting to shower daily drew a fair bit of mockery.

It was just as well we had started to get along. On day 7 Frank stepped back. That put me in charge. Not only of my handful of marines, but also of a dozen paras. They wouldn't even shake my hand when I arrived. Now they had to take my orders.

Well, this is going to be fun . . .

Actually, it was. The more we learned about each other the more good-natured the ribbing. The fact that I could match the paras in the field, and that I'd jumped out of as many planes as they had in training, helped. In fact – don't tell them – but of all the units I've worked with, aside from the SF units, the paras are the ones I'd most trust to have my back. They're not marines, but they're damn close.

Over the next week the rest of my team arrived and the last of the para departed. On day 13 I looked around the checkpoint and thought, *Well, it's my trainset now.*

Most of me was glad. Proud, even. But there was another thought. *What the hell have I let myself in for?*

CHAPTER EIGHT

WE NEED TO MOVE THE WATERMELONS

Even if I achieved nothing more as checkpoint commander, I had to protect my compound. That was the bare minimum expected of me. It wasn't straightforward. To do it properly meant creating almost two half-camps. In front of the CP was Dorset, the main road running north-west from Shazaad in an arrow-straight line. It was no more than a dusty track but as it was the only route between the checkpoints – and it was how all our deliveries from the FOB would be made – it was important. The barricaded tower that had greeted me when I arrived stood proud and grey. Called a 'super-sangar', it offered protection and a high vantage point for surveillance and returning fire. It was the first line of defence, permanently manned by at least one sentry. Further afield were barbed wire entanglements and a line of flares that would be set off if a wire was tripped. Behind the sangar there was a bridge over an irrigation ditch, a line of trees and then the main compound itself. Inside the CP we had two further sentry positions manned twenty-four hours day. In daylight there'd be one guy in each position, at night two.

Because we were living in and on what had been someone's private house and land and not a military installation, there were neighbours within a stone's throw either side. Our visibility was about thirty metres, no more. When I went up the sentry tower I could see the inhabitants going about their business on the other side of the walls that enclosed their own properties. If they were put out by our being there they didn't show it.

Our own 12-foot wall and the trees outside looked solid enough to keep most things out. An irrigation canal ran parallel to the road out the front and there was another smaller one at the rear of the compound. Beyond that were more trees and a field. Those trees had seen better days. The paras called them 'The Range' – because in darker times the Taliban had hidden in the field and fired at the CP, to be met with concentrated fire from the paras in return. We had to cover all of it, a job made easier by some high-definition telescopic CCTV cameras on telescopic mounts that we installed on the super-sangar. The cameras gave 360-degree views of the camp, in crystal-clear colour during daylight and via thermal imagery at night. Sitting in the little ops room at Mulladad I could even zoom in. These were impressive pieces of kit.

Inside the compound walls the checkpoint comprised a series of mud huts. Some of these we kept as storage facilities for the original family's stuff. Of the other huts, one became our ops room, another our canteen – and another our toilet block. Like everything else the British did, there was a policy. As there was no sewage system; we just dug four holes in the ground and balanced toilet seats over the top. It was all for show – or policy. Nothing we did ever touched that hole. We had all been issued with a set number of 'shit kits', which contained everything you needed. You'd put a hygienic plastic toilet cover over the seat, sit down, do your business, then wrap it up, sterilised wipes, toilet paper and all, then leave it in the sun for three days and the crystals inside the plastic would do something to your waste so that it would be dry enough to be burned.

Bossing the paras around would have been more fun if they hadn't looked so exhausted. There was fair amount of wisecracking each way but they all pulled their weight, even when it was a 'hat' calling the

CP MULLADAD

N

gate

sentry
point

burn pit

stores

toilets

MP

MP

MP

ops
room

fruit trees

bridge

stream

sangar

'Dorset' MSR (major supply route)

Key

razor wire   accommodation   MP mortar pit

shots. Even so, I was relieved when my guys began to filter in and the last of the soldiers left.

The military brass might not recognise individuals, but in theatre I did. The moment my 2ic arrived I began to feel more comfortable. Mac, a corporal and more importantly a sniper, was someone not only on my wavelength but a real friend. With him there I felt I could begin to relax.

With another corporal, Fergie, I could actually laugh. He had a great personality and was always full of optimism, despite having been shot through the leg during a previous tour in Afghan. He'd been hit in the rear of his right leg by a tracer round, which contains phosphorus; essentially, the bullet is on fire when it strikes. The round passed clean through the muscle but the chemicals remained and burned away part of his leg. He had a large hollow where there was once muscle and so he'd wear a prosthetic filler which he called his 'chicken fillet'. Once we had got our feet under the table at Mulladad anyone who cocked up something had to drink out of the fillet.

Fergie and Mac were both essential to my sanity, but you couldn't find two more different guys. They were almost opposites: Mac was straight down the line, no messing, and was engaged to be married. Fergie was covered in so many tattoos that you didn't know whether to talk to him or read him, and he was never, ever going to walk down, up or even near the aisle. He was colourful – literally – and left-field, but damned good at his job. I can honestly say that without him I would not be here today.

One of the most important components of a patrol, apart from the point man sweeping ahead for IEDs, is the MFC or mortar fire controller. It's his job when you come under enemy fire to call in mortar support from the CP. The rounds from these would kill anything within 30 metres and injure anyone within 100. So you have to be bloody sure where you're directing them, and it's the MFC's job to know exactly where you are on the map at all times. Every time you looked at Fergie on patrol he had his map and his compass out, ever ready to go. Another lad, 'Elvis', had the same gig. He was just as diligent, and just as essential.

The fourth most important person in the CP – although he wouldn't want to be remembered as that – was another sergeant. This guy was in charge of the mortar line. He would sit in the compound with his weapons – three 81mm tubes each with its own heavy steel base plate – and wait for information from Fergie out on patrol. From that he would calculate direction, elevation and the charge to fire the mortar bomb onto the target. The sixteen men under his command would do the rest. As much as Fergie and Elvis, he really had to know his shit. When you're firing high-explosive projectiles a kilometre into the air you have to be confident that you've got your angles right. We were of identical rank but he ran his team and I ran the CP, which I guess put me further up the command chain. It was never an issue. We were all there with a mission.

As my boys were arriving – Lance Corporals Sam, Snake and Fergie (no relation), Jonathan, Robbie our Vallon man, Duncs, Matt, Adz, Pinky, Dan and Space Cadet – I repeated the familiarisation process Frank had taken me through. When a good number arrived I took them out on a similar patrol, the familiar snakelike order, cascading the information I'd learned down to them. There was a lot to take in, but it did mean that we got to visit the other multiples – Al, Ollie Augustin, Si Jones – so it gave the guys the opportunity to see some of their friends. The mood, I have to say, was pretty good.

It's fair to say we all started our tour pretty optimistic. We were fresh and we were hungry. The only thing missing was action. When the last of the paras finally left they reminded me again of how they'd already won the war for us. They were still ribbing us as the vehicle picked them up.

'Enjoy your holiday, hats!'

Annoyingly, the first week was about as active as they had predicted. The only people I saw outside our compound were children. That made me laugh. There we were, out in our armour, walking single file with a 3-metre gap between us, sweeping the earth for IEDs, and all these kids would come running up, oblivious to the dangers. They just wanted to touch us and wave or watch. It was nice.

I noticed very quickly that the only men of working age I saw were in the fields harvesting the crops. And when I say crops, I mean opium. The Afghan government was trying to encourage farmers not to grow the poppies, but it was obvious that the financial rewards were too great to resist. The only other men we saw were village elders sitting outside their compounds chatting, watching the world go by.

Getting to know the populace was part of the ISAF mission. There's no such thing as a census in Afghan and births and deaths come and go unreported. So we were given these biometric HIIDE cameras – Handheld Interagency Identity Detection Equipment – to try to establish some order by taking fingerprints and retinal scans from everyone we encountered. It is a very long-winded and time-consuming process, and for obvious reasons the locals took some persuading. Working with our interpreter – another essential member of the team – I managed to get the majority of people onside. But every so often there'd be a bit of resistance. That's when the lads got to assert a bit of authority. In week 1 we found a young Afghan who was a bit nervous of being put through the system.

A couple of the guys stood just close enough behind him to offer encouragement. He went ahead and the machine started pinging (it contains a database for cross-checking details).

'That's interesting, Mohamed,' I said. 'You've already been catalogued and there are some people in Shazaad who would like to talk to you about some fingerprints found on an IED there.'

Said through the interpreter, obviously.

The lad tried to make a break for freedom but that's hard with six men blocking your path. He was forced, at gunpoint, down onto his knees and cuffed.

The interpreter wasn't required for *that*.

Even the ones who did cooperate fully posed problems. It seems almost unimaginable to us in the West, but a lot of these guys didn't know when they had been born. I had people tell me they were twenty years old when they were clearly no younger than eighty. They weren't lying. They honestly didn't know. Birthdays aren't exactly a priority for those growing up in a war zone.

And as for the names, if I met one Mohamed Mohamed I met a hundred. Often from the same family. It beggars belief, but you could easily find seven or eight people in the same family with exactly the same name. And I thought the military saw *us* as interchangeable.

We were also charged with continuing the paras' work of mapping the area. There are no street names or no house numbers, so, using a map, we'd ascribe numbers and names for our own reference. This meant that when we came across someone already in the system the entry might say, this bloke is called Mohamed Mohamed and he is twenty-four years old and lives in compound 136 on Dorset Road.

Once you map the population, then you can police it. That was the point of the mission. That's what ISAF and the Americans had promised the Afghan government. More proof, as if it were needed, that we were not there to fight. It was all about hearts and minds. Everything we did was focused on preparing the Afghans for self-rule – without Taliban influence.

We put word around that we wanted to have a meeting with as many of the locals as possible. The most influential, a man called Mullah Omar, suggested we host a *shura*, a word from Arabic meaning 'consultation'. Such meetings are common in Afghanistan, as they are a means for local people to air grievances or express other concerns to council members.

'Great idea.'

Outside our compound was a beautiful orchard where there were peaches and pears growing. We bought a load of rugs and set up an area in the orchard where we could all sit down, to speak to the locals and to hear what they had to say. Although it was outside we still set up a perimeter, and anyone who wanted to come in was scanned with a metal detector. This was a gun culture, after all.

I have to say that the shura went well. Through our interpreter, we explained that we weren't the bad guys. We were there at the behest of the Afghan government to help. We would, we told the assembled elders and others, help build schools, bridges, and if the canals get blocked just give us a shout, we're on it.

We also said that if anyone suffered damage as a result of our presence – for example, if we trampled crops during a march or maybe killed a cow during a firefight – then the owners would be compensated. And we also told them that we'd pay for intel on Taliban activity – the Americans had given ISAF forces money for such eventualities. I don't know about hearts and minds, but brains and wallets were won over. Two people immediately put in claims for ruined fields – despite the fact we hadn't gone anywhere near their properties yet. Another local man was more useful.

'You should check this compound because the man living there was a bad man.'

Without addresses I got him to point it out on a satellite image of the area. He was a bit shocked that we had access to such a high-resolution image, but he pointed to a compound.

'He's not there any more but check inside. I never trusted him.'

When we did search the compound, we discovered a load of material for building IEDs. So that went down as a win – and it only cost us a few US dollars.

That first shura was such a success that I decided the next one would be even bigger. This time we flyered the area with leaflets in the local language and told everyone we met to come along. Turnout was better than expected, but the results didn't match. I went through the same spiel about being there to help and asked, via the interpreter, if anyone had any concerns and – nothing. No one said a word. A few elders made as though to speak, but then I caught them looking across at other members of the audience, men I hadn't seen before. Only afterwards did someone tell us that the Taliban had infiltrated the meeting. We didn't recognise them, but the villagers did. They knew that if anyone had said a word there would have been repercussions. I wish one of them had given us a heads-up. They came, they drank our drinks, shook our hands, but nothing happened. It was a waste of a nice moon and a shitload of man hours.

We held other meetings, but even at the good ones not everything was always as it seemed. We received the odd tip-off that so-and-so was Taliban. When we investigated it transpired that so-and-so just happened to be an enemy of the complainant. We were being used by villagers to settle personal scores. It was like Pristina all over again.

The person who worked hardest at the shuras was my interpreter. Each CP had one and for some reason they all took British names. Mine called himself John. He was from northern Afghanistan and was very well-educated, for he had gone to university up there and spoke five languages. We couldn't have achieved anything without him. On patrols he'd have a short-wave radio glued to his ear, listening to find out whether insurgents were broadcasting anything of interest. They mostly communicated in code but we picked up the odd little thing, although nothing much happened as a result though.

In all the shuras we conducted during those first few weeks at the tail end of March and the start of April I never saw anyone I could state categorically was Taliban, which was pretty much the story of my tour. After a month in theatre the sum total of our action was the odd cache of weapons and a handful of wanted men caught by the biometrics cameras. For some reason a TV crew covering the war flew out to speak to us. They asked me if I thought the war had been won.

'Put it this way, I can't believe how quiet it is here. We're fortunate that it's given us time to learn the geography of the land and bed in.'

Off camera, I mentioned how disappointed the boys would be if it continued to stay quiet.

'We've come here to fight a war that people keep telling us is over. I'm not sure we can take another six months of this.'

Be careful what you wish for . . .

* * *

As we got through April and the temperatures started to pick up, I noticed a shift in the local demographic. For weeks we'd seen the odd young male walking around the area, but suddenly I was seeing more and more twenty-to-forty-year-olds sitting by the side of the road, just watching, chatting, shooting the breeze.

'The harvest in the fields is over,' our interpreter, John, explained. 'They've earned their money. Now they have come back to spend it.'

Plenty more of them began bombing up and down the roads on little mopeds. When we were on patrol I spotted a pattern. I got on the radio to the two corporals.

'Mac, Fergie, have you noticed a few of the same bikes going up and down?'

They each radioed back that they had.

'What do you think they're up to, Rob?'

'I don't know, but I intend to find out.'

As more men began to populate the village each day I noticed that the children who'd been so friendly were slowly disappearing into the background. We'd still see them and give a wave, but they stopped running over and playing. After a while they stopped waving back, too.

'It's the men,' I realised. 'They don't want the kids talking to us.'

It was only a small thing, but it changed the atmosphere of the place. It was like there was something in the air, I just couldn't put my finger on what. I wondered if I was imagining things.

That night I was just about to turn in when the road outside the CP turned into the Fourth of July. From the other side of the compound wall – from the direction of the super-sangar – flares were launching into the sky.

'Christ, it's the trip wire!'

Were we under attack?

Immediately everyone in the camp began to stand to. Weapons were grabbed, armour pulled hastily on. I grabbed my radio to call the tower.

'Sitrep?'

'Three unknowns.'

I flew into the ops room to get a view from the cameras. The thermal images of three adult males filled the screen. Their shocked faces were a picture. What they'd been doing trying to approach the CP was unclear. They were already turning back by the time our guys got down to question them.

Whether they were out for a ramble or just wanted to test our security, I couldn't say. It's possible that they were just young and curious. It's also plausible that they wanted to find out how quickly we responded. Whatever their motive, I do know it added to the slight sense of edginess in the air. By the time the camp stood down, satisfied there was no attack, we could all feel it.

* * *

We had so much food in the camp that we were never desperately short of it, but it was always good to see the truck coming with deliveries of water. An Ocado delivery it is not. Six or seven giant British Mastiff trucks, one filled with supplies, the rest there as security, would make the drop-offs. It was some security. Painted in desert livery, and with cameras at the front and back to scour for IEDs, the Mastiffs were armed to the teeth with fixed machine guns and grenade launchers, as well as a multiple of eight men ready to spring out and engage an enemy. The Mastiff has a top speed of 65 mph, but a golf cart could have overtaken them on delivery days. Even after months of inactivity from the insurgents they crawled up the track, on high alert for IEDs every single time.

The delivery trucks also provided a good way to get around. In early May – week 6 without incident – the OC J Company sent word he was visiting his troops. I couldn't wait. An audience with Major Steve McCulley. What wasn't to like?

We didn't go out on patrol. I sat with John in the ops room monitoring the convoy's progress. It was currently further north of us, between Taalander and Kamiabi, a checkpoint even further away on the dusty track.

While I was following the British radio reports, John was listening to the ICOM – the local chatter – on his walkie-talkie. There hadn't been much since we arrived. This day there was a buzz. Half a dozen different men with crazy call signs were pitching in. I didn't know what they were talking about.

John wasn't clear either.

'It's all in code, Rob.'

'Tell me what they're saying.'

'Lots of things.'

'Translate it, man!'

He did, and he was right. Not much of it made sense. For some reason they kept talking about watermelons.

'John, do you have any idea what this means?'

'No. But now they're saying they have to move them.'

'What?'

'"We have to move the watermelons."'

Within a few minutes we discovered what they were. I was tracking Major McCulley's progress onto the Dorset supply road when suddenly there was a huge explosion. I heard it over the radio but it resonated in the compound as well. A big plume of dust showed us where it had gone off.

'Contact IED! Contact IED!'

In layman's terms: 'We've been hit!'

Christ!

The convoy carrying Steve had come under attack. I didn't know how. I couldn't get on the radio because HQ would need all bandwidth. So I listened. One of the Mastiffs had rolled over a landmine. Of all the identical vehicles in that procession, the bomb had hit the one carrying Steve McCulley. It was no coincidence. He'd been targeted.

'Is Sunray safe?'

Sunray is the code name for a commanding officer: in this case, Steve. My heart was in my mouth.

'Sunray is okay. The Mastiff took the brunt. But we're going to need cover.'

That was my cue to scramble. We were one of two checkpoints near the convoy, one of the closest quick-reaction forces (QRF). We had to get out there.

We'd drilled this a hundred times in the UK. In the two minutes it took the lads to pull on their gear and assemble by the compound gate, my official orders from HQ to get out there and secure the convoy's safety came through. I was already on it. That's what my training had been for.

There was something else it had prepared me for: recognising signs. The gate swung open. As we made our way out, in customary single file, I thought, *I knew those bloody paras were wrong. They didn't finish anything. The Taliban were just taking a break.*

I didn't care what anyone else said. I knew in my bones that the break in insurgent activity had been drawing to a close for a while, and now it was well and truly over. After six weeks of pretend soldiering things had got serious.

'Hearts and minds my arse! This is a fucking war.'

CHAPTER NINE

IT'S ONE OF OURS

You could feel the eyes burning into you.

Around the stationary convoy and still-smoking Mastiff stood small groups of locals. Some of them children, some of them elders, the majority young men muttering into mobile phones. These people weren't there to rubberneck. They hadn't been attracted by the sound of an explosion. I got the distinct feeling they were observing. Observing and reporting via the mobiles. More than likely, at least one of them hadn't been surprised at all when the mine went off.

It had taken us about an hour to reach the convoy. As desperate as we were to get there, I couldn't stop my point man, Robbie, from doing his job. One false step and one or more of us would be blown into the air and land missing a few bits. It wouldn't help anyone in the Mastiffs if we suffered a single casualty. By the time we did arrive M'lord's's QRF from Taalander was already *in situ*. Their group had reacted more quickly than ours.

As soon as I arrived I went straight over to Steve. He was still in the Mastiff, which had taken the full brunt of the blast. It was wrecked, but its armour had protected everyone inside.

'Mate, are you all right?'

He actually giggled as he stepped out.

'I'm better than this Mastiff.' Then, seriously, 'It's two hundred thou up the Swanee but no casualties. Amazing, eh?'

It was only later that I realised why he was in such good spirits. It's one thing being assured that these vehicles are bombproof, but the engineers making those claims never drive them in anger. Realising the advantage we had in physical kit put a spring in everyone's step.

Normally I'd have given the order to sweep the area for evidence of how the mine had been triggered and whether or not any of the onlookers had played a part. But Steve had already called out an explosive ordnance team (EOT). When they arrived we would provide security. Until then I wanted to see what information we could get from the watching Afghans. Unsurprisingly, the answer was none.

The EOT had more luck with the ballistics. The track was particularly narrow where the explosion had occurred, and shielded from the majority of the nearby compounds by a bend in the road and by tree cover. The explosion had not happened there by accident. They discovered traces of a wire, which meant that someone had been hiding close enough to detonate the IED as soon as Steve's Mastiff was over the concealed mine. And, yes, it was pretty clear that the insurgents knew which vehicle he was travelling in. Those mobile-phone conversations had probably been happening at every CP on the convoy's route. Steve had been under observation almost from the start of the journey. The second he was seen getting into his vehicle, his card was marked.

If I'm honest, I knew that the attack marked day 1 in whatever war was about to follow. But I was actually relieved at how insubstantial it was. Casualties amounted to no more than a bit of whiplash in a couple of the Mastiff's passengers, although the vehicle was a write-off. I'd always assumed that when the first salvo was launched we'd be calling in helicopters to remove the body bags.

As I said to Fergie, 'We have to take this as a win.'

'How'd you work that out?'

'No casualties, plus a major insight into how the insurgents plan to operate. Also, it's just good to know we weren't imagining it. There is a war. And we're in it.'

* * *

Not everyone agreed. The word from the UK and down through the chain of command stayed resolutely familiar. We weren't in Helmand to fight a battle. What happened to the convoy was a one-off. We were there to continue the hearts-and-minds programme. We were there to stabilise and rebuild and help police the area.

If only someone would tell the locals . . .

If the brains at Shazaad and Bastion wouldn't take our situation seriously it was up to me to instil some rigour into the boys. I genuinely believed our lives depended on it. The day after the Mastiff incident we went out on patrol as usual. It was the standard snake formation with Robbie up front, an enthusiastic young marine behind him, me in third. We were maintaining a gap of 5 metres between each of us so all talking was done by radio. I didn't need the radio to hear the occasional bursts of laughter coming from further back. After about the tenth time, I thought, *This isn't right.* I radioed everyone to halt and then walked back down the line, careful to keep as close to Robbie's cleared path as possible.

I'm going to put it down to age. Some of these guys had been in the Marines no more than a year, and eight and a half months of that had been training. They hadn't had time to become attached to the number of men that I had. They hadn't yet experienced that sickness when you realise one of your mates has lost a limb or, worse, his life. How else to explain their not standing to, not walking in a line straight enough to be anywhere near Robbie's footsteps, and not wearing the correct protective clothing?

I couldn't believe it. Four of them had bare hands.

'Where the hell are your gloves?' I demanded.

The guy almost shrugged.

'In my pack.'

'Why aren't you wearing them?'

'It's too hot.'

This is when you learn what sort of commander you are. Before every patrol I gave the same instruction: 'Get yourself ready.' We'd all gone through the same training. We all knew what the instruction meant. I wasn't going to patronise marines by having kit inspections each time we left the compound. Maybe that was my error.

'It *is* hot,' I said. 'It's thirty-five degrees. But I'll tell you what's hotter. An IED ripping four layers of your skin off. If you want to get your fingers blown off do it on your own time, not mine. Now be a good boy and put your gloves on.'

Or words to that effect.

All four of them had their own excuses. All four of them soon changed their minds. It was the same for the guys not wearing protective goggles, or the ones who'd been kidding about when they should have been concentrating on potential threats around us.

'If you think keeping your mates safe is a joke, then we're going to have words. Sort it out or you'll be eating from Fergie's fillet for the next six months.'

Not everyone was slapdash. If anything, one guy was too eager. After the Mastiff explosion the lad second in the line behind Robbie started seeing enemies everywhere. If he'd been behind me I might not have noticed. But 5 metres ahead I could see every twitch, every little swivel he gave as he scanned the hedgerows on one side then the other like he was playing some zombie arcade game. I thought he was just being diligent, but then he said, 'Enemy in the undergrowth on the left. Permission to engage.'

I halted the line and we all dropped to our knees and into offensive shooting stance. The guy – I'll call him Space Cadet for reasons that will become clear – was rabid. 'There, there, he's moving. There!'

I moved up. Positioned myself next to him, followed his line of sight into the trees.

'Where?' I said.

Silence.

'He's gone.'

'Okay.'

We waited until I was confident no threat was imminent. Then we moved on. Over the next six hours Space Cadet didn't stop twitching. We were on the return leg of our patrol when he went into cocked-weapon mode again.

And this time I saw the movement as well.

'For fuck's sake, put your weapon down!' I screamed.

He didn't flinch.

'There's definitely someone there.'

By now I was running up to him.

'Yes, you idiot, it's one of ours.'

He was aiming his SA80 at the super-sangar outside Taalander. The enemy he wanted to engage was one of M'lord's sentries.

I'd like to say he got better. A few weeks later he was on night sentry duty. I was in the ops room filing sitreps to Shazaad. Fergie and John were with me when Space Cadet came on the radio.

'There's movement out the back. I don't like it. Permission to launch a schmooli?'

I looked at Fergie, who half laughed, half shrugged.

Once launched, a 'schmooli' floats down on its parachute from 1,000 metres illuminating a 300x300-metre area with the brightness of 40,000 candles. It's a brilliant device, literally, although to be used sparingly in such dry areas. Crop fires, I knew from our PDT, were a natural hazard in southern Afghan. Given the levels of compensation paid by ISAF, such fires were not cheap, either – but then nor is peace of mind.

'Okay,' I said. 'Keep me posted.'

I scanned the monitors for thermal images of bodies around the perimeter. Nothing that I could make out. Any moment I expected the area to be lit up like midday in Athens. Then we'd see the truth.

A few minutes passed and Fergie said, 'What's he playing at? Want me to go and check up on him?'

He'd barely finished speaking when the door to the ops room flew open and Space Cadet burst in.

'I can't get this bastard to work,' he said. 'Can you check it?'

As he went to hand it over to me, he must have flicked the switch. There was a fizz and then an explosion and then the bloody thing took off. It smashed against four walls before zooming through the window. For the next thirty seconds all we could hear was rocket-powered mayhem going on in the compound.

How the hell the three of us in that room weren't injured I'll never know. But Space Cadet was about to be. Fergie launched himself at the youngster. He had him by the neck before the noise outside had even subsided.

'You—'

I managed to get between them. If I hadn't been the boss I'm not sure that I would have done, though.

Needless to say, there was no threat outside. And Space Cadet kept his distance from me and Fergie for the next few days.

* * *

The night after Space Cadet's *son et lumière* stunt, the sentry out by the road reported another noise. This sentry I trusted.

'What do the thermals say?'

'Hang on, we're getting something.' Then a pause. 'Oh shit. Incoming!'

A second later there was a smash in the compound. I waited for the explosion that never came. It took a few seconds but I recognised the shattering sound. It was an empty bottle. It was harmless.

This time. We all knew it could have been a grenade.

We lit the perimeter up and spied a group of kids running off towards the bridge. They weren't exactly terrorists but they'd shown themselves fearless enough to get past our defences. In the dead of night the sangar boys would have been within their rights to have opened fire.

I didn't want it to come to that. Not for kids or anyone else. The next morning we fitted some fake cameras that I'd ordered on Amazon before we left the UK. Don't ask me why, but I was glad I had. We erected them at various points around the wall where there was no obvious surveillance. And we took our time doing it, as well. I wanted to get the message over to whichever mysterious group was watching that we were protected.

That night, as well as doubling the guard, I toured the various sentry points then walked around the whole wall listening out for insurgent activity. Sod's Law that I was at the point furthest from the gate when the sentries radioed that they could hear people outside. By the time I had run back they reported that no one had been spotted. The next morning, though, there was a trail of blood outside coming from the barbed wire.

That, and all the dummy cameras were missing.

The following night was a similar story. This time it was kids again. They threw metal at the sangar and laughed as it bounced off. It took an enormous amount of self-will for the guys not to respond with the level of violence permitted by Card Alpha. In genuine fear for our lives, we were permitted to respond with force.

It struck me that the kids didn't know what we were capable of, but the adults behind them almost certainly did. They also knew that we would never act.

On the previous Herrick tour, soldiers and marines had been issued with the order to follow a policy of 'courageous restraint'. Violence, it said, was to be used strictly as a last resort and only when an enemy had struck first. You may as well play Russian roulette. *Will this unidentified object lobbed over the wall kill me or just smash harmlessly?* How everyone managed to deal with the illogical terms of that policy is a source of pride to me. Like many others, I personally struggled with it. When I heard that one American strategist had gone so far as to say – and this is quoted online – that he would rather lose ten US soldiers than kill one innocent Afghan, I realised that we were fighting a war with at least one hand tied behind our backs.

Not that the brass accepted that there was a war.

What, I wondered, *will it take?*

* * *

A couple of nights after the thrown bottle incident, things escalated. Again, it was dark. This time the menace was not glass but lead. A number of bullets thudded into the compound wall, while many passed over the top. Although these fell harmlessly beyond the other perimeter, the threat was clear. The whole CP stood to, but no one knew where the attack was coming from. Not that time, anyway.

Night after night we endured some form of harassment. They weren't exactly attacks, although even the bottle had been capable of causing serious harm if it had hit someone. I considered each event as the insurgents testing our capabilities and perhaps our standard responses. What they didn't realise was that we were testing ourselves. It's one thing practising during training in the UK, it's another on operations under duress. The boys acquitted themselves brilliantly during this period. Even Space Cadet. He didn't cry wolf once.

I knew that, should things move up a notch, they wouldn't let me down.

* * *

Whether what we were engaged in was classed as a war or not, I do know that it was serious enough that there was no day of rest. Sunday, 15 May, was no exception. We went out on patrol that morning, successfully arrested a couple of people thrown up by the biometrics as persons of interest, then returned for some well-earned shade, water and rest. That is, except those who went straight onto sentry duty. I personally had a couple of hours of liaising with command at Shazaad to look forward to.

Our ops room wasn't well equipped by Shazaad standards, and compared to Bastion it ran on clockwork and pulleys, but we had enough tech for me to follow what was going on in the region. I knew, for example, that part of Lima Company, 42 Commando, were out with the Afghan National Security Forces doing a raid along a stretch I knew fairly well, the Loy Mandeh wadi in the Nad Ali district of Helmand, north-west of Lashkar Gah and not far from our area. I decided to keep an eye on it, as I would any bit of action.

I was plotting with Mac the route for our next patrol when suddenly all the comms in the room went black. That is to say, all non-tactical communication switched off. Local radios were up but emails and welfare phones were down.

'Generator?' Mac said.

I shook my head. 'I wish it were. Someone's been killed in Loy Mandeh. Or as good as.'

Standard military procedure when there's a fatality in theatre is to shut down all non-essential communication in the region until the facts are known. Otherwise, half of Taunton could suddenly learn about a serious injury, or worse, before the marine's family. Hence the blackout. Hence my knowing that something terrible had happened.

It came out that evening. The wadi raid had turned toxic. A firefight had broken out and during the action a young marine from L Company, had detonated an IED. He was killed instantly. Disengagement was the only option. I could only imagine the horror of his mates at having to gather his body to take back home. It's the least his family would expect.

This was in mid-May. We had been in theatre since March and it was 42 Commando's first fatality during that time. My lads all took a moment to reflect on the loss. I hadn't known the marine who'd died in the IED blast, but I was friends with plenty of the others who'd gone out with him that day. In that respect we're all brothers.

The fact that he was killed barely three miles from where I was sitting didn't shock me as much as it seemed to surprise the voices at Bastion. In my next report they seemed convinced the violence was a one-off.

Mac, sitting next to me, heard it all.

'It's like they're listening but they don't want to hear,' I vented afterwards. 'You can't tell me these are isolated incidents. Something's definitely kicking off and this is just the start. I can feel it.'

* * *

For the next few days I began to wonder if I'd let my imagination get the better of me. We patrolled every day, made a number of clean, satisfying arrests thanks to the biometrics, got some good intel from a shura and basically felt we were getting to grips with the territory. Then it was our turn to get our first serious test. Information from a concerned citizen fingered a guy near Taalander as part of the insurgency. Shazaad processed the intel and coordinated a response. At 0300 hours one morning I moved my full multiple – Robbie, Fergie, Mac, Space Cadet, Jonathan, Matt Kenneally, Jenny our Navy medic, and the others – out towards our next-door CP. The going was slow. When you can't see your feet it's hard to follow in anyone's footsteps.

There was a maize field directly to the north of the compound where the suspected insurgent lived. That's where we were headed. Our role was to hide in the field and be ready in case the target or targets tried to escape that way. Two other multiples took up a similar positions on the south and east sides of the property. A fourth team, led by Ollie Augustin, would be the ones doing 'the knock'.

It took me back to my SFSG days. Except this time we weren't securing the perimeter for the SF lads – we were doing it for the Afghan police.

It's to NATO's credit that they kept persevering with the idea that the local force could be a tool for good. On the ground we knew otherwise. So, while the order from Shazaad was explicit – namely, that the Afghans would arrest the suspects with Ollie and co. as support – no one trusted them not to sell the information beforehand to the interested party, or at least not to blab it out innocently. And so, on the morning of the raid, a section of OMLTs collected the police from their station and marched with them to the compound. Only when they stopped did the Afghans learn the location.

Apart from my work with the Special Forces I'd done so many missions that promised more than they delivered that it was hard to get too excited. So imagine our delight when, as dawn broke, Ollie et al. stormed the compound and we got the shout over the radio, 'They're heading out north.'

By May, a maize crop has grown to above waist height. After several hours of lying in the field completely hidden from view, it felt extremely liberating to be able to stand up. It felt even better to cock our weapons.

The two guys running towards us just stopped dead. You could see them thinking, *Where the hell did you guys come from?*

Faced with twelve SA80s aimed in their direction, the Afghans did the only possible thing.

And dived for cover.

That could have been very bad for me. With the crops at waist height they could quite comfortably have crawled away and been lost forever. The inquest into the mission would ask: 'Why didn't you take them out before they had the chance to escape? Do you know how many British and American lives you've put at risk because you didn't fire?'

I was annoyed, although not because we hadn't fired on the two Afghans. I was proud of my boys for showing restraint. Mind you, our Victorian principles of fair play are fine when you're winning. For a moment that didn't look to be the case. If those Afghans got away to kill innocent troops another day, all the principles in the world wouldn't make it right.

'We need to find them!'

There was a hell of a lot of shouting in English and broken Afghan as we fanned out to cut off any escape routes. John's voice was the one that mattered. He could explain coherently what was going on. It worked. Suddenly from exactly the spot the two Afghans had disappeared, four hands appeared above the tops of the maize.

'Hold fire!' I yelled. 'They're surrendering.'

After they were arrested the suspects maintained that they'd been framed by a neighbour who was after their fertile land. I have no idea whether their story held any water. What I did know is that my lads had shown a level of control that would make anyone back at the CTC proud. Card Alpha was safe in our hands.

* * *

The reputation of the Afghan police was second only to their behaviour. Some days later we were in a village following up a lead as a combined British-Afghan force and the compound owners actually requested my men search their property, rather than their compatriots.

Via John I said, 'This is not the way our partnership is meant to work. We are here to train the police.'

'You will never train them not to steal from our homes,' came the reply. 'We trust the British with our possessions, not the police.'

You couldn't blame them. On another patrol we came across a roadblock. Through John, I asked the policeman in charge what they were looking for. He said, simply, 'Insurgents.'

'Have you had a tip-off? Is that why you're blocking the road?'

'Yes. Very bad men are coming this way.'

Something about his demeanour didn't sit right. I went with John over to one of the cars that had just been released. The driver said he'd been forced to hand over all the money from his wallet.

I said, 'Why? What reason did the police give?'

'They said it was a tax.'

I could have arrested the lot of them there and then, but I knew it wouldn't go down well in Bastion. Every time I reported bad operations I was told they were the result of teething troubles. We must persevere. Trust in the programme. The programme I could believe in. The Afghan police? Not so much.

* * *

What with the bottle, the bullets and the blood trail from the barbed wire, the mood back at Mulladad was one of heightened awareness. It was no longer just me who sensed something in the air. The general air of peace and quiet had been gradually shifting for a while, ever since harvest finished. The attack on Steve's convoy had been the first salvo, as far as I was concerned. I fully expected more. I just didn't know how or when.

For all the training we marines get, the thing I found myself relying on most in mid-May was my instincts. And they were saying –

screaming in fact – 'Something has changed.' We went out on patrol one day and the village elders we came across blanked us. These are men who barely a week earlier had shared tea at one of our shuras. A few minutes later an angry farmer came up to John and demanded compensation for the destruction – by us, he said – of a significant swath of his crop. The fact that he approached John showed how familiar he was with us. The fact that he lied through his teeth about the degree of devastation proved that something was amiss.

We had a flat fee for crop damage: US $20. For death or injury to cattle it was higher. We were authorised to pay any such claims on the spot. For any higher claims we wrote a chit for the claimant and told them to take it up with Shazaad. For some reason, on this particular day we were inundated with vociferous Afghans desperate to prise their pound of flesh from ISAF. There was something off about the whole situation. Why would an entire village suddenly have a problem with our work? We'd physically helped many of them in one way or another during our time in the area. It didn't stack up.

Fergie nailed it. 'Shit's happening,' he said. 'And we're going to find out the hard way.'

Never a truer word . . .

The day got worse. A couple of men with whom we'd previously had decent contact almost went out of their way to get my back up. One in particular was doing his damnedest to provoke a reaction. I say 'men' because kids stop being kids much earlier in Afghan, but this guy was fourteen, fifteen and just would not stop irritating us. One minute he's trying to touch our weapons, the next he's running in between us, pretending to go in for a wrestling hold then pulling out at the last minute. I was amazed Space Cadet didn't ask to shoot him on the spot. But then, he'd been very restrained recently.

John approached the teen's dad to ask him to intervene and was shot down in flames.

'Why are you working with them? Why are you betraying your own kind? You should be ashamed of yourself.'

This was a guy who'd previously fed us intel – quality intel. It was as though the guy and his boy were trying to provoke some kind of physical response from us.

Today is not the day, I decided.

I also noticed women virtually running away from us when we approached even their vague direction. Again, many of them were known to us. Some had given us info. Why, suddenly, were they obeying the harsher reading of Islamic law and shunning strange men, when they'd never done so before?

The whole atmosphere was one of distance. I've never felt more unwelcome or more alien in any company. There was nothing we could do that made a difference. It was as though they wanted to put cultural miles between us. For what purpose I couldn't imagine.

* * *

The following day began as most of them did, with us on patrol. The only difference was that we set out at the crack of dawn so we could avoid the harsh midday sun.

We biometrically tested a few people, reported a couple of odd situations back to Shazaad, then made our way back to the CP. Like almost every other day so far there were no arrests and no gunfire. I was beginning to think I'd imagined the potential threat against us.

We were actually just walking through our compound gate when we heard it. Somewhere not too far away there was a firefight going on. A real one. A loud one. I could make out the distinctive sound of machine-gun fire. I had a map of the whole region in my head, for by now we'd walked every square yard. Concentrating, I managed to pinpoint the firefight's source. North-west of us.

'Lads, Kamiabi is under fire!'

A buzz went round the group. Yes, some of our colleagues were under attack. Yes, we had no idea of how serious it was. And, yes, it could end badly for some marines. But we all knew in our hearts that we'd swap places with H and his guys at Kamiabi in a heartbeat. This is what we'd trained for. As I looked round the group the vibe among everyone was unmistakably one of excitement. Even though we weren't involved.

Yet.

I got on the radio to speak to HQ. Major McCulley was thinking along the same lines as I was.

'I know you've just got back but the Kamiabi lads need help. Can you get there?'

'We're on our way.'

My guys were chomping at the bit. Any thought of tiredness or boredom from the day's exertions had vanished. We couldn't get going quickly enough. Unfortunately, I could see that one or two of the lads were running on fumes. Telling them to stay back was one of the hardest decisions I'd made. Two fresh pairs of legs joined the fray instead.

I'd never done a harder patrol. What had never been explained during training was how to do this in 40-degree heat while looking for IEDs at the same time.

Keeping to our own rules about distance between men tested everyone's self-control. We managed to keep the 5-metre gaps but we were all so eager that there was more than the occasional instance of concertina effect. Poor Robbie had never swept a path under so much pressure.

Even as we were jogging the firefight continued in the distance. Whatever was going on wasn't pretty. Our arrival could decide the fate of the whole checkpoint.

En route Steve got back in touch. The Kamiabi call sign were getting the upper hand. More importantly, they'd called in air support.

'The last thing you'll hear will be the Apaches.'

That was the great thing about air support. We had it and the Afghans didn't.

Good to know.

* * *

While we were moving I was trying to study the maps. There was a quick route, and there was a safe one. Today we needed to be quick.

Garnzi Street: one path with a small stream on the left and trees either side. On the other side of those are the mud walls and the doors and windows of homes. The street had been named by the paras – it was what Frank called it on my first recce patrol. We never actually went up it for the simple reason that the paras had never got from one end to the other without some kind of action. Sometimes it was stones, sometimes it was shit, sometimes it was bullets. But now we had no choice.

Let's see what they've got.

But first . . .

Because of the speed at which we'd covered the ground, my God we were hot! The second I saw the stream I just jumped in. Everyone, including Jenny, did the same. In, out in a matter of seconds. It was all the time we had and all the time we needed.

As we started up Garnzi Street, I noticed we were going against the flow. It's barely 2.5 metres wide; you couldn't get a car down it. But people were walking, rushing past us.

I couldn't watch everyone. We had enough problems with covering the trees and the houses. It was intense. Robbie had his eyes on the ground. Space Cadet was yelling, 'I've got the left-hand door.'

I took the right-hand door.

Shouts behind me told me the left-hand window, right-hand window, other doors, other windows, other trees, someone was covering everything. And all while locals were streaming past us in the opposite direction.

You're on high alert, you're exhausted, you're wet but drying at a rate of knots. And you know you could be fired on at any second.

And then you are.

The noise when it comes is horrendous. Mighty blasts of automatic gunfire. So deafening that we have no idea where it's coming from.

'Ditch!'

Even as I say it everyone is moving towards the stream. Lower than ground level, it provides natural cover. Scrambling into it is not pretty, but I am proud how quickly everyone makes it and gets ready to return fire.

That's when I get the call: 'The Ugly call sign has engaged.' That was the firing we'd heard – from the Apache helicopter that H had called in.

Looking back, it seems funny that it was the onslaught from our own side that made us all dive into a ditch. But that's how heightened the threat was. If we hadn't done it I'd have been disappointed. The survival instinct that comes after years of training isn't a switch you can flick off.

But now we have a mission. The Apache's 60mm cannon had taken out a number of insurgents but the pilots couldn't confirm a total kill. It was possible someone had made a break for the tree line. The call from HQ couldn't have been clearer.

'Move forwards and remove any further threats. Card Alpha is off.'

'Roger that.'

This is the big time. Suddenly we were to go from acting as a cut-off to support for the helicopter boys. They'd been sent in to annihilate the insurgents. It was our responsibility to finish the job.

When we leave Garnzi Street our adrenalin is pumping. We are about to step into a kinetic war zone. I call our machine guns – two 5.56mm Minimis – to the front of the snake for protection. More than ever I need the men in front and behind to radio back to me everything they see, hear and smell.

It's intense. The reports come in thick and fast. Everyone can see something. Everyone can hear a potential enemy just out of sight. No one more than the Space Cadet. At the same I'm trying to plot a route to the grid coordinates we've been given as well as work out where Ollie's lot is located. They're being led by his 2ic, Sam Alexander, a very, very capable marine. They were heading to the same place as we were from a different part of the pizza slice, from the west. I need to know exactly where they are, if only to keep Space Cadet from opening fire on them.

On top of all this the ICOM chatter is off the charts. Lots and lots of call signs – meaning lots of different insurgents – giving their views. John struggles to keep up. I want to know if there is any talk of survivors. He says, 'Yes.' He also adds, 'They are getting something called "The Big Gun" ready.'

'It makes more sense than watermelons.'

But it probably means the same thing.

I knew from the paras that the insurgency liked to engage a patrol then lead it towards an IED. It was essential that we stayed alert.

I followed the grid coordinates given. The land around us is flat, but high, dense hedgerows linie the path. Now the radio reports from my lads double. Everyone is seeing potential threats. Weapons are cocked. We are all ready to go.

Apart from Robbie. His eyes are firmly on the ground ahead. He has to rely on the man behind for protection. That man is the Space Cadet. If anyone is going to spot an insurgent, it's him.

We come to a fairly deep but very narrow canal. More of a ditch, really. That's on our right, a grass verge separating it from the path. On our left is a field and before that a low hedgerow running alongside a dried-up riverbed. It's what's ahead that counts: about 50 metres in front of us the earth is scorched and in places still burning. The point where the Apache's missile struck is a crater. Lying just beyond it are parts of a human body.

'Okay,' I radio everyone. 'The missing insurgents could be here. Let's move forwards.'

People are getting twitchy. Jittery. The word from the front is that there's definite movement off to the right. Beyond the canal. Beyond the hedgerow. Ten or more men.

I check my map.

'Hold your fire! They are friendlies, I repeat, *friendlies*.'

There's a slight incline and Robbie decides to avoid the path so we keep the ditch on our right and hug the grass verge. The road is slightly higher so for a while our sightlines are lower. As we begin to rise again I see something 15 metres ahead on the left, in the dried-out riverbed. I can't make it out but it's blue.

And I swear it's moving.

If it's 15 metres ahead of me, it's only 10 ahead of Space Cadet and 5 ahead of Robbie. Whatever it is, Space Cadet at least should be seeing it. Robbie's eyes are firmly on the ground. Space Cadet is looking anywhere but to the left. He's convinced he can see someone on our right. He's shouting down the radio for orders.

'For fuck's sake,' I yell, 'they are friendlies. Look to your left!'

That's when I see the flash of blue move. That's when I see it's a man. He's hiding, but he's not staying still. He's crawling forwards. He has a plan.

'Robbie,' I yell into the radio. 'You have movement on your left.'

Nothing.

'Robbie! Movement on your left!' I'm shouting now.

Fuck.

Robbie is a couple of metres away from the threat. The blue shirt could take him out with a knife, let alone an IED or a gun. I raise my rifle, line up the crosshairs and fire. Three times.

And I watch the man in the blue shirt die.

CHAPTER TEN

BLUE SHIRT'S DOWN

I knew I'd killed him.

It wasn't me and nineteen SFSG guys aiming at the same target. It wasn't infra-red lasers making it all feel like a computer game. It was three rounds – three bullets – fired from my SA80 into the chest (twice) and head of the man in the blue shirt. I, single-handedly, had caused the death of another human being.

But if I wasn't careful, other casualties were about to follow.

* * *

'Robbie!'

My heart was still pumping. My ears still ringing from firing three rounds into the undergrowth when I saw my Vallon man go down.

I screamed into the radio, 'Robbie! Are you hit? What's happened?'

There was no answer so I just broke protocol and sprinted forwards still screaming at him. Sod the IEDs. *There must be someone else in the river.* As I moved I could hear shouts from the other side of the path. My adrenalin was through the roof. It took a few seconds to process what was being said.

'Hold your fire! Hold your fire!'

My radio was going crazy with the same message.

'Eleven Lima, hold your fire. We are friendlies. Repeat: we are friendlies, hold your fire.'

I recognised the voice. It was Sam Alexander. I was aware of his position. None of it mattered in that moment. All I knew was that I had to reach Robbie.

When I got to him I saw fear in his eyes, but there was no blood.

'Robbie, are you all right?'

'Rob, what are you doing? We're under attack. Get down!'

Now it all made sense.

I stood up and shouted the same thing to my men and over the radio: there was an enemy in the undergrowth and he'd been eliminated. No one was shooting at us. I wasn't shooting at Ollie's patrol.

'It was just me, guys, just me. There was a threat in the hedgerow! All eyes on the hedgerow.'

It was barely thirty seconds since I'd pulled my trigger but the confusion reigned for minutes afterwards. I had Omar, Kamiabi and HQ all radioing, 'What the hell is going on?'

Honestly? I wanted the same answer.

I pointed to Blue Shirt lying barely five metres away from where Robbie and I were standing.

'Look – I was shouting you had movement on your left. He was crawling towards you. Why didn't you do something?'

'Rob, mate, I'm sorry. I didn't see him. Too many friendlies the other side of the hedgerow.'

Space Cadet approached us. 'Is he dead? Did you kill him?' He looked like he was going to explode with excitement. I soon punctured that.

'And you. You're meant to be Robbie's eyes and ears! You should have spotted him!'

He started saying about the other threats he had seen. 'I told you: they were friendlies.'

'But . . .'

'Just do your job.'

Pulling all those conversations into some kind of order now isn't easy because they were happening at once. My own men, the ones 40 metres back in the snake, were as in the dark as anyone. But we couldn't relax.

'He might not be alone. All eyes on the hedgerow.'

Despite the confusion going on all around, training kicked in. You can't assume a threat has been eliminated just because he's been shot. You have to do a 'dead check' and you have to do it carefully. The target could have bombs on him, he could have a suicide vest, he could have unpinned a grenade just before he died. Even if he's barely alive he could still detonate something serious. While we all scoured the ditch and provided armed cover, Robbie and Space Cadet worked their way over to the riverbed and Blue Shirt. Any hint of threat and they would have to take further action. They would have to finish the job the helicopter had started and I'd continued.

I was watching anxiously. They circled the man for what seemed like minutes, then Space Cadet turned round and gave me the thumbs-up.

Blue Shirt's down.

He's dead.

I was relieved. The insurgent threat had been eliminated. It had been a clean kill.

But the good news ended there.

While his partner stood a few feet back, Robbie laid himself down on the corpse: standard procedure for checking for weapons. Using the insurgent's own body as a shield, Robbie rolled them both over so Space Cadet could check underneath for grenades or bombs or other imminent threats.

'Clear!' he shouted out.

Robbie released the body, stood up and continued a manual search.

By now we'd combed the hedgerow from our side and Sam Alexander and his men had done it from theirs. There was no second man.

But there also weren't any weapons on Blue Shirt.

Robbie was almost apologetic when he told me.

'We couldn't find anything, Rob.'

'No gun? No rifle? He looked like he was lining up for a shot.'

'Sorry, sarge, we've double-checked. He isn't armed.'

'All he had on him was $30,' Fergie added. 'Probably what he was paid to kill everyone.'

Oh shit.

I wasn't on Dartmoor any more. I wasn't shooting squirrels or pop-up metal targets. I'd just fired three rounds into a living being because I thought he was a threat. The only damage Blue Shirt could have done to my men was if he'd thrown a pebble from the riverbed.

Was that now an offence punishable by death?

I tried to replay the whole thing in my mind. I'd seen movement, I'd seen colour, I'd seen a figure of Afghan descent crawling along a dry riverbed. I genuinely believed he was trying to cause harm to my men and so I had acted.

Fergie could see the world of doubt I was in.

'Rob, he's a wrong'un. He was hiding from us. You got him. End of story.'

'I don't know, mate. What if he was just a scared farmer?'

'For fuck's sake. Why would a scared farmer be crawling on his belly in a wadi? Listen to me: HQ wanted this bastard dead. The Apache was sent to annihilate him. They missed and you finished the job. It's a win.'

'We don't know for sure he was one of them.'

'Call the chopper, then.' He was getting exasperated. 'Ask them what the bastards looked like.'

Not a bad idea.

I had to go via HQ but after a few minutes the message came back.

'One of the insurgents fired at was wearing blue,' I was told. 'And we think he got away.'

Fergie slapped me on the back. 'Happy now?'

I was. And I was about to get happier.

There was a shout on the radio from one of the Kamiabi lads who had been involved in the initial firefight. They were further up the riverbed.

'What is it?'

'We've found a massive IED. We think it's where he was heading.'

'Yes!' I literally punched the air. I knew my instincts had been right. I knew Blue Shirt was moving with a purpose. I knew he was going to try to kill us – I just didn't know how.

But now I did. If he'd detonated a mine of that size he could have taken out two or three of my men, 5-metre gaps or not. Several others might have been seriously injured by the flying shrapnel packed into the bomb for maximum carnage.

We stayed at the site for a couple of hours. The Apache did its customary fly-past – partly to show off, partly to show solidarity, and partly to get photographs of its work. I also had to radio for an EOD (Explosive Ordnance Disposal) team to deal with this bomb we suddenly had on our hands.

In a spare moment I found myself walking over to Blue Shirt. It just seemed important. I don't know why. I wasn't paying my respects. I wasn't wishing I could turn back the clock. I actually found myself wondering if he would be missed. Would anyone mourn him? From what I'd seen of Afghan families, they didn't let themselves get too attached to their own kids. Not in a Western sense. Perhaps I was doing them a disservice by applying my European logic. The thing is, where family is concerned it's the only logic I've got.

I tried to put myself in the position of a Taliban fighter. How would he be feeling if he were in my shoes at that moment? I couldn't answer that but I did know, with unflinching certainty, what would have happened to the body. On my first tour of Afghan, and then later with the SFSG, I'd heard of ISAF forces being captured, killed and then mutilated. On one occasion the Americans had gone back to retrieve some fallen comrades and found their dismembered bodies displayed from a tree. Even while they were telling us this, just later that night, I found it hard to believe. What human being could do that to another? Even in war. It was too barbaric for words.

The worst fate that was going to befall our insurgency friend was a biometric test. Even as I stood over the body, young Robbie was doing the full retinal, fingerprint and DNA sweep. I can't imagine it's what he thought he'd be doing when he signed up, but he did the tests without question. I couldn't have been more proud.

Things got grimmer, however, when we had to attempt to do the same to the bits of body left by the Apache. First we had to collect it all up. It's not something you can train for.

A British military police officer attached to Kamiabi arrived to go over the scene. Under her guidance a few of the lads did a full bagging and tagging of all the remains, plus all the effects on Blue Shirt's and his mates' persons, and shoved it in their bergans. While this was going on Sam Alexander made his way over from his team on the other side of the hedgerow.

'I'm sorry, Rob, we should have seen him. We were closer than you.'

'It's okay. We got him.'

'But he could have got you lot. We're going to have to work on that.'

While the MP was working I went around the lads, checking they were okay.

I was interrogated by the officer and had to give Steve McCulley a full blow-by-blow account. We watched camera footage from the Apache. Before the day was out it had been declared a clean and proper kill and one that in all likelihood had saved the lives of several of the Green Berets under my watch. There was a mood of jubilation in Mulladad that night. All the men were buzzing, congratulating me.

I was buzzing, too. But the last thing I remember before falling asleep that night is the sight of that man's eyes as the life drained from him.

It was an image that I knew I would see again.

And again.

CHAPTER ELEVEN

DON'T YOU NEED AN OVEN TO COOK PIZZA?

War isn't always about winning. Sometimes surviving is a victory in itself. Watching the Afghan people go about their business was a source of some admiration. True, in many ways they didn't live by our standards, but they found a way to achieve things that I couldn't help but respect. I saw a few people riding pushbikes that had small motors welded on; I saw cars built entire from the shells of six or seven other cars. One guy we bumped into had found and repaired a dead television, then fashioned a satellite dish entirely out of tin cans, pointed it at the sky and was able to pick up TV from all around the region. And I saw entire compounds run by hydro-generators constructed from nothing more than cast-off bits and pieces from other people's waste. If you got close you could make out parts of car engine, bikes, anything they could lay their hands on. And then the compound owner would pull out his new iPhone. It was mindboggling really, this contrast between resourcefulness born of deprivation and state-of-the-art technology.

Much of the way in which the Afghans lived was anathema to us. But the lads were really inspired by this *Blue Peter* make-do-and-mend ethos. For the first few months at Mulladad our compound changed almost daily. Every time I came back from a patrol there was something new in play. They managed to build a decent, well-equipped gym out of bits of wood and stones; they fashioned hammocks, sofas, anything to make life a bit more comfortable. The level of invention was incredible. For my birthday, without my knowledge, they got one of the translators to buy and kill a goat, then bought vegetables. This was for a curry. But what is a curry without beer? It's not something that marines in the field are supplied with, but in our food packs we did have quantities of yeast to make our own bread. Mac and a few of the others decided that this would be better employed fermenting some peaches growing at the back of the compound. When they 'cheers-ed' me that night it was with the most amazing fruit lager from our own micro-brewery. They must have planned it for weeks.

Believe it or not, that wasn't the most impressive culinary feat. On another night Mac said, 'The lads are planning a beer and pizza party. Is that all right?'

'Yeah,' I said. 'We need to unwind. But don't you need an oven to cook pizza?'

'Yeah, you do.'

'Well, last time I looked we didn't have one.'

'No, we're going to build one.'

And they bloody did. It was the most incredible thing I've seen built. It was fully functioning. It had hotplates and everything. It must have taken hours to cut out the bits of steel alone. Then they had to get it working with the fire.

Necessity can drive you to great achievements. There's no rule to say they have to be positive ones. Very soon into our Afghan experience I learned the consequences of leaving anything behind. Whatever the item was, the insurgents would find a way to weaponise it, to use it against us. I remember coming across the remains of fires containing burned-out batteries. I asked Mac and Fergie why the locals would set fire to them.

'For the explosion,' Fergie explained. 'When the battery blows up you're left with the carbon rod, which is what they use to trigger the IEDs. Clever bastards, really.'

* * *

Something that PDT doesn't teach you is how you maintain your enthusiasm for protecting a populace that at worst wants to kill you, or which, at best, you simply don't respect. By mid-May I was already wrestling with this problem. The fact that our commanders at Bastion, or even further afield and higher up, in the UK, kept telling us that everything was under control didn't help. The people of Afghan weren't under anyone's control but the insurgents'. Why wasn't Command seeing that?

This feeling of disconnect only got worse. With the increase in temperature came a noticeable stepping-up in insurgent activity. We were out on patrol one day when suddenly a distant part of the field we were walking alongside fizzed into life. It took a moment to register the sound.

'Shells!' I shouted. 'Everyone – cover!'

In that situation I have three immediate tasks: get the men and women under my command to safety; log a 'bang rep' – a report on enemy fire – with Command; and work out where the hell the threat is coming from and whether it's ongoing.

We quickly established that a missile of some description had landed about 50 metres away, wiping out a sizeable chunk of someone's crop. Ten minutes later we saw another one, airborne this time, hissing through the sky. It's never nice seeing a massive shell heading in your direction, but again it landed some way off. Before the morning was done there were three or four more. The closest landed 25 metres from our nearest man.

If that was the worst thing that had happened to us in Helmand I'd have been terrified. The truth is, however, that those missiles were being launched from 6 to 7 kilometres away. The Afghans might be able to turn a toaster into a satellite dish but the finer aspects of missile guidance were still some way off. In short, their aim stank. Pinpoint artists like Fergie they were not.

Which was great for us. But shit for the villagers, whose livelihoods and, sometimes, homes they hit.

As soon as I was confident that the attack was over, I gave the order to head for the missiles' landing sites. The field was closest. Like the IEDs, it wasn't the blast of the explosion that did the damage, it was the amount of shrapnel expelled on impact. The crop had been shredded by bits of metal, stones, any old crap that the insurgents knew would cause damage at 300 kph.

It shakes you up thinking what would have happened to us if we'd been in the way.

When we tracked down the next missile, we got a clearer picture. It had landed in a compound where a couple of families were just going about their day. I won't go so far as to say the kids were outside playing because with some of these families you never know, but they'd definitely been exposed to the blast. I counted four children, all under the age of ten, with missing limbs, blinded eyes or debris embedded in them.

Jenny the medic was straight over to them, yelling to me, 'These kids need medevac.'

I knew they did. I also knew it wouldn't be sanctioned. Unless it was one of our munitions that had caused the damage we were not permitted to call in any military assets to help. That included helicopters for medical evacuation – 'medevac'. There was so much we were prepared to do for the Afghans, but helping injured kids went against 'policy'.

'I'm sorry, Jenny, we just have to patch them up as best we can here.'

We left a couple of men on guard and the rest of us dived in to help the wounded. I'm pretty sure we saved a couple of lives. Even so, the parents could offer no information on who might have launched the missiles. John couldn't even get them to speculate about possible local insurgent figures.

'No one will know you've told us,' he assured them. 'Write it down if you want to. Just give us a clue. Don't you want the people who did this to your children brought to justice?'

We got nothing.

Not only that, but a couple of days later, when we crossed with another patrol, I heard that all of those kids we'd treated had been marched to Taalander.

'Rob, they wanted compensation for the injuries your men caused.'

'Tell me you're joking.'

'Deadly serious, mate.'

'And these are the people we're trying to protect?'

'Tell me about it. But who wants to listen to us?'

* * *

As well as aspects of what we called Blue Shirt day, I'd raised reservations with Mac and Fergie about our man Space Cadet, and his being so wrapped up in looking at friendlies that he'd missed the real snake in the grass. Nobody likes to hang a fellow marine out to dry, so we agreed we'd keep an eye on him, help him where we could, and work out how to get the best from a kid so enthusiastic and, according to his test results, so clever.

We were readying ourselves to go on patrol. Since my meltdown earlier in the tour – when I'd discovered not all the guys were preparing themselves in the manner I expected – the multiple were drilled in having everything ready before we took a step outside. That meant goggles, gloves, full safety kit in place. It also meant weapons ready.

Space Cadet took that too literally.

I was a metre away, but that would not have mattered if the round from his Sharpshooter rifle had had my name on it. For reasons known only to him, he cocked the rifle as a test and instead of clearing the weapon he pulled the trigger.

The bullet hit the compound wall, missing seven men on its way.

Two seconds later, those same seven men had Space Cadet pinned to the ground and the blows were flying.

I had to intervene. Once I realised what the hell was going on, that is. My men had nearly taken friendly fire from a guy meant to be covering their arses. Everyone is entitled to one mistake, but there wasn't a person in Mulladad who believed that this was Space Cadet's first. Not everyone was aware of the incident with the Schermuly flare, but they all knew about his trying to take out the friendlies on one patrol and missing Blue Shirt on another. I like to think that I pulled the guys off before their fists caused any significant damage but I can't guarantee that. He was shaken, shocked and bloodied.

And he was on the next Mastiff out of there. It was out of my hands.

'You'll have a mutiny on your hands, Rob, if you don't ship him out,' Fergie said.

So that's what happened. Steve McCulley agreed to reposition him somewhere else and send a replacement.

I joked, 'If you send us no one it will be an improvement.'

It's funny how quickly words can come back to bite you.

* * *

I never thought I'd miss the Green Zone – our current area of operations – until I was flying somewhere worse.

The area ISAF covered was huge: 10,000 square kilometres at least. That still left plenty of areas beyond its purview. Steve McCulley decided to do something about this. There were entire desert regions to the north of us, he said, that we needed to process. They'd either prove to be inert or essential to the Taliban cause. It was worth a week of our time to find out which.

I always knew the poppy fields were big, but only from above do you grasp how vast they are. And how many. We flew for an hour over nothing but the base ingredient for heroin. Even when we landed, opium poppies were still among the green stuff, and the second we moved out of the poppy field we were on desert soil. On sand. It was like being in another country.

We were dropped in a poppy field. Three helicopters, sixty men. Quite the circus. No wonder dozens of locals appeared from nowhere. Actually, closer to hundreds. They were all curious, all acting as though they'd never seen people. Other people.

Steve McCulley headed the party. He'd identified, via satellite imagery, the perfect compound to house sixty marines and set off with an advance party to negotiate its rental. Negotiation was one of those quirks of 'helping' the locals that meant he was always going to get his way. It was purely a matter of price. I think, in the end, $500 covered it. Then it was time to move the troops in to occupy and reinforce this little mud property.

While this was going on, a convoy of Mastiffs was heading north to join us. I didn't know all the driving team but I'd trained with one lad, 'Damo', and had nothing but respect for him. If the rest of his men were as skilled we'd be okay. He and his team were carrying supplies and, crucially for a desert mission, water. You can easily drink five or six litres a day in the Green Zone. In the desert it's more.

The mission was twofold: to gain intel about the region, and to demonstrate that the ISAF's reach extended further than the Taliban realised. For the first couple of days it worked. We definitely had the upper hand. We patrolled, fifty of us and more, into territories never before touched by the allies. What we learned was inconsequential other than the fact that we weren't expected. In a sixty-hour period we didn't come across even a hint of an IED. At that time, in that region, in that country, that was unusual.

On day 3 things changed. We were on patrol and I noticed John was busier than usual. A translator is always by his commander's side so more often than not I knew what was troubling him. This time was different. This time, he said, there was no obvious message.

'Just a lot of noise, Rob. It's like they've just noticed we are here.'

One faction of the insurgency was shouting at another. Plans were being drafted, in code of course, and codenames were bandied about like emojis on a teenager's phone. Barely an hour into our patrol John said, 'I think I'm getting something.'

'What is it?'

'They want Jenny. They're talking about "female infidels".'

Women, to the Taliban, are second-class citizens. They are not permitted to study or drive. They certainly wouldn't be tolerated if they were to touch men other than a husband – even if they were medical staff saving lives. Apart from Jenny we had other FETs – 'female engagement teams' – among our number. For the reason of gender alone they were near the top of the Taliban target list.

But there was a higher target.

'Sir, they keep talking about the "Big Chief": "Big Chief" is doing this, "Big Chief" is moving there.'

'What do you think it means?'

'I think they want to kill Major McCulley.'

* * *

The compound had very little shade. On patrol there was less. We needed to break for water every five minutes but that was all we could afford. Despite the surprise factor we had gained from our unexpected arrival in the area, I didn't dare let my men rest in the shadows.

'That's the one place the insurgency will have planted IEDs.'

It was the same rule for everyone. Steve McCulley came on some patrols but not all. I told him about the ICOM threat but he just shrugged.

'They've got to find me first. And even if they do, there'll be another major taking my place. I'm not irreplaceable.'

Like everyone else, he was more interested in getting his ration of water.

I thought I was protecting my people by keeping them away from the obvious IED sites, and I'd make the same call today. But the truth is, there were casualties as a result. It came on so fast. A lad called Adam suddenly started acting completely delirious. One minute he was walking in our snake, then he was wandering about all over the place. It was like watching my mate Paul A. high on mystery painkillers during the final task of the Commando Test years ago. Like Paul, no one could talk to Adam. He was muttering to himself. When I was called over it was too late.

'Sunstroke,' I said. 'We need water and shade.'

Jenny appeared a second later.

'We need more than that.' She turned to the guy walking behind Adam. 'How long's he been in trouble?'

'Since the last stop. But this is the worst.'

'Shit.'

'Jenny,' I said. 'Tell me straight. What's going on with him?'

'Honestly, unless we get him back to the compound he's not going to survive out here much longer.'

We were a good hour's march from the compound. The route Robbie had cleared on the way out wasn't marked so he'd have to start again. I radioed Steve an update. He was as concerned as I was. More so.

'Rob, you need to be aware that ICOM chatter is off the charts. The usual call signs and then some. I don't know where the insurgents are but they know you're a man down. They're mobilising. We can hear them. You need to hurry on full alert.'

I didn't fancy our chances and I told Steve that. But the next voice on the comms wasn't his. It was one of the Mastiff drivers, Damo.

'Four Mastiffs heading to your position for medevac,' he said. 'Secure your position and hold. Confirm.'

And that was it. I don't think Command would have sanctioned the move, but we were all grateful he was doing it. The routes he'd taken had not been cleared by minesweepers. There was a viable threat to his life, his men's lives and the machines in his care. But he knew that. He also knew one of his fellow marines was in a critical condition and that the vultures were circling. So he acted.

After ten minutes he still hadn't reached us. During that time I heard for myself, via John, the toxic radio posts about us sent between the locals. The Taliban were definitely on the move. The question was: would they discover our position before Damo reached us?

John was approaching meltdown.

'Rob! Rob! I hear them. I hear the insurgents. They're almost here.'

I ordered the men to stand to. The crops around us provided cover, but only from the enemy's sight. Against bullets they'd be useless.

We were all on high alert. Only Adam was out of it, and keeping him still was the hardest job of all. Then suddenly we heard the growl of engines.

'Vehicles!' Mac called out. 'Coming at speed.'

I squinted through my rifle's optics.

'Mastiffs,' I said. 'Ours. It's Damo.'

'Thank Christ.'

We got back safely. After a good six hours of care Adam was restored to something close to his old self. He wasn't the only one affected. Several other people went down with heatstroke that day. Nothing serious.

CHAPTER TWELVE

THE AMERICANS HAVE LANDED

Even in a war zone, some things are almost more important than life and death. For example, it doesn't pay to forget your wife's birthday. Carly's happened to be on 23 May, a couple of weeks after mine, and so I rang her from the ops room. She wasn't celebrating with a slaughtered goat on a spit. She was taking the boys for a well-earned break to Spain. It was a bizarre conversation, if I'm honest. I was happy for her, I really was, although I'm not sure I showed it. I'm not sure I could have. The world she was describing seemed a million miles from where I'd been over the last weeks. The things I'd seen, the things I'd *done*. There was no way to share them down a dodgy phone line. Not in a way she'd understand. In fact, I wasn't sure she'd ever understand.

She was aware of the news in general but we danced around specifics.

'Are you all right?'

'Yes, I am.'

'Are you eating enough?'

'Food's not the problem. It's the bloody heat.'

'I don't know what you're moaning about. That's why we're going to Spain.'

I could see a clock from where I was sitting so I knew it was time to wrap up.

'Love to the boys.'

'Okay, be safe. Phone me in two weeks and I'll tell you all about it.'

And that was it. I hung up the phone, left the ops room and climbed on board a waiting helicopter.

Carly and the kids were going to the Costa Brava. I was going into battle.

* * *

While Carly had been packing her suntan lotion, I was packing my rifle. The one that had already taken a man's life. She wasn't the only one heading off. The whole of J Company was flying out to the region where the young marine had lost his life. The mission was simple. We were going, in numbers, to put a stop to the insurgent supremacy in that area.

And avenge a fallen comrade.

It was big deal. There were fifty-five of us flying in on a ten-day mission. The plan was for J Company to act as a lure, essentially, to engage with Taliban aggressors in one area while an engineering division could begin to secure the region and start to rebuild the villages and supply routes destroyed by the insurgents. Our destination was a compound in the Nad Ali part of Helmand, about four kilometres east of our usual area of responsibility, a long march or a short drive away. But our helicopters weren't to take us there. First we were going to Bastion for mission briefing and to ensure everyone knew their specific AORs (areas of responsibility). Nothing was left to chance.

All my lads were up for the fight. The loss of a marine to an IED was tragic and each of us was itching to right that wrong. None of us contemplated the same fate befalling us. I don't think you can if you're about to step into a live battlefield. Which is why I was actually a bit pissed off when the padre came to find us on our last night at Bastion.

Some guys do draw comfort from a man of the cloth reminding

them that there is more in Heaven and Hell than we experience on earth. I'm not one of them. As I said to Fergie, 'Someone doesn't think we're coming back alive. They may as well have sent a damn vulture.'

With the encouragement of knowing Command knew more about the scenario we were entering than they were letting on, we finally set off. It was a big deal. There were four groups made up of personnel from my lot, Kamiabi, M'lord's Taalander and Al's 2ic and Kaz, the Canadian medic, from Omar. Al stayed behind because of problems in his own area. There was also an HQ element present, including our Sunray Steve McCulley and his 2ic, Captain G-side, plus several FACs (forward air controllers). Obviously where we were going could require bombs being dropped from aircraft, and these were the guys who could do it on the hoof.

We flew at night, as 23 May turned into the 24th. I don't know how the helicopters took off. Each man was carrying so much – water, a roll mat, shovels, sleeping bag, tons of ammunition, surveillance equipment, extra batteries, extra clothing – we barely stumbled on board. A couple of guys had to be helped just to stand up. It was worse the other end. Because of the terrain the closest the choppers could land to the compound we were going to inhabit was still 600 metres away. Just the idea of the walk made you feel tired. Luckily, then, we got a rest as soon as the helicopters took off.

Just not the kind we were expecting.

No sooner were we on the ground than John, my translator, was tapping me on the shoulder. As usual his walkie-talkie was pinned to his ear.

'Rob, Rob, you need to listen. This is not good.'

He handed me the radio. It was going banzai. Even though I couldn't understand the language I could tell the tone was animated beyond belief. And the amount of chatter was off the charts. Someone had kicked the hornet's nest.

'John, tell me everything being said. I need codenames, everything. Something huge is going on.'

Sometimes the Taliban would jump on the radio and make threats just to intimidate us. On those occasions there'd be just a couple of voices doing the talking. You figured there weren't exactly troops waiting behind them.

This could not have been more different. I couldn't keep up with the stream of handles John started rattling off. I managed to scrawl a few on my glove but the list kept coming. Within minutes I had run out of space and had to use my sleeve.

This was not intimidation. This, whatever it was, was real.

John was repeating everything verbatim, not really processing the content in his own head. Suddenly he froze.

'They're saying the Americans have landed,' he said.

'Okay,' I said, 'where? We have to warn them.'

'Here,' he said. 'The Americans have landed *here*. They're talking about *us*. They can see us.'

Shit.

I radioed to the front of the group. All the leaders were hearing the same thing.

'Everyone down!'

Steve gave the command but we were all thinking it. Using NVGs in the darkness I saw we were in the middle of a field, surrounded at its perimeter by a thick cover of trees. There were taller crops where we needed to get to that offered some visual protection, but they would do nothing against bullets.

At the front Steve and his team had their heads down. How had the Taliban known we were coming? What were their plans? And how serious was the threat?

That soon became very clear.

'Rob, they're saying they need to "move the big thing",' John said. 'They're saying, "Get as many as we can. Don't let the Americans leave that field alive."'

We lay there for what seemed like an eternity, listening to Afghan chatter. Knowing that every unintelligible word spoken is a part of a threat against your own existence is an odd sensation. One of my lads snapped.

'This is ridiculous. Can't the checkpoint send transport?'

I laughed. 'No.'

'Why not?'

'Because there isn't a checkpoint till we get there.'

It was the same scenario as our desert jaunt. To keep intel about our movements to a minimum, no one had been informed of where we'd be staying. Not even the family currently living there. Unfortunately for them, the compound we were heading to had been identified by Bastion as the perfect size and location for our company. The plan was that an advance party, including translators and Afghan forces, would go and negotiate rental of the compound. That, we hoped, was going on while we were lying in the field. I wished it would all hurry up.

'If we're not careful this will be "watermelons" all over again.'

Nerves were becoming frayed. Sod the kit we were carrying, we all just wanted to run. Impossible weight versus impossible wait. As the dawn came up, it just made us more determined. I saw children and women beyond the trees, all rushing, all fleeing, desperate to head in the opposite direction to us. There was mad panic, no other words for it.

What the hell do they know that we don't?

Eventually we were given the order to move out. The residents at the compound had put up a good fight. But faced with moving out with generous compensation or being evicted at gunpoint by the Afghani forces with no compensation, they'd done the sensible thing.

This was good news, but for it to mean anything we had to get there before the heat got too great to walk in – and while we still had our lives. Not everyone was up for it. We'd barely made it to the cover of the crops when my 2ic for the operation, Snake, toppled forwards.

Your first instinct is attack but the only noises we heard came from him. Our medic Kaz broke the line and ran up.

'Stomach cramps,' he said. 'He needs water.'

Dehydration is a massive problem in normal conditions. Carrying the loads we were, it could kill you. While we were treating Snake I got a radio report that M'lord had gone down with the same complaint.

Two others followed moments later. They also had diarrhoea. No sooner did I hear this than Snake started suffering the same way.

'It's a virus,' Kaz announced. 'We need to get them quarantined.'

Before that we had to get them – and everyone else – to safety. It was already a challenge with just our baggage. Supporting four ailing teammates made it nigh on impossible to travel at any speed other than a shuffle.

When we finally emerged from the tall crop field I could see a dusty track, not dissimilar to what passed for a main road at Mulladad.

The walk along the track was on high alert. Guns were held at the ready, alternately pointed left and right, up and down. Extra men guarded the wounded and their helpers. It was like walking along Garnzi Street, except here we were not alone. Despite the early hour, dozens of young men on scooters bombed up and down the track, all of them craning their necks to get a good look at us as they passed.

'If we got biometrics on half this lot we'd win the war,' Fergie said. I didn't doubt him for a minute.

The atmosphere was as tense as the going was tough. When we finally made it inside the compound's 3-metre-thick walls I thought my knees were going to buckle. Some of the lads already there had gone one stage further. The compound was large – it needed to be to fit us – with an orchard at one end, and a stream on the outside of the walls. Where the owners had extended their plot beyond the stream it actually ran under the wall at one point and into the compound. I was still throwing my baggage down while a dozen or more guys were already jumping in. After the night we'd just had no one could blame them.

But it did mean that, when the first attack came, we were caught – quite literally – with our pants down.

* * *

Steve McCulley lined up the four multiple commanders and gave us each a quarter of the compound – now christened Checkpoint Toki – to look after. I immediately got to work organising my sentries on the mud buildings' roofs and building protective walls of sandbags around

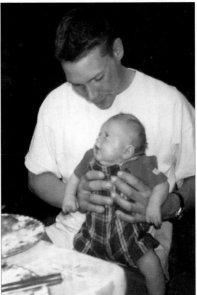

Above left: 'A pothead like me' – as a teenager, with my grandmother . . .

Above right: . . . and, after years of service in the Marines, with my nephew Luke.

Below: On exercise in Scotland during training. The yellow devices fitted to the muzzles of the SA80 rifles are blank-firing adaptors.

All photographs are from the author's collection

Left: Jungle training in Belize; we also did the Arctic warfare course.

Right: Having completed a signals course, I was one of the advance party sent out from RM Condor in Arbroath, Scotland, to Pristina in Kosovo, to maintain order in the war-ravaged country. Here I am showing off my living quarters.

Left: One of our tasks was to persuade local Kosovans to hand in any weapons, although they tended not to give up 'the good stuff'. This is me with a Second World War-vintage .45 Thompson sub-machine gun – the famous 'Tommy gun' beloved of American gangsters in the 1920s and 1930s.

Left: Searching a house in Kosovo – in fact, much of the action we saw seemed to be farmers shooting at each other as the result of some feud, on one occasion a quarrel over a stray cow. However, a culture of violent revenge undeniably permeated the country at that time.

Right: Me, exhausted, during the invasion of Iraq in March 2003; this was taken on D-plus-2.

Left: Heading northwards into Iraq following the invasion in March 2003 – I am standing up in the back of the Land Rover.

Left: Me during a house search while clearing villages south of Basra. I am holding up one of many portraits of Saddam Hussein that were to be found in all government offices and most homes.

Right: Sitting on the quad bike on which I reconnoitred much of the area south of Basra; note my SA80 strapped to the luggage carrier at the front

Left: Three comrades-in-arms, including Corporal Sibsy, and I (second from right) digging an emplacement in the Iraqi desert. We quickly learned that the desert is not only almost entirely sand, but is extremely cold at night or in bad or winter weather.

Left: When dawn broke after my arrival at Camp Bastion in Helmand Province, Afghanistan, the first thing I noticed were the encircling mountains. An RAF CH-47 Chinook on the airstrip at Bastion – we would fly in these amazing aircraft many times.

ight: 'Er, guys – I've ɔt a situation here' – e after discovering a ndmine while we were uilding our camp at astion, even though the ea was supposed to ave been swept.

Left: On operations in Tora Bora. This network of caves in eastern Afghanistan, close to the border with Pakistan, was a Taliban stronghold.

Top: J (Juliet) Company, 42 Commando RM, at Camp Bastion in Helmand Province, Afghanistan. Not all the men in this photograph would make it back home, and some would be terribly wounded.

Middle: Me (third from left) with members of my multiple, including Fergie, before we left Camp Bastion for our first CP. Neither we, nor our uniforms, would look so smart on our return some seven months later.

Right: 'Sunray' – Major Steve McCulley, commanding Juliet Company, in the ops room at CP Toki directing the ISAF response during an attack by insurgents – he had been bathing when the attack started, and only had time to throw on his body armour. Not long afterwards he was to be severely wounded by an IED.

Left: Me in full battle array during a compound search. The weight of our equipment, including body armour, combined with the heat to take its toll during long patrols.

ight: Patrolling
ongside one of the
any irrigation channels
at criss-cross the
untryside in that part
f Helmand. At times
e were glad to get into
em to cool down a little;
others, they provided
ver from Taliban fire.

Left: A patrol entering a compound to search it and question its inhabitants, while locals Afghans look on. Note the tall crop and the mud walls

Right: Me (left) and another of my patrol safely in cover after a prolonged firefight with the Taliban.

Below: Homecoming parade at Bickleigh Barracks, Devon, after 42 Commando's return to the UK from Afghanistan, late 2011. Proud Green Berets, but not all of them escaped unscathed, and some paid the ultimate price. The RSM (far left) stands at attention next to his injured marines; ahead of him, Kaz is in the wheelchair nearest the camera.

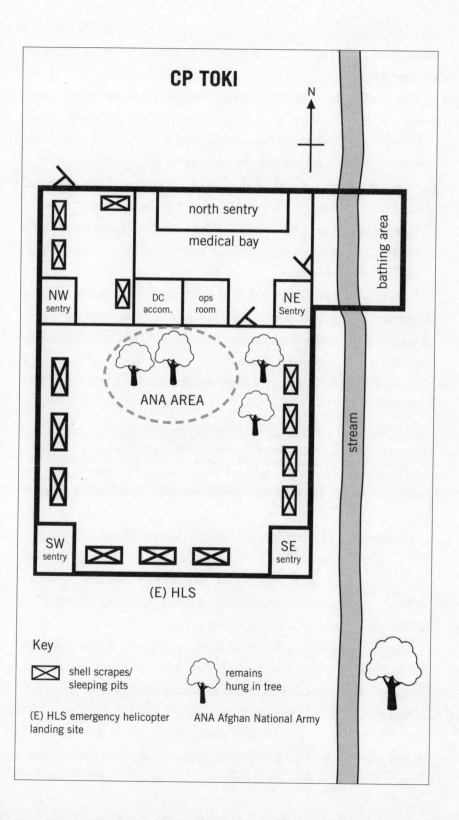

CP TOKI

north sentry

medical bay

NW sentry

DC accom.

ops room

NE Sentry

bathing area

ANA AREA

stream

SW sentry

SE sentry

(E) HLS

Key

shell scrapes/ sleeping pits

remains hung in tree

(E) HLS emergency helicopter landing site

ANA Afghan National Army

other virus casualties under a tree in the courtyard in the centre of the compound.

The sandbag nest was still under construction when the first shot came.

It missed everyone and everything, but it got our attention. The sentries and the lads building the walls dived for cover to return fire. At the same time I heard further shots coming in from points all around the compound. There was so much noise, so much shouting, so much confusion. One thing emerged: all the sentry points were being attacked at once.

This is not coincidence.

I ran to take a position on the roof of one of the buildings. Out of the corner of my eye I could make out Kaz and the other swimmers dragging their semi-naked carcasses out of the stream and grabbing their rifles and uniforms. What I didn't see was the RPG (rocket-propelled grenade) soaring in from the south. But I heard it. And I saw where it hit.

I've read and heard lots of accounts of the Taliban being a backward culture – and, in my opinion, they largely are. But not militarily. There were occasions in Afghan where I would have doffed my cap at some of the tactical decisions they made if I hadn't been trying to kill them.

This was one of those times.

The initial rounds fired at all four sentries at once drove every able-bodied marksman onto higher ground to return fire. That was precisely the moment at which the insurgents launched a series of RPGs into the centre of the compound.

The grenades themselves landed far away from anyone. But the reach of the explosion was massive. The shrapnel spray flew in every direction. White-hot shards of metal scarred the walls, the trees.

And our men.

Snake, M'lord and the others resting in the shade were all caught by the wave of metal. M'lord was struck in the neck. Snake was hit from behind, between the shoulders. One of the engineers clearing the compound got shrapnel in his foot. They weren't fatal injuries but they were all nasty and all required medical attention. Plus, the attack was still going on.

Confusion reigned. We had no idea where the threat was coming from. We hadn't got our bearings, we hadn't patrolled, I personally hadn't even looked at a map since Bastion. And, unlike the insurgents, we were afraid of hitting civilians. We needed a target, plain and simple.

The distinctive muzzle flash of a rifle flared from just above a wall about 30 metres in front of us. That was enough to go on. The lads opened fire. As we did, other shots came in from new positions. They were 360 degrees around us and maximising the advantage. Even the bullets that missed us ricocheted off the compound walls like a deadly pinball. At least each time they fired we gained new targets. For two hours it was all-out shooting, total mayhem. We were lighting up the entire area. No wonder the women and children had been fleeing earlier. This had all been planned down to the second.

In the first sixty minutes I was confident that we had superior technology and training. In the second sixty I remained resolute. As we entered our third hour, however, the doubts started to creep in. Our machine guns were awesome weapons, but they were tearing through the rounds.

'Lads,' I said, 'you need to slow down. Much more of this and we're going to run out of ammo.'

'You're not wrong,' Fergie said. 'We need to end this.'

As darkness began to fall I contacted Steve.

'One of my snipers has seen muzzle flash about 200 metres north. Permission to engage with the 66?'

'Hold fire,' he said. 'I'm bringing in air support.'

A couple of minutes of later there was the familiar roar of a French Air Force Mirage jet overhead. I assumed it was going to drop a bomb. It banked for a couple of seconds, then levelled out and opened fire with a massive 90-degree strafing run of cannon fire across the tower building.

It was devastating and loud and it did the trick. After that everything went very, very quiet.

* * *

I'm not saying for a second that the Mirage killed the entire opposition during that manoeuvre. But it did demonstrate the almighty power at our disposal. That coupled with the knowledge that our NVGs were far superior to theirs, encouraged the insurgents to put away their guns.

At least for the time being.

We needed to patch up the wounded, so as many men as the medics needed jumped on that. There were also fires that needed to be extinguished, inside and outside of the compound, and ball-bearing bombs that had hit but not detonated requiring attention. The majority of the men, led by Damo and his boys, were on security detail. Steve McCulley was superb at directing the best people to the right jobs. For me he had another task.

'I need someone to go out and do a battle damage estimate.'

We need to check if we killed anyone.

'Are you up for it, Rob?'

'Yeah.'

'Great. Get going.'

I took six men. All marines, no interpreters, no medics. It's the minimum we needed and the maximum we could spare. I decided to leave behind the ECMs (electronic countermeasures). They were too heavy and we all had jelly legs from the morning. Also, they might not survive the route I was planning.

The insurgents may have packed up shop for the night but there wasn't a man in Toki who didn't believe that IEDs would have been installed outside the main gate the second we'd all locked ourselves in. There was no way of leaving in a hurry without major risk.

'What about the stream?' I suggested. 'We could all swim out there.'

Sometimes the worst ideas are the best. And we'd get to cool down.

I led the boys into the courtyard, we stepped into the stream and waded towards the wall. Then I held my breath, dived under and swam. It was barely two strokes but knowing you can't come up because there's a fucking great wall above your head adds that frisson of pressure. The risk that twenty Taliban rifles will be pointing at your head when you pop up adds to that frisson.

I emerged the other side unscathed. I looked up and saw the reassuring sight of three snipers on top of the wall covering our exit. As we waded upstream, they were with us every inch of the way.

I thought I knew alertness. I thought Garnzi Street had pushed me to the limits of my awareness. This was different. Different class. Different scale. If I had a 'Spider-Sense', Spider-Man's hyper-awareness, it was operational. I was aware of every insect hovering over me, every bird chirruping behind my back, every rustle of leaves as the wind picked up.

Slowly we inched our way up to where the jet had made its strafing run. I couldn't help being impressed. There were massive holes the size of two fists where each round had gone through the walls. If I say that our bullets were just bouncing off these same targets you will have an idea of how powerful a Mirage's armoury is.

Using just hand signals – like you see in the movies – we inched cautiously around the building. Weapons ready, postures aggressive, Spider-Sense turned up to the max. As we approached the north-east – and final – corner of the building I put my hand up.

Stop.

I could hear something. Someone.

I turned to face the lads. 'Around that corner,' I whispered, 'could be an insurgent. On your toes.'

I counted down from three with my fingers, then we swung around the corner en masse, rifles hot.

And saw an old woman peeling fruit.

She was just sitting there. An old lady in rags, minding her own business. Obviously it looked like a trap. We scoured the ground for tripwires, the walls for IEDs, the windows for snipers. Nothing. I radioed in that I wanted an interpreter. In the meantime, with one lad remaining with the woman, the rest of us turned the building inside out.

Nothing. No one. Not a single body.

You don't like to think of anyone being killed but, when you've got four good mates with serious injuries back at base, part of you wants – needs – some payback. We just didn't have any. There were no blood trails, no signs of injury even. The Mirage had ended the fight, but the score stayed resolutely the same: Taliban 4–Royal Marines 0.

By the time we'd searched the building some locals had started to appear. They were trying to talk to us but I kept them all at a safe distance. Friend or foe? When you don't share a language it's impossible to tell. Only when the recce lads arrived with an interpreter could I begin to relax.

The old woman said, 'The Taliban were here.'

'I know that,' I said, through the interpreter. 'Tell me about them.'

She shrugged, still shaving her pears. 'They come and go when they please. I don't stop them, they don't hurt me. These people –' she gestured to her neighbours – 'they don't help them but they don't oppose them either.'

'Are you on our side or not?' I said.

'I'm not for you or against you. But I do wish you hadn't come.'

Other villagers said the same thing.

'Go home. We don't need you. We are safer when you're not here.'

'But the Taliban want to rule you with violence.'

'It is what it is. But they don't have helicopters.'

I told the old woman and everyone else the same thing: 'We are here to help. We are here to rebuild your village, to guard your safety, to protect your rights as Afghans. We don't want anything from you. Trust us, please. We are not the enemy.'

We weren't – I believed that. But almost everything else was a lie. L Company would do all the good deeds I promised. The purpose of my lads, and J Company as a whole, was very different. But I could hardly tell the locals that. How do you explain 'We're here to draw fire away from our colleagues?' Or 'We're here to put your lives in danger.'

And, I was about to discover, *our own.*

CHAPTER THIRTEEN

WE USED TO BE THE HUNTERS

The sun is shining, there's the sound of splashing water and men's laughter, and the smell of fried food and beer in the air.

God, I wish I was in Spain.

It was hard to imagine that twenty-four hours earlier I had been speaking to my wife on her birthday without a care in the world. One of us without a care, anyway. A day later and she and the boys were doubtless enjoying the best Costa Brava beaches while several of my good friends had been badly wounded. I'd had my nerves shredded. And the Taliban had learned a good deal more intel about our fighting capability and methods than we had learned about them. And yet . . .

And yet it was a good result. Our brief was to stir up trouble. To draw the fire away from the north. We just hadn't expected it to happen so quickly.

Steve McCulley can inspire anyone. He's almost American in the way he can whip up a crowd, get the blood pumping. Ten minutes in his company and you're convinced you can take on the world. So, even though the lads with metal sticking out of their dehydrated backs might disagree, 24 May was a 'win' for us. A weird kind of victory but a victory none the less.

Now, as a new day dawned, we needed another.

The morning of the 25th started with me on sentry duty. Usually Toki would've been a four-post site. Because of what had happened the day before Steve had upped it to six positions, a minimum of two men each, all in constant radio contact. It could have been worse. I was sharing my shift with my corporal, Fergie. The man could speak but you had to be judicious in your listening. He was 50 per cent full of wisdom, 50 per cent full of shit. This watch, it was more the former.

'There's something odd about this situation,' he said.

'What? You and me getting the early shift? Tell me about it.'

'You did the rota, you wanker. I mean this war. Everything. It's all wrong. It's nothing like what we've been trained for.'

'I know what you mean. CTC is all about us being the superior force. And on paper we still are. It just doesn't feel like it. We're meant to be gathering intel on these bastards. It feels like they're gathering gen on us.'

'It's this simple,' he said. 'In the old days we used to be the hunters. In this hellhole we're the hunted.'

Our shift ended and we had breakfast with a few of the other lads. It was only whatever we had in our rations but it's nicer to eat with other people. My old mucker from Bickleigh Barracks, Plymouth, Ollie Augustin, was sitting with his 2ic, Sam Alexander, and a few of their men, so Fergie and I dropped in. I ran Fergie's theory by the lot of them. Some agreed, some didn't. It was mostly a split based on age and experience. To my mind Fergie, with his 'chicken fillet' a constant reminder, was the voice of reason. I was somewhere between the two.

Sam was another interesting guy. Just marine rank but at twenty-eight very experienced. He'd already been awarded a Military Cross for single-handedly saving some of his comrades on an earlier tour. Given the day we'd all just had, I said, 'Do you worry we're rolling the dice a few too many times here?'

'We've all got to go some time.'

It was just small talk, no one meant anything. But the mood in the camp and outside tended to give everything said a little extra weight.

As we tidied up, Kaz, the medic, was just sitting down so I stayed to chew the fat with him. To check that he was okay after the previous day. It was what Al Blackman, his multiple leader, would have wanted.

I shouldn't have worried. Canadians, in my experience, rarely let the world influence them if they can help it. It's their special power. Kaz would rather not have been busy that Tuesday, but to him, it was what it was. He lit a cigarette and offered it to me. I'd not smoked much before arriving at Mulladad. By now I was virtually a chain smoker. I took a drag before taking out one of my own and lighting it. Then he said casually, 'We're all in this together, Rob. Let's just see if we can get out of it in the same state.'

Shortly before 8 a.m. Steve McCulley called me and the other multiple leaders into his makeshift office. He wanted to push out some patrols. Show the locals who's boss. And, more important, draw the fire.

The first patrols were myself and Damo. We pushed north-east. Steve had picked a few compounds of interest, no more than 4 kilometres away, so that was our agenda. We were all wary as we stepped out of the main gate, but my trusty Vallon man, Robbie, swept the way and off we went.

I was only too aware of being watched. Mopeds zoomed up and down, back and forth, many times without any sort of purpose other than making sure they were seen. If it was an attempt at intimidation, it failed. All I took from it was multiple chances to remember their riders' faces. Beards can only hide so much.

To the west, the wounded M'lord's 2ic led a patrol with similar results. A lot of two-wheeled busybodies, a lot of chit-chat on the ICOM, but nothing of note. Certainly no engagements. We spoke to dozens of locals, performed twice as many biometric logs as usual; then, late in the afternoon, returned to Toki, exhausted but relieved.

And then, as dusk approached, came the first shots.

The attack was exactly the opposite to that of the previous day. We should have expected it. The Taliban were testing us. They'd seen what we could and would do during daylight. How would we respond in darkness?

This time, however, it was nothing like the long-drawn-out onslaught of the previous day. Thank God! Just enough to rattle everyone and keep us on our toes. The firers popped up one place, then another, then another, and then sodded off. I swear they were checking out our positions and timing our response. Job done, they drifted away for their tea or their assignations with goats, or whatever it was they did in their spare time.

When we realised they'd jacked it in for the night I suggested to Steve that I take a team out for a recce.

'Just a hundred metres forward, in the dark. You never know what we'll find.'

I took a skeleton squad. We followed the stream for about 100 metres. It cut through a field giving zero visibility to anyone watching. When we'd gone far enough, Robbie, Matt Kenneally and I broke cover and fired a Schermuly into the air. There was some general chatter when it lit up the area but no response, armed or otherwise, from locals. Thermal imaging revealed a few people but no one of interest. Confident we'd gone as far as we needed, we headed back.

Back at Toki one of the guys said what a few of us were thinking: 'Was that it?'

Our collective Spider-Sense said not.

* * *

The next morning, Thursday, 26 May 2011, we agreed with Steve to push out further and further from all round the compound, like petals on a flower. The plan was to cover 1,000 metres from the base in every direction.

My guys stayed back for the first shift while Damo's Recce guys went out on their own. They followed a similar patrol path to the one we had taken the day before. Back at camp I listened to the chatter. The interpreters had made a little area of the orchard their own slice of Afghan. By coincidence it was within listening distance of where Fergie and I were sleeping. Everyone had their own 'shell scrape' – your own little trench you slept in. Usually around a foot deep, I ordered my team to go down two feet. They provided warmth from the soil, but also, the idea was, if a bomb went off at surface level, you'd be just low enough to escape injury. After our first day at Toki it seemed practical.

Because the trenches were in the shade we often went there in down time, to relax. And so I heard the translators talking about what they were picking up from the field. The Recce lads weren't having an easy time. They had been pursuing a target. Then they were in a firefight. Then they were retiring. One of their lads was injured, badly. The more I heard, the more I knew we had to get involved. I summoned my lads out of the stream, out of their shell scrapes, wherever they were, and said, 'We need to stand to. It's only a matter of time before we're ordered out.'

As it happened, it didn't come to that. The Recce troop handled everything. They summoned air support and, while the Mirage flew menacingly close, they regrouped and dealt with their casualties. Then, with the aircraft still present, they called in a helicopter for a full-scale 'dust-off' or casevac – 'casualty evacuation'. That was it. They went, they fought, they returned, but in smaller numbers. They were obviously shaken up.

'They're definitely out there,' Damo said of the insurgents. 'And all they want is us. Dead.'

* * *

Friday, 27 May. Day 4 at Toki.

'It's time to step things up,' Steve McCulley said. 'Three teams, all pushing east, all within shouting distance, all tackling different targets.'

It made sense. East was where most the kinetic action was originating. He showed us multiple leaders a map marked with compounds or areas of interest and indicated where he felt each team should be in relation to the others. He wanted one team moving east from a slightly north position – that would be Damo with Steve's HQ boys attached.

Another team – led by me – would move in the same direction on a more central axis, and a third team, led by Ollie Augustin, would start in the south. So, three multiples marching in the same direction on different routes.

The territory was deemed so dangerous that any more than 40 metres between the teams' operational lines could be fatal. We each needed to provide 'overwatch' for our neighbours. That was the plan as Steve unfurled it.

The thing about Steve, though, is that he never orders you to do anything. Not if you're one of his respected few. So, as multiple leaders, we all got an opportunity to input. After a bit of to-ing and fro-ing we decided that the overwatch was too narrow, so why not extend the operational line to about 300 metres? That way we could cover more territory and still be in shouting contact with each other. One party would advance, declare it safe, then the others would follow and overtake. We'd concertina our way through the territory. It might be slow but it would be safe.

'Agreed!' Steve clapped his hands. 'Let's do this.'

By the time we set off, the temperature had already hit 40 degrees – and this was in the morning. By lunchtime we'd be roasting. And knackered to boot. We had a 9-square-kilometre area to cover.

The northern strand of the operational line included Steve, his FAC, his radio operators and other staff. In total they bolstered Damo's group to thirteen. My multiple began as eight, then we borrowed another two guys from M'lord's patrol, taking us to ten; Ollie's party was twenty – eight of them plus a dozen Afghans. We were a reasonably large force, for a patrol.

Numbers mean nothing against the Taliban. We knew that. The threat of IEDs and snipers behind every tree made the going slow. Monitoring each patrol's progress as well as my own just added to the wading-through-treacle effect. To explain: on a map you have northings, which are vertical lines on the page, and you have eastings, which go from the left of the page to the right. Navigation is via GPS. So when we moved 1,000 metres from easting 87 we would arrive at easting 88 and everyone else could pinpoint it on a map. That's how we stayed roughly in line.

While I had my eyes down in cartography land, my ears were full of ICOM chatter. John translated as much as he could but the sheer volume of material would have taxed a dozen translators. Luckily, there was no urgency. After two hours we were still a good way from our first compound of note. And it was to be another hour before we made contact with another living soul.

When we did arrive at the target compound my guys were flagging. I gave them a minute to take on water, then we knocked on the compound door in the wall. There is a whole list of measures you can take if an inhabitant doesn't open. This one did, first time. He even smiled when he saw me.

'Hello, Mister. How may I help you?' he asked, through John.

Every Afghan we spoke to, despite being perfectly placed to have seen or heard something, had nothing to say. It was almost as though an enemy force had beaten us to it and threatened repercussions if they so much as uttered a word. Looking around the family in that first compound, it was possible even that one of the so-called sons was an insurgent interloper. With Afghans, given their brown clothes and black hair and beards, it could be very hard to tell one from another.

The other patrols weren't faring any better.

I was so relieved to reach our last compound. We were all exhausted and boiling alive. If it weren't for a bit of intel from an informant, we would never have bothered going that far.

This had better be worth it.

We stopped 300 metres short of the target compound and waited for confirmation from the others that they were overwatching. Then we made our advance.

After a long, hot, tiring and fruitless day, it was tempting to go easy on the methodology, but there's no way I'd let men under my watch take their feet off the gas. If we go in, we go in as British Royal Marines. That means doing it by the book: full regalia, full respect, full training procedure. We did all this and, to a man, were disappointed to discover no more than a family. It was so frustrating. I wanted to wring the neck of the local who'd tipped us off about this gig. I was that angry.

'Maybe we should push on further?' I suggested. The lads agreed. More importantly, so did Steve. His own patrol was proving just as fruitless. He was happy for any initiative.

We decided we would go to the limit of our exploitation area, about 200 metres east of our latest position. Ollie and his patrol were running slightly behind us on the eastings line: they'd come across a complicated set of compounds, maybe four or five, all linked. At the same time Damo had reached a small compound to the north that didn't sit right with him. By the time we reached our final destination we felt the same bad vibes coming off it. It appeared to be defended like Fort Knox. And yet there were no people to be seen.

'Same story here,' Ollie said.

'Ditto,' we got from Damo.

'Nothing else for it then,' Steve said. 'Move in.'

Like everything else in the Marines, there's a policy for entering a building 'of interest'. We call it the 'quiet knock'. You start by banging on the door as normal. If no one answers but you are certain people are home, then they get a 'flash-bang' (stun grenade) through the window. It's a method that the police use before they enter a room. The flash-bang does what it says on the tin: it flashes and makes a lot of noise, usually leaving anyone in the vicinity in no state to put up a fight. Nine times out of ten, however, they will open the door, looking all disorientated. This was one of the one-out-of-ten occasions.

We knocked on the door: nothing.

I ordered John to speak through the loudhailer in case the family were in the rear of the compound. Nothing.

In the meantime the guys were working around the compound to check for hidden IEDs. Matt Kenneally came back to me and said, 'Do you want me to get up on the roof for a better look?'

'Good idea.'

We always carry assault ladders with us so Matt and a couple of others got up on the compound wall and hopped onto the closest roof.

'Christ, Rob,' he called back, 'there's loads of people in here.'

'Do they look deaf to you?'

'They look surprised.'

'Good.' I grabbed John. 'Tell them this is their last chance to open the door or we're taking it off its hinges.'

John did as I asked and eventually an old guy came out. Like so many Afghans he was incredibly hospitable and invited as in to enjoy some water and a bit of shade.

I didn't buy it.

'John, find out why they didn't let us in.'

The old guy came back with a cock-and-bull story about being scared. 'He thought we were the Taliban.'

'Do the Taliban normally knock?'

The old man shrugged.

I said, 'We need to know who's here.'

'Just me and my wife.'

We knew that was bollocks. What else was he lying about?

'Okay,' I said, 'that's enough reason for me to want to search this place top to bottom. Lads, in you go!'

You've never seen a fella look so worried. But whatever he was hiding didn't want to be found. After an hour we'd uncovered nothing in the house or the outbuildings. What we did see was a standard of living far higher than was usual in any other compound. It was bloody fishy, but there was nothing to pin on the old guy – yet. We still had one place to search, an air-raid shelter the man had built in his yard.

By coincidence, the old geezer couldn't find the key. My patience was wearing thin. I said, 'You've got five minutes. Then you won't need a key.'

While the seconds ticked down, I got in touch with Sunray to update him on progress. His party likewise had yet to unearth anything of note.

'What about Ollie's lot?' I asked.

Whatever he said in response I didn't hear. All anyone heard was the sound of a massive explosion.

It was the unmistakable sound of an IED. It came from the south. Judging by the plume of dust in the distance, I'd say about 500 metres away. I glanced at my map.

'Christ, that's where Ollie is.'

I started to send a bang rep to Steve. Suddenly the radio crackled with the sound of Ollie's 2ic trying to get off a nine-liner and struggling.

A nine-liner is the sequence in which you send nine pieces of information to arrange a casevac. Anyone with radio training knows the drill: via a series of letters and sequential numbers you categorise the extent of injuries, your location, how many wounded, how many dead, and so on. For anyone listening who knows the code it's a microburst of information. For the rest, it's like listening to a game of Battleships.

From his voice he was in a bad way. They all were, according to his report. In the end he gave up on protocol and just said, 'We've stepped on something.'

I immediately got off the radio. Sunray and Command needed the airwaves to speak to the patrol. But I was already lining up my guys. As soon as there was a break in transmission I got onto Sunray.

'We're closer than you. I'm going over.'

'Roger that,' Steve said. 'We'll be right behind.'

That's when I heard the second explosion.

This one was from the north – Steve and Damo's location.

'Oh my God!'

There was silence for about ten seconds. It felt like an hour. Then a voice came back on the air. It was Steve.

'The good news is it was just a goat,' he said. 'The bad news is the area is obviously littered with IEDs. We're not going anywhere very quickly. It's all up to you now.'

My instinct was to get everyone running south to help Ollie asap. My training said something different.

If both those patrols in the middle of nowhere have found IEDs, then what are the odds that we're surrounded by them as well?

High. And the lads knew it. They were all itching to get going but there was anger at the risks we'd have to take.

John the interpreter came up with an idea.

'This old man will know where the IEDs are for sure.'

'You're right.' He hadn't looked at all fazed by the explosions. He knew more than he was letting on. I went up to him and poked him hard in the chest.

'Tell me where the IEDs are buried,' I made John ask.

'There are no IEDs here,' he protested.

I was doing my best to remain professional, but it was hard. While I was speaking to him the radio hissed again. It was Ollie's man.

'I think there are four serious casualties. No, five. Including our medic.'

Kaz!

I was losing my patience. 'I haven't got time to play games, old man. Please tell me what I need to know. Men's lives are at stake.'

'No, no, no, I speak the truth. There are no bombs here.'

John was insistent. 'He's lying, boss. He's definitely lying.'

The radio came alive again: 'I think one of them has just died.'

At that point our medic for the mission, a Navy lad I'll call Jonesy, on loan to us from M'lord's multiple at Taalander, came up to me. 'Come on, Rob, I've got to get over there.'

'You're right, fuck it.' I turned to John and said, as coolly as I could, 'Tell this piece of shit that if he doesn't tell me where those IEDs are buried I will march his entire family out of this compound, over to Ollie and let them find the mines for us.'

There was no way in a million years that I would ever have done that. But I needed the old man to believe it. Judging by John's animated expression I think he embellished my threat even further. Whatever was said, the old man bought the story.

He said, 'As long as you stay near my compound and stay clear of the path you won't tread on anything.'

John wasn't satisfied. He said to me, 'Get your men. This pig is going to lead us to safety whether he wants to or not.'

Slowly but surely we walked out of the compound, down to a hedge.

Beyond it was a weird stretch of land, arid and raised in places.

'It's a burial site,' the old man said. 'Walk through the middle and you'll be safe.'

'If we're not, your compound is getting a visit from the Mirages,' John said. 'I promise you that.'

I looked at the map. Ollie's team were directly opposite, on the other side of this field.

'Fergie,' I said, 'what do you reckon?'

'I reckon we fucking go for it.'

'Agreed. Robbie – can you get us there?'

The nineteen-year-old was already in front of me. 'I'm on it, Rob.'

And off he went, at a run, at the same time clearing every inch of ground as best he could. One by one we filed after him, all running not for our lives, but for those of our mates on the other side of the burial ground.

The second we set off, John's radio started up. Interpreters are nowhere near as fit as marines but the guy did his best to shout out what he he was getting from ICOM in between panting.

'"The Americans are leaving. We have to catch them before they reach the trees."'

This day just gets worse.

'They can see us,' John said. 'It's probably those pigs at the compound.'

I knew he was right.

'Everyone,' I yelled into the radio, 'we have a viable threat around us. Weapons hot!'

We were running full pelt in heat of 55 degrees, with the possibility of landmines at every step – and now there was the very real danger of being shot at as well.

Can this fucking day get any worse?

The answer, I would soon discover, was *yes*.

CHAPTER FOURTEEN

HAVE I GOT EVERYTHING I NEED?

I wish being shot at was the only worry on my mind.

As we sprinted into the unknown across the burial site I was also in contact with Ollie's 2ic. If we made it over to them in one piece I needed to know what we were going to be met with. It didn't sound good. *He* didn't sound good. The whole patrol had found a gate inside a deep arch in a wall and, with temperatures at 55 degrees, they'd all gone in to escape the sun for a few minutes.

And, of course, that's where the IED had been hidden.

Someone, he said, had trodden on it. Sam Alexander, Ollie Augustin, JJ Chalmers, an interpreter and another marine were caught in the direct blast. Others, like Kaz, were felled by the shrapnel. Even as we spoke, the 2ic said they were still pulling the injured from the rubble.

'Have you ordered a medevac?'

'Yeah,' he said. 'First thing I did.'

I just hope you can stay alive long enough to need it.

As prepared as I was when we arrived, breathless, seeing the carnage with my own eyes was something else. While my brain began to slowly digest the scene in front of me, a blur of khaki ran past. It was Jonesy. His medipack was already off by the time he reached the first casualty.

The boy was terrific: straight in, no panic, no hesitation. A great addition to the patrol.

'That man needs a tourniquet – get on it!'

'Someone, elevate this leg.'

While Jonesy took control of the medical side of things, I went straight into overwatch mode. We knew for certain that enemy eyes had been on us. If they'd followed us here we'd be sitting ducks. All men not helping Jonesy I stationed in a sentry ring around the group. We might not able to stop an RPG, but we might stand a chance of shooting its operator before he pulled the trigger.

It was bloody tense. *I* was bloody tense. We had trees one way, fields another. Everywhere else was compounds. The threat could come from anywhere, but it was most likely to be from inside one of those buildings. The sweat was pouring down my face, not all of it from the oven-like temperatures. I was aware that just behind me were men in a condition I hoped never to see.

As everyone settled into their roles I allowed myself a chance to look around at the bomb site. Considering that I knew all these men, I was shocked that I couldn't recognise half of them. Blood was everywhere. On everything, on everyone. Body parts were scattered over the area. It was sickening.

I saw Jonesy leave one of the bodies. He'd been too late. The man had no legs. It must have been him who stepped on the bomb. It took me a significant period of staring to realise it was Sam Alexander. I felt sick. Two days earlier we'd been talking about our luck running out. No one truly believed it would. Certainly not Sam. Yet here he was.

Further round was another mess of missing parts. This was Ollie. He was only twenty-three, already a lieutenant, and destined for greatness. From the way Jonesy was frantically working on him I guessed he was still alive. But it didn't look promising. Near by, Lance Corporal JJ Chalmers was another one in a bad way. His right arm was in pieces. His left hand had fingers missing. His head looked like it was pointing the wrong way. Everywhere I looked was like a horror film.

Eventually I noticed the wounded man closest to me. The blood made it hard to distinguish who it was. *Bloody hell, it's Kaz!* Just eight hours earlier we'd shared a smoke together. Now one of his eyes was looking the wrong way, his face was totally messed up and his right foot was nowhere to be seen. Still keeping a watch in the distance, I knelt down next to him and took his hand. It was pure instinct.

'Mate,' I said, '. . . ' But the words just didn't come. What do you say?

Kaz groaned. At least he was alive. His good eye stared at me. He knew he was in a shit state.

'Rob,' he croaked. 'You've got to tell me: have I got everything I need?'

'Everything you . . .?'

He was looking towards his feet now.

Oh, I know what you're talking about.

I glanced at his groin. All intact as far as I could see.

'Yeah, you randy bastard, you've still got everything you need.'

He smiled. At that moment the morphine being pumped into him couldn't have made him feel better.

'What about the others?' he said.

'You just worry about yourself.'

I didn't want to tell him that one of the interpreters had not been so lucky. Even from where I was kneeling I could see the man was missing his genitalia and much else. Weirdly, he appeared to be in less pain than Kaz, thanks to the morphine the lads had already pumped into him.

'How are we doing on that chopper?' Jonesy called out. Calm but firm.

I made contact with Captain G-side, Steve's 2ic at Toki, who contacted Bastion.

'Five minutes,' I relayed back.

It was the longest five minutes. To make it worse people started coming out of the compounds. *With cameras.* There we were, surrounded by our dead and wounded friends, and barely 70 metres away from us there were people taking photos.

So many things go through your mind at a time like that.

On a tactical level I'm thinking, *Are they recording our responses to see how we operate?*

On a cynical level, I'm thinking, Is this just going up on YouTube for the hits and likes?

But on a human level I'm thinking, *These ambulance chasers disgust me.*

I radioed Sunray a sitrep.

'Permission to fire warning shots.'

'Confirmed.'

On my command the few of us guarding the area facing the crowd raised our weapons and fired above the heads of the rubberneckers. At the same time John was yelling through the loudhailer for them to go back home. Some went. Most just backed off. At least the filming stopped.

What really got them moving, though, had nothing to do with me. The sound of two American Pavehawk helicopters – 'Pedros', as they're known – buzzed over us from nowhere. They'd been sent for a reason. British MERT birds – medical emergency rescue teams – aren't armed. You didn't have to be a military expert to see that these were bristling with machine guns. After one pass the front chopper hovered over us and rotated, firing as it turned. We were in no danger. It was pivoting on a 50-metre arc. But it bloody cleared those Afghans out of our way.

Job done, the first bird began to land 20 metres from us. I'd already helped get the injured onto stretchers that were part of the patrols' kit. 'As soon as the dust settles, we get them out of here.'

As knackered and hot as everyone was, the lads tending the victims found the energy to sprint towards the Pedro. The second it landed I wanted those casualties on board and out of here. The longer they were on the ground the more danger they were in from the assembling Taliban threat.

But it didn't work out like that.

The Pedro's rails barely touched down when a paramedic leapt out. He took one look at the men haring towards him with stretchers and said, 'They're not going anywhere.' Then he gave a shout and the chopper just took off again. It barely bounced on the earth before springing back out of reach.

I was straight over there. I proper wanted to smash that guy in the face.

'What the fuck are you playing at? Get these men to safety!'

I was ready to square up. I was ready to do God knows what, if I'm honest. A combination of the heat, the pressure of running the whole site and seeing my mates badly wounded all burst out. The Yank looked stunned. Somehow, I got myself back under control.

He said simply, 'That's not how we do things.'

The British MERT technique is simple: you throw all casualties on board and deal with them on the fly. American medical practice was: send out a doctor, perform triage as best you can and prioritise the evacuation. They both have their merits but what the US system doesn't take into account is that the threat from local aggressors was only going to get worse the longer we were there. The ICOM was in meltdown. Tons of voices were talking about us. I had barely half a dozen men guarding the site, with the injured, the dead and those tending them. If just half those chattering on the radio appeared with guns we'd be outnumbered. Outnumbered and exposed trying to protect our comrades.

This makes no fucking sense.

The medic flew round the group. Jonesy had done as much as any man could. There was little else the Yank could offer. Except 'wit'. When he checked Kaz over he said, 'Is he American?'

'No, he's Canadian.'

'Ah,' he smiled. 'Fucking idiot.'

Kaz opened his good eye. 'Fuck you.'

The American wasn't finished. He took one look at Kaz's stump and said, 'Your dancing days are over, I'm afraid.' (Which proved to be ironic, because five years later Kaz would win a special Christmas edition of *Strictly Come Dancing*.)

Eventually the expert had seen enough. He whistled the birds back down and we got the lads on. As they pulled away Steve McCulley and his team emerged from the trees.

'Rob,' he said, 'you look like shit.'

'I feel like it, sir.'

'You know this is just the beginning, don't you?'

'All too well.'

* * *

It was a relief to hand over the burden of responsibility to Steve. Whatever happened now wouldn't just be on my own shoulders.

At least, that was the idea.

Mentally I was on my last legs. So many decisions, all those men counting on me. But, as Steve said, it was far from over. We'd only packed off the injured. I still had to maintain the integrity of the explosion site until the investigation team arrived. And, of course, they'd need protecting as well.

By now we'd been on our feet for seven hours. In the blazing sun. We were drained and, I realised, dangerously close to dehydration. When you're so determined to help others you forget to look after yourself. Luckily, the investigation boys brought a shitload of water with them. One by one I called the lads in to get their fill, then it was back to the day's work.

Robbie, as usual, was the first to lose any downtime – the curse of being the best at his job.

'We need to sweep the compound where the IED went off,' I said. 'Can you get us a path?'

'I'm on it.'

Amazing kid.

Suddenly there were four operations going on. The big tidy-up process was the one I liked least. There were body parts scattered around, among the helmets and blood-stained armour. That all needed to be bagged and tagged. The investigators worked the bomb crater for clues as to how it had been caused. Half the available men from both patrols began the search of the compound, while the rest stayed

Off we went, this ragtag group. There was me, a few Afghan soldiers, a couple of OMLT men, people drawn from all quarters. We'd all been in the field for ten hours. By the time we got home it would be a full twelve.

John was still keeping me updated about the ICOM. I was beginning to feel that the chatter was more bluff and bullshit. For most the afternoon we'd been ripe for the picking. I definitely would have launched an attack if I had been the Taliban.

But I wasn't 'them'. I didn't think like them or act like them. The longer I stayed in that country the more I realised that I never could or would. The Taliban were prepared to do things I couldn't contemplate. For that reason we couldn't afford to relax for a second. Any movement at a window, behind a hedge, in a field, was a potential deadly threat.

After a wearisome 3-kilometre march Toki was finally in sight. Just two fields and a bit of track lay between us and safety, probably about 300 metres. We kept to the fields. They were less likely to have been mined. They also offered the most direct route. It meant going near some abandoned farm machinery and towards a quiet compound. But it did keep us away from the road, where, once again, the sight and sound of mopeds bombing along, then stopping, turning round and bombing back, again filled the air. They were all ridden by men with mobile phones or walkie-talkies pressed to their ears.

Fergie radioed from the back of the line.

'I've got a bad feeling about this.'

'You're not the only one,' I said. The Afghan soldiers in our group had been twitchy as hell for the last ten minutes. Obviously they knew the people we were dealing with. They could also hear the activity on John's walkie-talkie.

I looked around us. Where were the women and children? Where were the farmers? Where were the normal people?

'Full alert, guys!' I instructed. 'Something could kick off here.'

No sooner had the words left my mouth than Matt came on the radio.

'Halt!'

We all dropped instinctively to a kneeling position, weapons poised. Shattered as we were, training just takes over.

'Talk to me, Matt,' I said.

'Change of direction,' he said. 'Just looking for the safest route.'

We had been walking predominantly westwards, but the layout of the land and compounds meant that we needed to shimmy through a chicane between two buildings before picking up our route.

'Did Sunray come this way?' I asked.

'I don't think so. Their trail went cold a while back.'

Robbie and Matt set off, me 15 metres behind the front man. When the three of us were through the chicane most of the rest of the lads hadn't yet entered it. Half our patrol were on the southern wall of the building and the other half had turned at a right angle and were already on the western side of the building. Not ideal.

I was carrying so much extra armour that I barely made it through the alleyway without scraping the sides. When I did emerge I could still see our camp faintly in the distance, about 120 metres away, partly obscured by the tall field crops. I could also see a compound much closer. Matt was standing by its wall outside, next to a farmer and a boy. All three were staring at what looked to me like a big oak tree on a patch of open land bare of crops.

I followed Matt's gaze and realised there was something in the tree. Objects dangling like Christmas decorations. But decorations don't usually wear British military camouflage gear.

The more I focused the more I managed to discern the various bits and pieces of armour identical to that on my back. I was faintly amused to make out the unmistakable shape of one of our regulation groin protectors – 'bulletproof nappies', we call them – strung up. Yet what was next to it was no laughing matter.

'Shit!' I said. 'That's not just a uniform. That's a leg.'

First rule: sitrep. On the radio: 'Steve, you're not going to believe this: there are body parts, belonging to one of ours, hanging in a tree. We're going to be back late.'

'Do not approach it,' Steve said. 'The land underneath could well be mined. We've had reports of similar.'

Most of my men hadn't seen it yet because the patrol snake was still back through the chicane. But suddenly I was surrounded by the Afghan deployment. They weren't particularly in a mood to follow blindly whatever we did. They were straight over to the farmer, shouting in his face. It was reckless but I admired their instincts.

'John,' I said to my interpreter, 'we need to question this guy before they do something silly.'

I thought I'd met the height of head-in-the-sand liars at that compound earlier in the week. This guy was just as evasive. More so, even.

'Who hung that up?'

'I don't know.'

'This is your field?'

'Yes, this is my field.'

'You have a tree in your field?'

'Yes, I have a tree in my field.'

'Who put these objects in it?'

'I don't know.'

'Where are the Taliban? Which compound do they live in?'

'There aren't any Taliban around here.'

'In that case,' I said, 'you'll be in no danger cutting those things down.'

He knew I meant business. He spoke to the young boy, who then ran over to the tree, shinned up it and started tearing away at the knots until every piece had fallen down. Then he dragged the whole lot over and dumped it at my feet. I thought I'd already experienced the worst thing I would that day, but this was something else. I actually apologised to the lads I asked to bag it up. I'm not sure I could have gone that close.

Fergie was at my shoulder.

'This is fucked up,' he said. 'We need to get out of here!'

I approached the old man. I was about to say that I'd be back later to search his compound when I heard a kerfuffle behind me as one of the Afghan soldiers just cracked the old man on the head with his rifle butt. He'd run from about ten metres back, and the force of the blow sent the old man sideways into the wall and down onto the ground. The boy looked scared for his life so I intervened. If I hadn't we'd have had a murder on our hands, Afghan on Afghan. That was something I could not allow.

I was shouting at John to order the Afghans to stand down when suddenly there was a loud fizzing noise. I turned, looked to my left at the field next to us. There, a metre from me, fizzing in a small furrow was a round black object.

'Grena—'

It all happened so quickly. A wall of warm air lifted me off my feet and dropped me face down among the crops. The sound of the explosion lingered long after the blast had died.

I was already dehydrated, weak. Now disorientated. Ears ringing, I pushed myself up and was aware of another noise. Gunfire.

All hell was breaking loose.

Shots were coming from the compound behind us. Robbie and Matt were returning fire. The Afghans had spotted another target, which they were engaging. Another one of my men was staggering, firing wildly in a north-westerly direction.

Directly at Toki.

I wanted to pick up my gun but, as multiple leader, I had one job at that moment. Same one I always had. Get a report off up the chain. Let them know that we were under attack from Compound 49, according to my map, and could require medical assistance. But mainly I had to ensure they didn't think we were firing at them – even though one of us was! If they got confused and launched one of their heavy weapons we were all toast.

The report was over in a matter of seconds, then I took stock of the situation. I realised that not one but two grenades had landed. Several men were down with shrapnel wounds. Fergie was nearest me. I went to check on him and realised he was just groggy, like me, from being thrown by the blast. Superficial damage only.

The worst hit were the old man and the boy. Each had serious stomach injuries. I couldn't work out why they were so badly hurt and Fergie and I were scratch-free. We'd been standing directly next to the grenades. Then I noticed a bit of metal sticking out of the extra armour over Fergie's shoulder.

Of course.

Fergie and I were so laden with the kit from Sam, Ollie and the rest, it had protected us from the blast.

As it should have done for them.

My priority was to rein in the maverick shooter who had risen out of the mud and was firing at the compound. I managed to grab, calm and disarm him and pull him to safety. Then it was a question of getting everyone organised while adding my own weight to the firefight.

Our primary threat was whoever was inside the compound. I manoeuvred the men to where they would cause maximum damage from the safest positions.

We returned fire for thirty minutes with no casualties on our side. The last thing I wanted was for the insurgents to regroup. The constant flow of mopeds from earlier had to be going somewhere.

We need to get out of here.

Normally I'd be straight on the radio: 'Fire and manoeuvre, lads.' Ollie's 2ic was already making it happen.

It was textbook stuff. While we covered Robbie, he ran out, drawing fire. He dropped into a shooting position then opened up. The moment he was in place another man ran 5 metres in advance of him and did the same. We were going to crawl our way out or die trying.

Slowly this weird caterpillar took shape. I was the last to go. I still had the armour, and now we had two seriously injured civilians and the remains of a fallen marine.

Fire-and-manoeuvre is a laborious process, but it ensures the widest coverage against an enemy that won't let up in its attack. Every step of the way I was in contact with Steve McCulley. When we'd put 100 metres between us and the compound, he said, 'Be prepared to take cover. I have a Pred on station.'

The beast in question, the Predator, is a drone, an unmanned aircraft designed for, among other purposes, stealthy destruction. Unlike the Mirages and the Chinooks, you don't hear the Predator. And you definitely don't hear what it releases.

Not before, not during and – if you're the target – not after.

'That is the first bit of good news I've heard all day!'

'Guys,' I shouted, 'prepare for an airstrike.'

Hellfire missiles travel faster than the speed of sound and their payload is devastating.

Even from 100 metres the shock wave from the explosions was immense. My ears still hadn't stopped ringing from the grenades, but this noise was something else. When it cleared I heard a new sound.

Silence.

'Enemy neutralised,' I reported. 'Or near enough.'

That was it. No more engagement. No more insurgent activity. Time to go home.

* * *

We'd left Toki that morning at 5.30 a.m. Twelve and a half hours later we were on our last legs, dragging ourselves and our baggage the final 50 metres along the dirt track to the compound. We were absolutely licked. I think the sentries saw this. A minute later the gate opened and half a dozen lads, wearing shorts and as much body armour as they could sling on as they ran, sprinted over to help us. Someone took the excess armour off me. Someone else saw to Fergie. Others picked up the wounded Afghans and the bags of body parts. Whatever they could do to ease our last few steps back.

I got in the compound and heard the gate shut and saw the sentries move the ballast into place to stop it being rammed. But I didn't feel safe. The day had changed me. It took a few moments to realise we'd come back with five men fewer than the group had set out with. That seemed like the work of another day entirely.

Sleep, though, wasn't an option. The sentry points still had to be maintained throughout the night. The old farmer needed to be seen to by a doctor and interrogated, and the boy too needed urgent medical attention. I needed someone to log the body parts from the tree and get them to Bastion for analysis, and Sunray needed a full briefing on what had happened. Perhaps more important, we all needed a moment to reflect on our own.

I remember sitting round the fire to eat. Fergie cooked my dinner. He was the closest I had to a confidant. We ate for a while in silence. Usually one of us would find the humour in the situation. This wasn't one of those times. Eventually I said, 'What the hell happened out there today?'

'We got fucked, that's what.'

'That we did.'

'But at least we're doing our job.'

'What do you mean?'

'We're the bait, remember?'

'Well, they're getting results. I don't know how long we'll last.'

The couple of guys I'd borrowed from M'lord's multiple came over to sit with us. One of them was an RMR – Royal Marine Reservist. Amazingly, he was holding up brilliantly, but then his 'day job', if you like, was a fireman. Stress, pressure, hideous odds, terrible injuries – nothing new for him there. Take out the IEDs and the bullets and today was just another shout. His mate was a different proposition. He was younger, much younger than me, and I honestly think he'd seen too much. I actually made a point of finding M'lord after and saying, 'I think he needs some time away from the patrols.'

Everywhere I looked there were men trying to clean the blood off their kit. Basically just trying to normalise the day. Get back into a rhythm.

The last people I spoke to before turning in were the interpreters. They were all pretty shaken up, even John, who'd remained solid in the field. One of their guys had been among the most serious casualties. I think it brought home the futility of what we were trying to do among their own people.

'Look how the Taliban treat their own people,' one of them said. 'You can't let them win. Promise us you won't.'

'Don't worry about that,' I said. 'Tomorrow the Taliban pay.'

Famous last words.

CHAPTER FIFTEEN

LET IT BURN

'**C**ome on, let's do this.'

We were at the gate, ready to go. I'd had a shake-up of personnel. Some of the lads who hadn't come out the day before were in the team. Others, like Fergie and the younger of M'lord's lads, I judged would be better served by staying back at camp. The rest were volunteers – as we all were, actually. At our 'council of war' with Steve McCulley after the previous patrol he had said, 'I'm not going to make anyone go back out there.'

He was addressing us multiple leaders. To a man we were all determined to go.

'We've got unfinished business,' I said. 'The Taliban gave us a bloody nose today. If we don't get back out there and try to even the score then our friends have died for nothing.' I wasn't going to let the ringing still in my ears put me off going back.

Everyone said a version of the same thing: to us, 27 May would be remembered as a loss. We'd been badly wounded without ourselves having touched a hair on the Taliban's beards. They'd injured more of their own than we had. We all took small comfort that the Predator might have balanced the books.

'If we don't go out we leave the north exposed,' Steve said.

Damo was more blunt. 'Lads, if we don't go out we may as well stop calling ourselves marines.'

We went out in two teams. Matt Kenneally had outperformed himself, spotting the body parts and getting us into the compound, so his reward was to be asked to go again. The same with Jonesy. I asked him if he wanted to come and he had no hesitation. Robbie, of course, could not be stopped. There was another lad I'll call 'Ted', plus a few others I won't name. They all wanted what I wanted. Revenge.

The other patrol was the Recce squad plus Steve's own HQ team and the FAC, who, if any big toys were required up above, could order them in minutes.

The plan was to take a very similar route to the previous day's, with the objective being to gain a good understanding of the compound and main buildings involved in the carnage. This is called a 'standing patrol', and it's as much an intelligence gathering exercise as anything. You go out and look around, and if you trigger an event then you can react.

And we were *desperate* to react.

In light of the hammering we'd taken, Steve said, 'For the purposes of this patrol we are moving to more aggressive rules.' He also revealed he would have air support on standby.

For the first time since March the senior management were acknowledging that their boys were not equipped well enough for the terrain they – we – had been sent to subdue. The Taliban had no rules. We had rules about shaving and shitting. In a bloody fight to the death, who would you put your money on? The highly trained bloke with hi-tech weaponry who has one hand tied behind his back? Or the survivalist who will do anything to win?

The amended rules of engagement didn't mean we were going to walk around murdering civilians. But we didn't have to wait until colleagues' legs were flying off in the opposite direction to their bodies before we could take lethal action.

I've got a good feeling about this . . .

* * *

Once again we were on the move before 6 a.m. I thought we'd have a clear run but the farmers were already up. The proper farmers, not the fake kids posing with tools while beaming their reports to insurgent leaders. These old guys didn't look at us twice. They were driving their animals, following the sun as they had done for generations.

We had fields to cross, little waterways to navigate. It was largely the same route, but by a different path. Retrace your own footsteps at your peril – IEDs were always planted where they guessed you would walk.

Travelling parallel to the Recce team along the eastings but slightly more to the south, we got ourselves to within 200 metres from the group of compounds that had caused all the trouble. A small incline gave us natural cover. Ted and I climbed up onto a stack of hay bales for an unobstructed view. We lay for a couple of hours, watching, monitoring, checking in with Sunray to see what his group was observing. I remember the radio signal was poor. Steve kept breaking up. Then he'd move position along the tree line and suddenly sound clear as a bell. Neither of us had anything to report. It was hot and we were totally exposed as the temperatures crept up. Everything was quiet.

This is not good . . . What are we missing?

And then I heard it. We all did. The horrible, deafening crackle and blast of an IED.

I rolled over on the hay to check the lads. It was none of us. I flicked the radio and contacted Steve.

'Ten A? Sunray? IED explosion to the north of our position.'

Unusually I got nothing back. For thirty seconds I kept trying all the frequencies for the Recce troop. Nothing. Then Captain G-side, Steve's 2ic, came online.

'Thank God,' I said – and then I remembered. He hadn't come out today. He was back at Toki.

'What's going on?' I asked.

'You tell me. I can't raise Sunray.'

'Do you need me to investigate?'

'Do you have a position?'

'I will in two seconds.'

We had started moving north when suddenly the radio crackled.

'Sunray!'

It was one of the Recce lads.

'Sunray's been hit,' he said. 'I repeat, Sunray's been hit.'

Oh, shit!

I got off the line to let him co-ordinate directly with Toki to get a MERT.

Just don't send the fucking Americans this time . . .

Listening to the nine-liner being despatched I knew things were rough. Even as it was being transmitted I got the guys ready to move. 'Do you need help?' I asked Steve's man.

'Absolutely,' he said. 'We've got a load of ICOM active near us. We think people are positioning themselves. This could get nasty.'

They were around the other side of the compound, about 400 metres from us. There was a straight-line route but as soon as we set off I heard machine guns. They weren't targeting us – yet. If we went the direct route, though, we'd be totally exposed for five or six minutes. Instead I kept the lads to the low ground to try to sneak up from behind.

As we neared the treeline the firing intensified. The Recce lads were under enormous pressure. At the rate we were moving I wasn't convinced we'd get there in time to be of any help.

Luckily, we didn't have to.

If the detonation of an IED is loud and unexpected, the sudden appearance of a Mirage directly overhead is ten times worse. I thought a bomb had gone off next to my head. The jet could only have been a few metres above the tallest tree. The noise was immense and the sight terrifying.

And I was on the same side.

The Mirage slowed almost to stalling point, then the nose lifted and its engines roared as the afterburners engaged. With the aircraft's tail pointed downwards, the heat where we were was like a furnace. What the compound must have felt would have been like a volcano. This was the modern equivalent of a dragon swooping down and threatening to torch a village, and I reckon it had the same effect. The shooting stopped, absolutely. The Mirage did one more circuit as a show of force before disappearing as suddenly as it had arrived. I was surprised it hadn't opened fire. I think maybe the insurgents were, too. They knew they'd had their warning though. Next time the Mirage wouldn't just bare its teeth.

We were still 200 metres south. A stream on our left was heading in the direction we needed to follow so I ordered everyone in. On top of cooling us down it was the safest way for us to travel. The streambed is below ground level and it doesn't have IEDs. But moving through the water can be hard work. The stream was 3 metres wide and came up to waist level at its deepest, so the going was slow. We were moving against the flow. I was also checking GPS co-ordinates all the way, as we were too low for visual contact. The last thing I needed was to overshoot the Recces.

Eventually we made it.

'Lads, we're here.'

We started climbing the bank.

Click-click-click.

Click-click-click.

Click-click-click.

'Break contact!'

We all fell back in the stream, guns at the ready. Someone was waiting for us to emerge. The giveaway triple clicks of sniper rounds aimed at our heads drew cover fire from the Recces.

Click-click-click.

Click-click-click.

I could hear the exchange of rounds, placing the two sides.

I summoned my team. 'I'm going out. I'll take two volunteers. The rest wait for the all-clear then get on with the casevac.'

I'm not losing any more men today.

In the next lull in the firing, I and two others leapt out of the stream – as much as you can leap carrying near your own weight in soaked equipment – and pelted towards the GPS reference I'd been given. Within a couple strides we got visuals on the Recce guys lined up. Two more strides and the shots began raining down again. The ground in front of me exploded in puffs of dust. The tree behind me splintered. The Recces opened fire to the max and silenced the attack. But I knew we'd cut it fine.

I ran straight over to Steve. This was my friend, my boss and my mentor. The nine-liner told you only so much. I had no real idea how seriously he was injured. I prayed he wasn't another Ollie or Sam.

He was lying on one of our black roll-up stretchers. They look a bit like an industrial bin bag and weigh about as much. The bag was as wet as I was, but not with stream water. He was lying in an inch of his own blood, and it was getting higher.

With the bullets pinging around it's hard to focus but all I could see was holes. His armour was pitted like a crumpet, his flesh looked like a pin cushion. But he had his legs.

The men working on him were doing a fantastic job.

'What did he step on?' I asked.

Without looking up, one of them said, 'He didn't step on anything. It was detonated when he walked past.' He pointed towards the trees. The remains of an oil drum were strewn around a scorched patch of earth. Its contents would have been blasted out of it at thousands of metres per second. The trees around it bore the proof. So did three of Steve's men being treated by comrades. The man himself had taken the lion's share.

'Shit luck,' I said.

'Nah.' The guy shook his head. 'This was organised. Three of the patrol walked past before Sunray. They knew who he was. He was targeted.'

Shit! How the fuck were they doing this? Steve was dressed identically to the rest of us. With the helmet he was indistinguishable from any of the others. This time he'd been fourth in the line. Another day he'd be sixth or eighth or third. Could it have been luck?

'They saw me.'

I did a double take. The voice sounded like a kid's who had sucked helium from a balloon. But it was coming from Steve. Somehow he was awake and he was following the conversation.

I dropped to my knees.

'Don't speak. We're going to get you out of here.'

He ignored me. *He's the boss.*

'I couldn't get a signal,' he squeaked. 'I had to stand up when everyone was lying down. They were watching. They had to be.'

For Christ's sake!

How were they doing it? We were part of the biggest military machine in history. They were a jumble sale of an opposition yet they were running rings round us. They saw us when we didn't see them. And they consistently racked up big points when we were scoring ducks.

The more I studied Steve the more holes in him I saw. The guys were cutting away clothes everywhere there was damage and finding more wounds each time. I think his eardrums must have perforated as well. He didn't always hear us and his answers were shouted. The high-pitched voice was explained by the cavern where his back used to be. Obviously the blast had caught his lungs.

'What's wrong with me?' he asked.

It was like listening to the voice of Mickey Mouse. To me, after everything I'd seen, it was just funny – at the darkest moments the blackest humour is what works. He kept saying his leg hurt. I checked. He had everything he needed, including both feet. The upper right side of his body had taken the full brunt of the blast. His mind, I think, was covering up the true pain.

Every cut we made in his clothing revealed a new horror. Under Steve's right armpit there was a huge hole, and it was pulsating. Jonesy was busy elsewhere. The rest of us knew just basic triage. This was out of our comfort zone.

'Where's that fucking helicopter?'

One of the lads called over.

'It's here but it won't land till we can guarantee safety.'

I wasn't doing anything useful with Steve, so I ran over to co-ordinate the HLS – helicopter landing site. With the rest of us providing cover by continuous fire, I got Robbie and three of the Recce lads to go out with mine detectors to clear a space. Downdraught from the rotors is enough to set off an IED so we needed a clearing measuring at least 15 x 30 metres.

Click-click-click.

Click-click-click.

Everything the insurgents fired at us we doubled in our reply. Still they kept pecking away and still our four boys kept sweeping that space. When Robbie gave me the thumbs-up I was straight on the comms.

'We've cleared the HLS. Get that bird down. Now.'

I was standing among the trees on the higher ground to the east of the stream. Toki was on the other side, to the west. The stream ran north to south. Between us and the water was a sloping field. That's where the lads were sweeping for IEDs. It could have been better; it could have been worse. It was the best we had.

Out of nowhere I heard rotor blades. A voice on the radio: 'Pop some smoke.'

'Roger that,' Damo said. 'Purple.'

Textbook procedure at a time of crisis. We throw out a grenade which streams out smoke. The smoke directs a helicopter to a precise spot and indicates wind direction. The colour of the smoke confirms it's a friendly. Use the same colour each time and the Taliban quickly start doing the same in order to encourage false landings. My choice of purple on that occasion was random – and safer.

Choppers always land into the wind. Watching from the ground is like watching an eerie *X-Factor* intro as this magnificent machine slowly emerges from the haze. But there was no time to be impressed. The second the Chinook touched earth four of us were sprinting towards it with Steve, each of us holding a corner of the stretcher. We had 15 metres to cover and we probably broke the record getting there. In a handicap race, anyway. The threat of enemy bullets at any moment added extra zip.

Just as we reached the Chinook its back door lowered and a medic dashed out directing us up the ramp and inside. Then he ran out to make sure the other casualties were being shipped in as well. Medevac is chaotic, it's noisy, it's dangerous and it's a little bit brilliant. All these tiny cogs in a well-oiled machine working without fault. And, I have to admit, without any regard to their own lives. A stray bullet could have taken down any one of us. It didn't enter our minds. We had to get our mates on board that bird at any cost.

That didn't mean we got it right.

The CH-47 is massive, but it's also designed to be flown in combat areas. The ramp is where the gunner would normally sit with a mounted machine gun. As this was a medevac he wasn't there – but the weapon was. We ran full pelt blindly up the ramp and straight into the machine gun.

'Ow!' Steve squealed. 'My leg!'

Him and his fucking leg. You couldn't make it up.

'Sorry, mate!' and on we went.

We dumped him down and sprinted back out for the next casualty, managing to avoid the gun this time. As I turned to leave, I took a look at Steve and hoped it wouldn't be my last.

His back was missing.

In the time it took for the next man to be delivered, the Chinook doctors had anaesthetised Sunray, rolled him onto his front and cut his back wide open from the neck downwards. Right before my eyes they were massaging his heart from behind.

Absolutely incredible. While the rest of us had our heads in the sky, high on adrenalin, these surgeons were cooler than ice. I knew Steve and the others were in the best hands. All around them were guns, grenades, ammo, armour and the sound of bullets mere feet away. And there they were, oblivious to the dangers, doing what they were trained to do.

With the last wounded man on, we jumped off and literally dived on top of one another. The second we were off the ramp, the Chinook started to rise as the rotors whirred. Seconds later the dust storm they kicked up made vision impossible. The real threat, though, was the downward pressure. Only the fact we were clinging onto each other stopped us from being blown away, possibly onto IEDs.

It took a minute or so for the dust to settle. Literally and figuratively. We looked like desert rats. Everyone else was still firing at the compound. When would it end?

* * *

Getting Steve and the others to safety felt like the threat was over, but for those on the ground it was just beginning. Not just for the day, but the rest of the tour.

The march back home was eventful. I had twenty-two men from the combined patrols, all moving with 5 metres between each of them in this giant snake configuration. What the front guys saw the back guys didn't. Sometimes the rear encountered threats not in place when Robbie et al., at the head, had gone through. We fired at every conceivable target as we went. The gloves were well and truly off.

Enemy fire came often when we least expected it. We would all drop to our knees and respond. At the penultimate treeline before Toki one compound got particularly spicy. Shots were falling mere metres from me. I gave the order to unleash an RPG.

The rocket shot into the house and the firing ended – and along with it several lives, I imagine.

But the rocket-launch system's backblast kicks up a hell of a lot of dust. Throw in the loud explosion as the grenade detonated and all those men not listening to their radio messages freaked out. A second after the blast, Jonesy came flying past me with the same vigour with which he'd leapt to tend to Ollie and Sam.

'Where's the bomb? Where's the bomb?' He thought we were the ones under attack.

It wasn't just the medic. All our nerves were on edge. Some of the men I barely recognised. They were twitching at crop stems like Space

Cadet used to, seeing enemy eyes in a gust of wind. I couldn't blame them. Most of the time they were wrong. Then suddenly a tree would appear to fire at us and you'd realise there was a moped parked in the track behind it. The shooter would let off a few rounds then disappear. There wasn't a moment's grace. A moment's peace. Our nerves were being worn down.

For two kilometres we moved with bullets rattling past us every hundred steps. The danger was everywhere and ever-present. And that was without the threat of IEDs. Your instinct when shot at is to dive for low ground. If that low ground hasn't been cleared by the Vallon man you could be leaping into more trouble.

Click-click-click.

Click-click-click.

I dropped to my knees and attempted to establish the origin of fire. Then I returned it with interest. It came from a compound 40 metres to our left. Just one position above the wall, so not an army. Just one person who recognised an enemy on his uppers. A week earlier we would have changed course and ripped that perp out of his eyrie. Right then, we just wanted to get home.

The problem with being in a hurry is that it makes you predictable. For the last 2 kilometres we'd been moving in a line as true as an arrow's flight. It was the most direct passage to base. It was also the easiest to predict. After breaking the back of the journey without injury, about 80 metres from Toki, salvation in sight, Robbie halted. If the point man stops, everyone stops. No one has to say a word. The second man stops and if the second man stops the third man stops, and so on. At the same time you adopt the firing position, so you have this ripple effect where everyone slowly but surely drops into a kneeling position.

I radioed Robbie: 'What's the matter?'

'I am literally stood over an IED.'

'You're joking?'

'Wish I was.'

'Okay, don't move.'

'Cheers – wasn't planning to . . .'

It's a fluke he found it. Sweeping the Vallon left and right, he'd happened to knock a large tuft of grass over where the IED had been hurriedly buried. Within seconds I had men there, taking control of the mine detector and checking there were no other devices in the immediate vicinity. Then we got to work establishing whether Robbie was on it, or '*on*' it.

I could have kicked myself. We'd been in one field surrounded by head-high crops, then in a forest, then back in another field, never deviating from our path. We already knew for certain that the insurgents had us within their sights. Obviously, they would have tried to plant IEDs along the course on which we were heading. And with the foliage and land undulation there's no way we could have seen them doing so, even if they had been only 100 metres in front of us.

I had to radio in a report. I asked HQ for permission to get Robbie safe, then detonate the device.

'Negative, Eleven Lima. Higher want analysis.'

Well, you get out here and spend a day under fire, I wanted to say.

In the end we established that Robbie was over but not *on* the trigger plate and managed to rush him to safety. While I didn't disobey orders and detonate the IED with a grenade, neither did I instruct my men to hang around for the bomb squad. We'd been targets enough for one day. We were going home.

I would put my life on the line for a colleague any day of the week. Any of us would. But hang around and protect an IED? That was ridiculous – procedure gone mad. Flesh and blood is what matters, not wires and explosive. I was determined to get my boys home.

I'll deal with the flak later.

I'm not sure I'd ever disobeyed an order before. I don't even know whether I accepted it as genuine. I had twenty-two men under my command. They'd all been shot at or bombed for the majority of the day. They deserved as incident-free a journey as possible. Asking them to hang around while the geeks got their shit together was just mean. I didn't want any part of it and so we kept going. We all just marched around the IED, leaving a marker so the support team could find it, and continued our journey home.

It wasn't without incident. The second we broke cover from the tree line there came the *crack-crack-crack* of a solitary machine gun.

What followed was a mad dash for the compound, returning fire as we went. The snipers in the sentry positions at Toki provided cover. We all made it by the skin of our teeth, with bullets ricocheting off the track to left and right of our path.

* * *

My patrol made it back alive. This was small potatoes, though, when you looked at the bigger picture. Twenty-seven men had gone out that day. Twenty-three had returned. We had been in Toki for four days. In that time the Taliban had reduced our number from fifty-five to forty-two able bodies. I started doing the sums and didn't like what I worked out.

If we stay twelve more days there'll be no one left.

That wasn't defeatism. It was maths.

It was hard to accept. What made it less digestible was the knowledge that we'd been outflanked at every turn. Card Alpha or not, we were taking a beating every time we stepped outside the compound.

The more I reflected on the last few days and speculated about what was to come, the more I realised that I had to admit a truth I'd never had to confront in all my military years.

I'm scared. I'm scared of what's going to happen to me.

I'm scared of not getting out of here alive.

* * *

Too often commanders in the British military lose sight of the needs of their troops. This was not one of those times. We had been back at camp two hours when the news came over the radio that the CO was going to visit. Immediately.

We barely had time to process the news before the helicopter landed in the compound. Out stepped the commanding officer of 42 Commando – the lieutenant-colonel – plus the regimental sergeant-major, the highest non-commissioned rank in the unit. It was a true honour. No other checkpoints were getting this attention, but then no other checkpoints were suffering to the degree that we were. Moments before they landed, all I had cared about was the insurgent threat I saw every time I closed my eyes. One look at the visitors in their pristine uniforms and I realised how all of us had four days of beard growth, four days of blood, sweat and tears on our uniforms. And, behind our eyes, four days of learning not to give a shit about certain things.

To my relief and their credit, they didn't comment. All the CO wanted to do was praise us for our invaluable efforts. The fact that he'd risked his life and those of helicopter pilots landing in a war zone emphasised his words. The RSM took a more direct route. As soon as the speeches concluded he handed out twenty boxes of 200-packs of cigarettes – paid for, I have no doubt, out of his own pocket. Warrant officers know how to respect the troops. I had always admired our CO and this small gesture meant a lot.

They also had news. Steve McCulley, they said, had been stabilised and was en route to hospital in England. They also had information for me about the body parts we'd rescued.

'They belong to the marine who was killed,' the CO said. 'It's a tragic case.'

Tragic and complicated. The lad who'd detonated an IED, our first fatality of the month. I knew that his family had already conducted a funeral. As far as they were concerned their boy was in the ground, ready to take the next step in his spiritual journey. The return of his actual remains later was never going to sit well, based on the reaction of previous families in a similar position.

The CO commended our recovery of the remains, adding, 'We've heard of IEDs being loaded with body parts. Some of our men have been injured by the bones of their own colleagues.'

I knew at that moment I'd done the right thing in burning those other remains.

Before our visitors left I asked if they believed we were making a difference. The CO said, 'Yes,' but I suspected he wasn't sure. Even the top brass have people above them making decisions.

* * *

Halfway through our ten-day operation I was glad to get twenty-four hours inside the compound. The following day we patrolled but no further than the area covered by the sentry. There just wasn't the heart for it among the men, me included. It's not that we were scared of stepping outside; we just didn't see the point. If I had had my way, a squadron of Mirages would have been called in to wipe every compound off the face of the earth. I defy anyone dealing with the losses we had suffered to think differently. It's only human.

Yet the powers that be did disagree. The air support never came, despite its war-winning capabilities. But then, according to the politicians, we weren't at war.

All these years later, I'm still not certain whether they had their heads in the sand, whether it was a political decision not to be 'at war', or whether we – that is, the troops on the ground – were just unlucky. There's no doubt that previous wars in Afghanistan involved the whole of the UK – not even the most blinkered MP could have ignored them. The fact that this tour just involved small pockets of activity, little patches of Helmand Province that wouldn't be quieted, made it easier to dismiss as insignificant, if that was your agenda. Yet try telling the families of the dead marines, or those who had suffered life-changing injuries, that it wasn't a war. To my mind it would be disrespectful to their memories.

I also believe that this policy put my life and those of my men under unnecessary threat. Our patrol on 30 May 2011 was a case in point, but you could have picked any day in Toki. Compared to the other days it was successful – we didn't lose anyone. But I'm not naïve enough to deny that luck played its part. Breaking through a treeline on the way to camp and being confronted by five blokes lying there firing at you with assault rifles can go very differently, depending on the day. This time we got away with it. How they didn't hit us before we realised the threat I still don't know.

Faced with such aggression, the first thing you do is shoot back. The Americans call it the 'Wall of Lead'. Everyone fired off sixty rounds in the general direction while we tried to isolate the exact position of the threat. Some of our guys had machine guns so retaliated at an even higher rate. Then suddenly a shot came from another angle so we turned our attention there. Then it was back to the original target. Before we knew it everyone had used 5 magazines – 150 rounds – and we hadn't even moved.

Shit, we're playing into their hands.

We'd been ambushed so many times on the way back to the CP that it couldn't be a coincidence. Between the young men on mopeds and all the unseen prying eyes in each compound, our position was always known, as was our destination on the homeward leg. The volume of hurriedly planted IEDs discovered on our routes was testament to that. I'd always assumed the firefight attacks were about more than trying to pick us off. By putting us under pressure they were attempting to push us towards where the mines were scattered, like a shepherd manoeuvring his sheep.

But there's something else . . .

I used to take with me 8 magazines holding 30 rounds each, which is 240 rounds. I would then have another 3 magazines in my bag so that's 330 rounds, plus two bandoliers of 300 rounds so 930 rounds altogether. When you do the maths, in building a wall of lead unloading at a rate of 30 shots in 20 seconds, the ammunition doesn't last long.

'Lads, lads – watch the ammo!'

The last thing I needed was a panic on my hands but the fear of being in a firefight without the means to fire back will destroy you as quickly as a bullet. In a full combat scenario, in which we would be supported with a constant resupply of ammunition, we'd have sufficient for the task. Yet here we were, in the heart of a combat offensive with the standard equipment of a recce tour, which meant just the weapons and ammunition we could carry.

There was no choice for it but to throw up the biggest wall of fire we dared and move out. Normal protocol is you fire then run.

'Lads,' I said, 'we've just got to run.'

Fire and manoeuvre, fire and move, fire and move. It's practised, rehearsed and drilled. But never with unseen forces trying to take you out. Not for the first time that week I found myself praying to all sorts of imaginary gods. *Get us out of this and I'll be a better person. I'll stop smoking, I'll give more to charity, I'll let my kids win at football . . .*

This time someone listened.

We got away with our lives that day. But I resented the fact that we had to take such risks just to do that. Where was the support? Where was even the acknowledgement that we were in a battle situation?

Yet, getting angry at the policy-makers was a fight for another day. Right there and then it wouldn't help me or my men on the ground. All I could do was adapt the things within my sphere of influence. I would already spend an hour or ninety minutes plotting each patrol. Now I'd spend double that. It wasn't enough to have a route and a back-up. I needed back-ups for the back-ups. I needed to be aware of every back door, every stream, every tree that could provide cover. And my God, we were going to practise running while firing backwards.

Screw the rule book . . .

* * *

It had become a struggle to engage with the local Afghans on anything other than antagonistic terms. I wasn't violent or rude, I just stopped giving them the benefit of the doubt as I would have just days earlier. We'd been betrayed by kids and old men. I couldn't trust anyone. Not even the people we were sworn to save. Each day that I didn't have to look into their eyes and know they were lying was a good one.

I don't think the locals care if we die or not.

On 30 May I was co-opted for night sentry duty. Even commanders had to muck in, that was the rule. It was a very windy night and I was sitting with another battle-weary mate, desperately trying to get a cigarette lit. Suddenly we heard a commotion from the south-east.

'Do we have any men out there?' my mate asked.

'Not that I'm aware of. Let's throw up a Schermuly.'

Two minutes later our flare launched into the pitch-black sky. Usually it would rise and rise. This time, because of the wind, it barely went up 50 metres before it was blown off course. By the time the gusts released it, it was pretty much where the commotion was coming from. In a field. One that hadn't seen rain for months.

The device landed with a crash and the explosive propellant used to send it skywards spilled out onto the arid crops. It might as well have been a spark onto dry tinder. The area where the flare landed went up. And, boy, did it spread! Within minutes we had this almighty fire. Whatever the crops were, they were toasted within minutes.

I looked at my companion. He looked at me. Then we just laughed.

I still didn't know what the bother had been. I still didn't know who was taking part nor whether it was an innocent civilian altercation. What I did know is that the last few days of my life had been the adult equivalent of watching a child rip the limbs off a daddy-long-legs. And somewhere deep inside me I was craving revenge.

'Do you think we should wake anyone and tell them what's going on with this fire?' I asked my mate.

'Nah,' he said. 'Let it burn.'

So we did. We watched as compound after compound emptied, with men, women and children coming out to beat the flames down. There were no casualties and no injuries. There were also no qualms from us.

'You know,' I said, 'I'm beginning to dislike the Afghans.'

These men and women, all polite enough to our faces, had stayed in their homes while the insurgents had tried to blow us up. The only time they ever came to us was to demand compensation for some cow or goat. I'm not proud of thinking it. That's how low the previous few days had brought me.

My mate agreed. 'Don't sweat it,' he said. 'Every one of those fuckers would sell us out to the Taliban tomorrow.'

'I know. Even though we're here to help.'

'*Because* we're here to help. They don't respect us. They don't want our help. We're being killed for nothing.'

I hated having to accept that he might be right. But at that moment I truly believed he was.

Not extinguishing that field fire was my last act in Toki. What should have been a ten-day operation was curtailed into a seven-day session. We were leaving.

Considering the hell we'd experienced at Mulladad I was surprised to find myself eager to return. That happiness was short-lived. When my papers came through, they didn't mention Mulladad at all but a different checkpoint, one called Daqhiqh.

At that point I couldn't care less.

'Anywhere has got to be better than Toki.'

Hasn't it?

CHAPTER SIXTEEN

MOHAMED MOHAMED

We flew from Toki to Bastion for a full debrief about the deaths and woundings, and other incidents. There's something odd about how military reports summarise the facts. What I took away from Toki was the horror, the terror, the sense of loss, fear and degradation. None of that was reflected in black and white. They wanted facts and nothing but the facts. Opinions and emotions were for another time. At least the men on the ground knew the truth. I bumped into an old SBS mate who said, 'I hear you lot have been up against it.'

'I think you Poole boys would have struggled. How's your war going?'

'Bloody boring, if I'm honest. Just a load of antinarcotics business. I could do with a bit of action.'

'That's what I thought until I went to Toki. Trust me, it's a place you don't want to go.' I couldn't believe it. I was *this close* to giving him old George's 'Be careful what you wish for' speech. How quickly things change.

We were all able to call home from Bastion. When I spoke to Carly she gave me blow-by-blow details of the Spanish expedition. I'd been really worried that she would have been concerned about me but she was none the wiser about our exploits. If the deaths had been carried on the news back home, they had passed her by. Mum was a bit more clued up but it was only Dad, really, who knew my exact company and location. He was horrified that we'd lost so many men but so relieved that I wasn't one of them. Even so, I couldn't bring myself to share more than a flavour of the cesspit we'd come from. It wouldn't have been fair to worry him.

I can't tell him I was scared.

He could hear that I'd had enough. 'Look,' he said, 'just keep your head down till your R&R. Everything will be all right after that.'

On a seven-month tour every member was entitled to two weeks back home for rest and recuperation. Mine was due at the end of July.

It couldn't come soon enough.

* * *

From Bastion we shipped to Shazaad, then on to Mulladad to pack things up there. Nothing had happened in our absence, so Command was winding it down as a checkpoint. The mortar line was moving north-west to Kamiabi. As for the checkpoint itself, it needed to be transformed back into a family compound. It's more work than you can imagine, especially as my men were being moved out a few at a time. We had to take down the super-sangars, our defences, even our oven. Nothing could be left for possible use by insurgents. Luckily, a mate of mine, Pinky, volunteered to come and help. I knew him from various courses and my first tour to Afghan. While we were finding guns aimed at us every step we took, Pinky's war was slightly more glamorous. He was security for the combat cameramen covering the war. In his own words he was little more than a 'ruggedised' *Hello!* photographer – and it was pissing him off. Yes, he'd seen action with Brigade Reconnaissance Force (BRF) in the desert, tagged along with the SFSG, but he'd also witnessed the calm of the southern AO (area of operation). For a man like Pinky that was dull. He wanted to be shooting bullets not pictures. Hanging out with us seemed a good place to realise that dream.

Regardless of title, it was great to have an extra pair of hands, let alone a pair that belonged to someone so qualified. Come the last night in camp, I was even more relieved to have him with us. Just because there was nothing left to guard didn't mean we weren't a target. The powers that be disagreed. They decided that three of us – with no heavy artillery or military defences – were enough to guard a compound that three times our number had long struggled to defend. Thank God for Pinky!

More by luck than judgement we made it through the night and the next morning we handed Mulladad back to the family. They were all set to be annoyed at the changes we made until they walked in and found their home in a 1-million per cent better state than that in which they'd handed it over to us. We'd repaired walls roofs and plumbing, and done the garden. And they'd been paid for the trouble.

* * *

The decision to move us meant a 2-square-kilometre region without a patrol. The road that stretched directly north from Shazaad to Taalander, with Mulladad between them, had been one of the easiest to guard. Abandoning the CP was a gamble, but in light of Toki, Command wanted to move personnel closer to the action. So it was that by the end of June my multiple was moving into Daqhiqh, about 3 kilometres north of Al Blackman's Omar. Considering Devon and Dorset had already seen significant kinetic activity, with the attack on Steve McCulley's convoy and the Kamiabi raid, all the intel said Cornwall was a valuable target. If you can imagine a dual carriageway with the central reservation being a 5-metre-wide canal, over 3.5 metres deep in places, an attack along there would cut off supply to a lot of places. Visibility from Omar was good. With clear skies they could see about 3 kilometres in all directions. At the other end of the stretch, Daqhiqh should be able to take up the slack.

Daqhiqh wasn't a new checkpoint, although it was new to the British. If you think of a clockface, with Shazaad in the centre, the area of British responsibility ran from about midnight around to 2.15. All the CPs under our jurisdiction were within that segment.

The Americans, Afghans and troops from other NATO countries controlled elsewhere. The place we were moving into had previously been under Estonian authority.

We were driven from Shazaad in a couple of Mastiffs and a reinforced HGV with wheels taller than me and metal plating a foot deep. We had a ton of heavy artillery and surveillance kit. I was met by the Estonian commander, a gorilla of a man – 6 foot 7 if he was an inch – and with a thick accent that made him sound like a James Bond villain. If he'd wanted to make us feel as welcome as the paras at Mulladad had made me feel, it could have got sticky, but he was nice enough. I'd go so far as to say all the Estonians were happy to see us, relieved even. Then I realised why: our tour length was seven months including a break. The Estonians were stationed for a whole year – with no let-off. Several of them were on their third or fourth tour. And I thought we had it bad. No wonder they looked like shit. But I couldn't talk. The change in me and the rest of the lads after three months was noticeable. We were all becoming those ghosts that haunted Camp Bastion.

'While you get yourself sorted,' the commander said, 'we're going on patrol.'

They hadn't been gone long when we heard an explosion.

'IED!'

I jumped on the radio to the commander. 'Is everything okay? Are you under attack?'

'It was just a mine,' he said, totally chilled.

'Did someone step on it?'

'No, we detonated it with a grenade. It shouldn't bother anyone else now.'

Wow. That makes perfect sense.

I thought back to the to-ing and fro-ing of messages when we discovered an IED. Not only couldn't we destroy the thing, but we had to guard it until the investigators could come and sieve it for evidence.

On reflection? *Give me the Estonian model any day . . .*

* * *

The compound was big, about the size of two football pitches. Obviously the owners were pretty wealthy, although the ISAF forces had pushed the boundaries out here and there to include one of the jerubs (fields) and part of a stream. It even had room on the far east for a gravel area that served as a helicopter landing site (HLS).

It needed to be big. In the short term at least. As well as my multiple of fifteen men we had our two translators, a new Navy medic (for Jonesy had returned to Taalander), a Recce troop with us plus a team of engineers who were going to build further security walls from Hesco bastion as well as offices, canteens, sanitary blocks and numerous other buildings. Throw in the Estonians as well and we would have swamped a lot of the other CPs.

Across the road from us was a small compound. Beyond that, stretching to the west of us, were fields. Fields and more fields, all bordered with trees. Like so much of the region, viewed from above it's a patchwork quilt of a place.

The western side of the CP housed our work space, all the living accommodation, our vehicles and the super-sangar. If you imagine that as bottom left of the CP, there was another sangar at top right. The engineers erected an ops room and meeting rooms and dorms out of sea containers, powered by generators they installed. It was not modern by any means, but coming from the mud hut we were used to it felt state-of-the-art. I actually chose to pitch a 9 x 9 tent with some of the other senior guys between the super-sangar and the ops room. If anything happened, I wanted to be able to roll out of bed and into the fray. Until the handover we'd be looking after the south of the compound and the Estonians the north. We couldn't wait to get the whole lot – their bit had the cool, refreshing river.

While the 'makeover' of the compound was going on, and with so many bodies guarding the camp, I took the lads out on a recce to our local CPs. The first one had to be Omar, which had now become an internal CP. They'd suffered such casualties in Toki and this was the first chance my lads and Al Blackman's had got to talk about it. I didn't know what to say to Al himself. He was gutted he hadn't gone. I think

CP DAQHIQH

N

Route Cornwall

canal

Route Cornwall

S

galley

interp. room

DR

accom. tent

toilets

med.

arm.

gen.

HQ tent

CP SS

vehicle →

H L S

Key

blast wall

Afghan compound wall

SS super sangar

CP command post

DR 'desert rose' (latrines)

razor wire defences

HLS helicopter landing site

S sangar

gen. generator

only so many times you can say, 'There's nothing anyone could have done.' We're all brothers, but Sam Alexander – a member of his troop – and Kaz – from his multiple – were two of his good friends.

Another reason for dropping in, obviously, was because Al was able to talk us through the entire region. He had the full tactical picture: terrain to watch out for, compounds of interest, locals not to trust.

'Wouldn't it be easier to tell us who to trust?'

'Yeah. And as soon as I think of someone I'll tell you.'

He never did.

* * *

When the makeover was done, the engineers and transport disappeared leaving us and twenty Estonians. Before we could take over completely the Estonians needed to move out their kit. This had to be done extremely clinically. As their machine gun and mount came out, ours needed to be ready to go in. You can't afford to be without defences for a second in that place. It wasn't a quick job. They would say, 'At ten o'clock we will remove the two heavy machine guns from the north-western sangar,' so at 10 o'clock one of my guys would be standing there with two of our GPMGs to replace the Estonians' weapons.

It was incredibly well worked-out, so I had to take my hat off to the Estonians for that. But I don't think they appreciated quite how different – or how advanced – some of the equipment we had brought was. As we gradually took over the majority of the camp there was little else for the Estonians to do than patrol. For their penultimate sortie, the friendly gorilla took me to their ops room and showed me a map on the wall.

He said, 'We're going to go to this compound first, moving on to this compound, then this compound and these three.' They were basically doing a full 360-degree patrol, hitting all the nearest compounds on the perimeter of the camp.

'Good to know,' I said. 'We will keep an eye on you.'

From the enthusiasm with which he said 'Yes', I imagine he just thought that our sentries would be watching out for them.

Even with a camera mounted 3 metres above the 5-metre super-sangar giving the best visibility I'd ever known in a CP, because of the trees lining every field we could only see so far. Which is where our high-tech heat-recognition surveillance system came in very handy.

I went over to the particular sea container that passed for our ops room. We weren't planning on being sneaky, but it soon felt like it. Using the surveillance system, we watched the Estonians set off for the first compound. They obviously knew the area better than we did. Even so, compounds can be very dangerous places so we kept a close eye on the thermal imagery.

Suddenly Fergie said, 'Is something wrong?'

'Why?'

'They're coming back.'

I studied the screen. 'Are they under attack?'

A pause.

'I can't see anyone else. Can you?'

No one could. Yet there were the twenty Estonians all walking away from the compound without having so much as knocked on the door.

'What are they up to?' Fergie said. 'Do you want me to call them?'

(At Toki we'd had full-time radio ops. Back at a smaller CP it was more DIY.)

'No,' I said. 'Let's see how this plays out.'

For the next thirty minutes we watched on the screen as the giant commander and his team moved parallel with our compound wall while keeping firmly on the other side of the trees.

'It's almost like they don't want to be seen . . .'

Not only did they not go into the first compound, they didn't even bother heading to the second, the third, or any of the others. Instead they made a beeline for the point of Daqhiqh closest to the trees, and made a bolt for the wall. Then following it like a handrail, they walked around to the south of the compound – the furthest point from the sentries and our men – and sat down. And that's where they stayed for three hours, smoking, laughing and sleeping.

Eventually they took up a southern route towards the direction of the last compound, then turned sharply and eventually arrived at the CP door proclaiming, 'Everything's fine, nothing of interest out there.'

I can't even begin to list the rules those guys had broken but, you know what? Even before they returned, I said to the lads in the command room, 'It's been a giggle. We don't know what shit they've had to put up with the last year. Let's just keep this to ourselves.'

According to all the Estonian reports, Daqhiqh had been a particularly benign posting for the last four or five months. That is, if they'd actually undertaken any patrols at all. *Even Toki might look harmless if you never set foot outside.*

For my own sanity, I had to believe the Estonians were telling the truth. The alternative didn't bear thinking about.

* * *

The Estonians were in a sense unlucky in that they caught us on a relatively cool day. Within a few weeks we'd discover that the heat cameras couldn't cope with the local temperatures. Looking south it didn't matter because we had a virtually unobstructed view along Cornwall to Omar thanks to the straight-as-a-die canal running along the west side of the road. All other directions were obscured by the trees and vegetation. Not even our 5-metre super-sangar could see clearly over those.

But the Estonians didn't lie about everything. On their final night they promised us a feast, and they delivered on that promise. We had barbecued goat, a surprising number of different vegetables plus some of the harshest paint stripper posing as alcohol you can imagine. It was hard on the lads I had to keep on sentry watch but at least they didn't get gut rot from the liquor.

The next day the Estonians drove off in their interesting-looking vehicles, resembling a procession from *Star Wars*. They'd been gone barely an hour when a few of the more creative lads had transformed the narrow stream into a large pool by a damming part it, slowing the water flow and causing it to flood. The result was a large, cool pool – perfect for June temperatures in the 50s. It didn't stop there. The next day they spray-painted palm trees on the walls of the compound and later found wood to make a decking area. Overnight this grim corner of a war zone was transformed into a little oasis.

All we need now is the pizza oven.

* * *

Estonian forces in Afghanistan had been under-strength, but the multiple housed at Daqhiqh was much larger than ours. When they left, the number of us for such a huge camp felt positively paltry. Throw in the fact that it was now July and the R&R season was in full swing, and I was seriously worried about being able to maintain security at the CP as well as conduct patrols. There were only fifteen of us to start with. Suddenly we were in a cycle where at any time two men would be missing, and not just for their allotted fortnight back home. Throw in the journey time to Bastion and back and you were looking at another four or five days. Virtually another week.

It stank. I don't believe it should have been sanctioned. Look at the numbers: during the night we had four people on sentry. We had one guy in the ops room and others getting ready to come on for their shifts, so at any given time you have six people or more working or getting ready to work. That's tight when your multiple is fifteen. Knock that down to thirteen and suddenly if you want to patrol you're splitting your manpower 50/50. And what if someone gets ill? Or injured? Forget about the craziness of setting foot into the Green Zone with barely half a dozen men, how are you meant to relieve the guards if you've just got back from patrol? Either we gave up the patrols, we gave up sentry duty or we gave up our sleep.

One of those would make us ill, but the other two could get us killed. No, scratch that – *all* of those options could get us killed. Eventually.

My plea for additional bodies fell on deaf ears at Shazaad, and even at Bastion.

'You'll just have to make do,' I was told.

* * *

Regardless of numbers, at least with no other agencies at the CP I could get on with my programme. We collated all previous reports on one side of the ops room and had ongoing intel mapped out on the other. The plan was to map the area and identify the buildings and bridges and communities, as we'd done in Mulladad, and bring our badass biometrics to bear on the local population. It was all about collecting and collating intelligence.

If we got the chance . . .

On the first day I thought, *Okay, we are a bit light on the ground so we're not going to stretch ourselves.* I picked the local mosque as a destination. It was no more than 600 metres away, reachable at snake pace in an hour. That passed without incident. I had two interpreters this time, so 'Max' came out while John stayed behind. He located and introduced me to the local elders. I explained our mission and asked for their help in passing on any information they had about local insurgents or suspicious behaviour. They all agreed, each man Jack of them. As we walked away Fergie radioed me.

'You're never hearing from them again.'

'I know.'

For the journey back I decided to get a feel for the area. Daqhiqh had two main gates plus another three improvised entry points so we could do a clockface tour anywhere up to 360 degrees and still get in relatively quickly. It was harder to guard but it did mean that the insurgents couldn't predict where we'd be exiting when they were setting up their IEDs.

It was as we were in sight of the CP on our way back that the ICOM started going crazy. This wasn't one voice shouting obscenities at us. It was dozens.

The CP was only 200 metres away but it might as well have been a mile. I gave the order to increase vigilance and step up the pace within safe boundaries. It was hard-going, stressful. At moments like that the extra 18 kilos (40 pounds) on your back weighs nothing compared with the pressures on your mind.

We made it back into the compound without incident, although it didn't feel that way. We were knackered, drained and confused.

'What the fuck was that about?' I said. 'Did we just get away with something massive?'

'Are they messing with us?' Robbie asked.

'No,' Max said. 'They were there. They were planning something. I think they ran out of time.'

'That should make tomorrow interesting,' Fergie laughed.

Which was one word for it . . .

* * *

Instead of going 600 metres the next day, I decided to follow a similar route but push out to 800 metres instead, into an area designated on our maps as 'Green 13', then patrol back the other way. Green 13, according to aerial intel, was a junction on Route Devon although no one I met had been there personally.

En route we met quite a few friendly locals who didn't seem to mind our being among them. They were used to patrols from Daqhiqh. Mind you, they said, 'We liked the Estonians. The Estonians did things right.'

After the thermal imagery cock-up, I was pleased to hear it.

It was only later that I came to suspect what they actually meant. We were making our way towards a large compound that was on our map but about which we had no information. Obviously the Estonians hadn't got that far. Biometrically testing as we went, I asked one local who was being logged if he knew the compound owners.

'You don't want to bother going there,' he said. 'There's nothing of interest there. Everyone will tell you that.'

The funny thing is, everyone *did* tell us that. Every person we spoke to seemed pre-programmed to trot out the same line. 'Nothing to see here, move along . . .'

Obviously that just made the place more interesting to us.

It took a while to gain access but eventually a gate opened and we were invited into the yard. It was full of people, predominantly young men. Max and John got busy telling everyone that we needed to check their IDs and that seemed to go down okay. There were just a couple of lads, typical Afghan-looking fellas with black hair, black beards, little caps, who seemed agitated by our presence. We got everyone in a line and started the process. Two guys on kit, two guys standing on collapsible ladders checking north and south for movement, the rest standing guard – however docile the scene may seem, you let your guard down at your peril. While that was under way I began mapping the compound and speaking to the owner. Sometimes they would offer you tea. This was not one of those times. When I returned to the line it hadn't moved. I thought, *Bloody hell, they're taking their time.*

'Come on, lads, speed it up,' I said. 'Don't keep these good people waiting all day.'

'What are you talking about?' Matt Kenneally said. 'We've never gone faster.'

'So why has this guy been at the back for so long?' It was one of the two I'd identified as acting warily earlier.

Even as the words came out of my mouth I fathomed the answer. I decided to conduct a little test. I memorised who was around him, then turned to talk to someone. When I looked back, the guy in question was still at the rear but those around him were well forward.

The bastard's moving back along the line.

'Lads,' I called out, 'I reckon this guy's confusing us with the Afghan police. He seems to think if he keeps changing his place we'll get bored before we get to him.'

'Does he now?' Matt said. 'Let's bump him up the queue, shall we?'

The second his DNA hit the machine, it responded, although not in a way the man would notice, so Matt had time to utter the pass code. Suddenly this Afghan had three rifles a foot from his chest. Wordlessly, my lads gestured for him to kneel down, hands behind his back. It went like clockwork. In the thirty seconds it took me to walk over his hands were already cuffed in plastic ties.

'What have we got?' I asked.

'Mohamed Mohamed,' Matt replied.

'*Original.* What's his story?'

'Wanted by Bastion. High-value target, it says.'

Certainly the contents of his clothes were high-value. They included fistfuls of local and US currency. He also had a modern mobile phone, as well as a new motorbike.

'Whatever he's up to pays well,' I said. 'Anyway, let's get him back.'

There were other tests we could perform at Daqhiqh. We slapped a pair of blacked-out goggles on him and set off. Progress was necessarily slow, but it gave Max time to translate the whirlwind of ICOM.

'The Americans have him! The Americans have him!'

'Hold your fire! They have one of ours.'

'Get the Big Thing ready in case he escapes.'

We managed to get home unscathed, ran the tests on MM, who passed each one of them – if that meant having explosive residue on his hands and clothes and a criminal record going back years. I put in a call to Bastion and said we had a prisoner, quite a big fish I guessed. They said they'd send transport for extraction – the next day.

Obviously I wasn't going to hang around waiting for that – I got the sense that there was more to be shaken out of Mohamed Mohamed. We managed to find out that he had connections with a petrol garage near Route Cornwall. I thought, *Okay, that's in our new area of responsibility. Let's see what's going on there.*

And so, for the second time that day, we went out, seven Green Berets plus one translator and the medic. I'll admit that when he arrived a bit of me was relieved he was indeed a 'he'. Jenny, whom we'd had before Jonesy, had been fantastic but on some level I suppose I felt a man would be 'safer' for everyone. Was it my imagination, though, or did our medical man not seem too keen?

He's Navy, he'll be fine. After all, what's the worst that could happen?

CHAPTER SEVENTEEN

NOT THE CAVALRY

We walked north up Cornwall for thirty minutes, then crossed through the canal, which was great because that cooled us down. When you're running on two or three hours' sleep – more often than not taken in forty-five-minute bursts – keeping your temperature under control gets that bit harder. Then it was up a very steep bank and over the other side into a line of trees. It was the usual formation. Robbie, Matt, then me and Max and so on. After Toki I couldn't imagine a more combat-tested, more efficient patrol.

I was watching our GPS every second of the way, overlaying it onto the basic map I had of Green 13 and its surrounding area. When we broke through the treeline into the middle of a field, the move was intentional. We could have crossed the canal earlier, where the field started, but that was where the IEDs were more likely to be hidden. With that in mind I plotted a diagonal course. 'Yes, it will ruin a few crops, but we can pay for that later.'

We were marching in a straight line towards a small wall that hid the road on the other side. The sun was blazing, the birds were singing. There was the occasional engine hum from somewhere behind the trees and the distant noise of day-to-day life. It was serene. In fact, our footsteps landing on the broken-down crops was the loudest thing in the area.

And then that all changed.

We could only have had another 12 metres to go. Twelve metres until we reached a tree-lined road and no longer be exposed in a cornfield that offered no more protection than an ear of corn.

Ten metres away from my point man, head down in my charts, I was slow to see the two young Afghan men rise from behind the perimeter wall. I was slow to acknowledge the threat as they raised their weapons while I dropped my map and swung up my rifle. But I saw the fall-out as quickly as anyone.

Click-click-click.

Click-click-click.

I was still bringing my gun to position when Robbie went down backwards.

Shit, shit, shit!

Five metres behind him Matt Kenneally was already returning fire. By the time I joined him the shooters had dived back behind the wall and we heard the sound of moped engines. To my rear the snake of men, all unsighted from the chaos, were shouting, 'What's going on?'

Without taking my eyes off the wall for a second I screamed, 'Matt? Is Robbie all right?' At the same time I was radioing a contact report to Shazaad in case another patrol was near by.

I was still on the radio when I heard shots from a different direction. The rear of the snake was being attacked. According to the lads, two more men firing at us. I made another report: more shooters, Robbie down, even our medic is having to return fire – unheard of. It's not looking great.

Suddenly Robbie begins to move. Not only does he move, he pulls himself up and starts crawling back towards Matt and me.

'I spotted the shooters, tried to backpedal and tripped,' he said. He sounded embarrassed.

'Don't sweat it,' I said. 'That stumble probably saved your life.'

With everyone able-bodied, that changed things. We couldn't go back because of the shooters. We had to go onwards towards the original threat.

I gave the command to fire and run. The man at the back of the snake would fire and sprint to the front before the new 'last man' did the same. I wanted two men returning fire at all times. I wanted half the others looking left and the rest right. We'd already been tapped from two ends. There was no knowing whether the insurgents had anything planned elsewhere.

It requires a vast degree of discipline to run with your back to the target but the lads did it. We all did, including me, Max and a puffing medic, all with no regard for IEDs. And just as well. We were three metres from the wall when shots started coming in from the left.

And the right.

Which went totally against Western military logic. If you're at 3 o'clock and your mates are at 9 o'clock you don't both shoot at a target directly between you for fear of hitting each other – so-called friendly fire. It's bloody obvious. Not to the Taliban, apparently. They'd clearly skipped class the day that lesson was taught. They weren't letting up, for suddenly I realised that shots were coming in from a third direction. Now we were on the defensive on three sides.

Max was getting really worried. He'd probably had twice as much sleep as any of us over the last few nights but that was still only four or five hours.

'I don't like this, I don't like this. There are a lot more than three shooters out there.'

'We need to get to cover,' I said. It was only a matter of time before we took a casualty, and if we remained exposed as we were now we'd be picked off in no time. I located a nearby compound on the map and pointed the front man in its direction. When we arrived he booted in the metal door and we piled in to find a frightened family cowering in a corner of the yard.

'Max, get over there and explain we're not the enemy.'

I scoured my map for an exit strategy while yelling at Fergie to get bodies on the roof, at Max to ask if there was another way out of the compound, and radioing our new Sunray at Shazaad all at the same time. By the time I got a connection, the men on the roof were already being engaged.

'We are in serious trouble. There's only seven of us plus auxiliaries. We've got contact from at least three separate directions.'

An explosion interrupted my broadcast.

'Sergeant? Sergeant? Are you all right?'

I scanned the compound. 'Grenade, sir. No damage. *Shit* – another one.'

The big fat wall took the brunt of the blast and shrapnel. Taking advantage of the confusion, I said, 'Everyone, time to go.'

A back door led directly into a tiny, narrow alley that had 'disaster' written all over it. We had no choice.

The lads were at my shoulder, alert but anxious.

'Rob, what do you want us to do?'

We were all experiencing something we'd never been trained for. We were drilled in how to attack, not retreat. How to find aggressors, not shake them off. How to overpower, not be a Mickey Mouse half-pint force pretending to be a patrol. I was no better equipped than any of them, but the men trusted me to lead them out of this particular hellhole whether I knew how to or not.

'I'll tell you what you're going to do,' I said. 'You're going to clear this shitty old alleyway as quickly as possible because that's where we're going.'

Robbie and a couple of others went out, checked it was clear, and we piled up the alleyway, to hell with the snake formation. We just needed to put distance between us and the unseen numbers behind.

We emerged at the other end of the alley into a bit of a metropolis. It was indicated on the map as the top end of Route Devon, but I had no idea how ordinary it would look. There were cars and shops and people going about their day, not in huge numbers, but definitely without a care in the world.

'You'd think they'd be able to hear the gunshots,' Matt said.

'They can hear. They just don't care.'

I scanned the road. Clear. We began to cross and out of nowhere bullets started pinging off the dusty track. Half the men were on one side of the road, half on the other, and no one had a clue where the shooter was. There was only one option. 'On my command, rapid fire and we run over.'

We made it intact. Two minutes later we were inside another compound, terrorising another trembling family. It was exactly the same as before. No time to breathe before the first grenade appeared from nowhere. We had no choice, we had to keep moving.

We moved like termites through wood, charging through one compound, then another, then another. But still the grenades and bullets rained down on us. Every time we returned fire we pushed our supplies of ammunition closer to dangerous levels.

One compound backed onto a stream a bit over a metre wide, so in we jumped. According to my map the stream flowed towards the canal.

'Let's go.'

It was hard work wading through the water but it provided a welcome respite from the noise of the threat. Information was coming at me from all sides. Max was telling me about the ICOM plotting, Shazaad were relaying messages about five or six motorbikes going up and down Cornwall while Bastion said that air support was thirty minutes away. I should have been petrified but the adrenalin had long taken over.

I passed the intel about Cornwall down to the men. They needed to be prepared. Fergie, his 'chicken fillet' ever present in his thoughts, just said, 'Rob, this isn't right. I want to get back to camp.'

We continued to follow the river in pure creepy-crawly mode. Max was on my shoulder constantly, saying, 'There are eight of them, all with guns, all scouring the area for us. It's only a matter of time.'

I was grateful for the updates but I didn't really need them. The stream was running parallel with Dorset, and I could hear the mopeds buzzing up and down with my own ears. Occasionally, I even heard one stop, and its rider contact his people by mobile phone.

We eventually got far enough to break cover. By my calculations if we made it into the field which should be opposite we'd be on a straight course of 600 metres back to Daqhiqh. But first we had to cross Devon.

The last time we tried, bullets had appeared out of nowhere and we'd fired back blindly. This time I wanted to level the playing field. I decided to put down some smoke that would obscure our passage across the road. Obviously, however, it would also give away our location.

The smoke canister makes a hell of a noise when it detonates. But, thirty seconds after it goes up, you've got a dense pea-souper that Superman would struggle to see through. Even so, I put two men on the side of the road, one facing north, one south, before I ran over. Immediately I covered the south from that side, the guy who followed behind me took the north, and everyone else piled over.

I said, 'That was easy.'

'Too easy,' Fergie muttered.

Now we just had a few fields to cross to get back on to Route Cornwall and the canal, 600 metres north of our camp. I started to feel a bit more positive. We set off, jumping into the various nasty irrigation ditches along the way for cover. Eventually, we got eyes on Cornwall. We were metres away from the raised straight road back home.

That's when the shots started coming again.

Click-click-click.

Click-click-click.

We all dived down into the field. I checked my perimeter. There were no dust clouds from bullets anywhere near me.

'Where's it coming from?' I demanded. 'Anyone have eyes on the shooters?'

A lad at the back of the snake, some thirty-odd metres from me, said the threat was behind him. He was returning fire.

'It's from our left,' someone else behind me said.

I couldn't support because I couldn't see either target. They were too far away down the snake. Then Robbie said, 'There's one in front of me.'

That one I was close enough to see.

Christ, it's another triple assault. Our ammo is low already.

'Fergie, can you do anything?' I asked. He was our mortar man.

'I thought you'd never ask.'

He shouted some co-ordinates into his radio, and back at the mortar line at Daqhiqh they were translated into action. Less than a minute later there was a godawful explosion to the rear of our snake. I didn't know whether the mortar round had caused any casualties – at the end of the day it's a fairly crude weapons system – and the odds of a direct hit were low, but one set of shooters stopped.

'What about the bastards in front of us? If we don't get back to camp we're cooked.'

'I'm on it,' Fergie replied.

'He sent off the fresh co-ordinates. Our man at Daqhiqh confirmed the order. Suddenly there was a new voice on the line. It was the HQ in Shazaad.

'Request for mortar denied,' the man said. 'There's a chance it could hit a native compound.'

'What about us?' I snapped. 'There's a damn sight better chance we won't make it home alive without help.'

I used to be a signaller. That is not how you speak to a command centre on the radio. But it is when you're operating on four hours' sleep in the last forty-eight hours, in 55-degree heat and 70 per cent humidity. Nothing more came.

We were all firing somewhere. Depending on where you were in the line the target could be in any of three directions. Even above the symphony of *click-click-clicks* I was suddenly aware of a commotion to my rear. I didn't dare take my sights off the threat in front but the noise got louder. Suddenly our medic burst past me, screaming,

'I've just killed a man! I've just killed a man.'

'Get back to your position!' I shouted.

'I'm out of ammo!'

Jesus! One damn thing after another.

I threw him several magazines from my own belt. That left me dangerously exposed. Worse, the guy was getting beyond my control. I wasn't sure I could keep him with us voluntarily; I certainly didn't want him with us. It was no good, we had to move or risk the enemy picking us off.

I radioed Mac back at the CP. 'Mate, we are so light on ammo we're going to make a dash for it.'

'We'll provide cover,' he said. 'Ready when you are.'

'Cover' meant fire from our snipers in the super-sangar plus Mac himself. Any number of weapons from Daqhiqh. All trained on our adversaries.

I gathered the lads. 'We've been lucky today but if we're going to make it we'll need that luck to continue. We've got no choice but to bolt.'

On my command we moved. At pace. *Upwards.* The earth that had been excavated to build the canal meant that Cornwall was raised 1.5 metres above ground level. I felt sick to my stomach as we emerged from the cover of the field to the exposed raised ground. Up there we were about as camouflaged as the bride and groom dolls on a wedding cake.

We may as well have targets painted on our backs.

The second I showed my face I saw a bullet ricochet off the earth a couple of metres to my right. If the Taliban were better shots I'd be dead already. A second later I saw the flash of shots fired from our super-sangar. They must have ID'd a shooter. For a couple of seconds at least the firing wasn't at us.

The CP was 400 metres ahead of us and getting closer. On the west side of the road, on our left-hand side, was the canal. On our right were compounds, fields, trees – all hiding the men trying to kill us.

The next few minutes are like a bad dream. I'm sprinting full pelt, oblivious to the danger of IEDs, and to my tiredness. I've got one goal. Get. Us. Home.

Three hundred and fifty metres to go and no casualties.

I've done runs like this a hundred times, often carrying more weight. Just never with live ammunition being fired at me.

Three hundred metres.

I never trained for this. None of us did. All the months and years I've spent loaded onto this course or that, and we never once imagined a scenario where Royal Marine Commandos would be fleeing for their lives, out of ammo, out of options and out of time.

Two hundred and eighty metres.

The bullets are pinging up stones all around me. The guys in front are still going. I pray the lads behind are as well.

Two hundred and fifty metres.

I'm aware of every step I take. Every thundering shudder vibrating through my boot.

I can do this. I can do this. I can do this.

Two hundred and thirty metres to go. Above the constant *click-click-clicks* I hear a shout on my comms.

'Are you all right?' I call back. But I don't stop.

'It's the medic.'

Of course it is.

I dare to turn and see two lads dragging a limp, crying Navy boy along as fast as they can. My guys are fit, and they're strong, but even they are being slowed down significantly by the useless dead weight dragging its feet between them.

'Do you need help?'

'Just go on,' they say. 'We can do it.'

Two hundred metres. The pace is slowing.

A hundred and fifty metres. My heart feels like it's going to burst. Not with fatigue: with stress. It's not my fault we're understaffed and underequipped, but these men are all under my protection. And right now I'm giving them fuck all.

A hundred metres.

Ninety.

Fifty.

I swear a bullet hits Matt in front of me, but he keeps going. We all do. We can smell the compound. We can hear our guys shouting encouragement to us.

Thirty metres.

One man has left the sentry post. He's at the door. It's only plywood on a stupid hinge. The Estonians spray-painted 'Daqhiqh' on it. It's amateurish. But it's open. It's waiting for us. He's shouting, 'Come on, lads, come on, nearly here.'

Twenty.

Not far. Nearly there. The little rickety bridge over the canal into the compound is right there. Right there. Right . . .

Come on, Rob, ten more metres.

Nine.

Eight.

We pile onto the bridge and then suddenly the enemy fire intensifies. They know it's their last chance. The other side of the canal is lower, out of sight, and the insurgents know it. Our snipers retaliate. There is now a wall of lead in both directions. I know who my money's on, but we only need to be unlucky once.

Seven.

Six.

Five.

I've never been more pleased to see an ugly mountain of Hesco bastion.

Four.

Three.

Two.

I stop and wait for the lads with the medic. I'm not alone. After the selfless job they've just done I don't want them felled at the final hurdle.

Everyone falls into the compound and collapses against the walls. The sniper fight is still raging.

I stare around the group. Heroes, all but one of them. I can't believe no one is carrying an injury.

But that's the thing with adrenalin. You can be hit and not actually feel it. Some serious injuries, life-threatening if untreated, can go undetected for a surprisingly long period when you're engaged in something as dramatic as what we'd just experienced. In these situations, like almost everything, there's a protocol.

'Lads, we need to do a naked injury check.'

Slowly, as we got our breath back, everyone started to unload their kit.

'Shit, Matt,' someone said, 'you've got bullet holes in your bergan.'

So he was hit.

Matt wasn't alone. Several of the boys had sinister little craters in their kit. How none of the rounds had made it through to the fleshier targets remains a mystery to this day. But I am never going to play cards again, because I know we used all our luck up that day.

The naked physical is pretty straightforward. You basically just check yourself over and each other for wounds. A couple of lads had sprained ankles, there was the odd bit of blood from cuts and scratches caused by diving to the ground, but no bullet wounds.

Normally I'd send the lads to the medic but he was already clogging up his own sick bay. Two of the lads he had been enrolled to help were actually nursing him.

'Is there anything actually wrong with him?' I asked one of them.

'I'd say so.'

'What is it?'

'He's out of shape.' He turned to the patient. 'Aren't you, son?'

What the hell were Bastion thinking sending me an unfit medic? His physical condition endangered two of my men. There were only seven of us. If he or one of those had been hit there wouldn't have been enough bodies to protect them.

I knew I had to evacuate him, and as soon as things quietened down I would. At that moment, however, I was just happy to be alive.

* * *

I'd like to say things quietened down after that. I'd really love to say that. But it would be a lie. We were attacked almost every day that we set foot outside the compound. We were attacked almost every day *inside* the compound. We were attacked so often that sometimes we didn't realise we had been. Because Daqhiqh was a big piece of real estate, it was crucial to maintain sentries and check the monitors in the ops room. At least once a day we'd receive incoming rounds, but either the shooters were interrupted or their aim was poor. The only time it was interesting was when grenades came over. The sentries would normally be able to pick off an insurgent before he got close enough to lob something over the wall. It was harder when the enemy fired grenades from a UGL (underslung grenade launcher, fitted beneath the barrel of a rifle) from a distance. More often than not these would land outside the mud walls. Even so, we still had to stand to each time, flinging on the body armour as if it didn't weigh half our own weight.

That was another problem. The heat, the stress, the workload, the total craving for sleep – they were all taking their toll physically. By mid-July I had lost two stone (over twelve and a half kilograms). Others, like Robbie, had dropped from thirteen stone (eighty-two and a half kilograms) to below ten (sixty-three and a half). You could see it in our bodies when we took those precious moments to unwind in the dammed oasis. There hadn't been an ounce of fat on us before, you'd think – we were that fit. But the weight had gone from somewhere. And, while our body weight went down, the weight of the loads we had to carry did not.

The guys never complained about tiredness. I couldn't have blamed them if they had, but that doesn't mean there weren't side effects. I took a tour of every sentry duty. More than once I found guys – my guys, well drilled by me, who'd experienced the horrors of the Green Zone – wearing shorts and a vest in the super-sangar.

'For fuck's sake, where's your armour?'

'It's too hot.'

'I'll tell you what's too hot – a grenade at your feet. Now get your gear on!'

Tiredness leads to all sorts of issues. I became so drained that my alarm clock wasn't enough to wake me up – although it had no trouble rousing Fergie or Mac, the men sleeping closest to me.

Most nights I'd be shaken awake by one of them. 'I don't know how you sleep through it,' Fergie said. 'They can hear this fucking clock in Shazaad.'

Exhaustion causes tempers to fray. That's a fact. Fights erupted every now and again – serious ones, sometimes – although they were always ended with a firm handshake and a commitment to 'move on'. Whatever else was being eroded, our camaraderie was still intact.

Apart from in one area.

The medic was still a concern. After our second day's patrol, when he'd cracked, he asked me to conduct a 'trim' on him. A trim is a medical procedure, a form of risk-assessment, to establish mental well-being. Usually this will be conducted by a medic, so, there was no one among us who knew its ins and outs better than him.

The outcome? He was so traumatised by killing a man that there was no way he could be included in the sentry rota. Even bearing in mind that he absolutely could not have killed anyone – he couldn't aim a rifle within ten feet of his target – I agreed to let him into the radio room – unheard of given his lowly rank.

He radioed the senior doctor at Bastion and reported he'd been trimmed. 'What for?'

'I killed a man in defence of the troops.'

Bang – a citation for bravery, just like that. I can't recall another case in which the original actor has cited himself.

I couldn't do anything about that – other than beg Shazaad every day for a replacement. What I could do, though, was put him on a course of immediate physical-fitness training. He moaned, he swore, he shouted. But he bloody did it – *or else*.

A few days after the big firefight we were out again and, this time, under no pressure from enemy fire, the medic just passed out and needed to be carried back to the CP. We had to carry him 1,500 metres back to camp. When we got there he came to.

I had to stand him down. He was too unfit to patrol with us. We'd be safer without a medic than having to literally physically carry one.

I thought things couldn't get any worse when one day, just before my R&R was due to kick in, I added him to the personnel for the day's patrol. We were all standing inside the gate. As usual the lads got their weapons ready to fire – we never knew what was on the other side once we went out. That means having a full magazine in and cocking the weapon, ready to take the safety catch off. To his credit, the medic did some of this.

Then he pulled the trigger.

A single round shot from his rifle and into the back of the man in front of him. By sheer good fortune it went through the bergan, skimmed off the armour and embedded itself in the wall. The medic just stared, his mouth wide open. The lads soon filled it.

With their fists.

Part of me wanted to let them continue. By God, he deserved it. He'd nearly killed a man. Begrudgingly, I had to intervene and separate the wanker from the heroes. That night he refused to sleep in the normal quarters for fear of his own life. Against my better judgement I agreed to let him move.

'Why don't you just burn him?' Fergie said.

'What can I do? We're so light on the ground.'

By rights I had the power to report the medic for an illegal and dangerous discharge, which would see him at worst expelled from his position and at best penalised his operational bonus of £3,000. I knew he had earmarked that money for his forthcoming wedding.

I said, 'If you take extra training I will overlook this issue.'

Reluctantly, he agreed – even if it meant training conducted by the guy he'd nearly murdered. Obviously the pace was fast. He was physically thrashed every day. He moaned constantly. That wasn't new. And then he stopped moaning. One day I came back from patrol and Mac said, 'The helicopter will be here in an hour.'

'What helicopter?'

'For the medic. His evac. Didn't you order it?'

I had not, but he'd got himself evacuated.

But as July progressed were any of us any better? I remember a lad – a good lad, one of my best – coming up to me.

'Sarge, I'm due home on R&R in two days. Can I give patrol tomorrow a miss?'

My gut reaction was *You're bailing on us?* But after a few seconds of reflection I realised, *You've seen enough. You can smell England and you don't want to fuck it up getting injured on patrol.*

One by one, the other lads offered a variation of the same line. The closer they got to freedom the fewer risks they wanted to take. They were paranoid about tripping up at the last fence. I tried to establish myself above all that, to lead by example, patrol right up to the last second. Then my own R&R crept up on the horizon and I finally understood what the Estonians must have gone through to take the short cuts they did on the eve of shipping out.

On 23 July I was leading a patrol but thinking only of my escape three days later. Yes, it would mean a slow slog to Shazaad, an overnight stay, then a flight to Bastion whenever they could arrange it. But anything was better than what I was going through. Then on the 24th a team of engineers flew in to begin repairs to our HLS (helicopter landing site), which for some reason was where the grenades lobbed over the wall often seemed to land. When they were about to leave the captain asked if I needed anything shipped to Bastion.

I fought the urge, I really did. But I was in a place where I'd been shot at every day since I arrived. I'd lost weight, I'd lost my love of the country I was meant to be protecting.

I just want to go home.

'Actually, I'm due to head out for my R&R.'

'Do you want to come with us?'

'Yes,' I said. 'Yes, I really do.'

CHAPTER EIGHTEEN

THAT WOULD BE ILLEGAL

'I'm going to the pub.'

I'd been home four days and that's all I could think of doing. Carly and the boys had met me at the airport and my heart had burst at how much I'd missed them, and how much of their lives I'd missed. Sam, Ollie, Will – I just wanted to hug them and never let go. The journey home passed in a haze. The questions came at me thick and fast and when I didn't answer Carly filled the silence with stories about their lives. That was when it struck me: *I don't belong here.*

I was barely home and I was wishing I'd not come. What made it worse was looking at Sam and Ollie and seeing the faces of Sam Alexander and Ollie Augustin, killed on the same dreadful day. It's a stupid thing. They just shared names, that's all. But I couldn't help thinking, *Are you going to follow in my footsteps? Are you going to enlist? Are you going to end up like some of my best mates?*

As a father that's the hardest thing you can imagine.

Crazy thoughts started pervading my brain. I started getting fearful for anyone I knew called Will. Another time we all went into London to visit Dad. We were in a car park and a car backfired. The kids squealed, Dad didn't bat an eyelid, and I virtually went into full kneel-

and-shoot pose. It was ridiculous. I didn't know how to behave in the normal world.

I was hopeless with Carly, too. When the two of us were together she would tell me about our family, herself, our friends, and most of the time I struggled to tune in. I made the right noises the best I could. But all I was thinking was, *What has this crap got to do with anything? I've got mates dying in Afghanistan.*

I wasn't angry at her. I felt guilty because I wasn't with *them.*

Several times during my fortnight at home Fergie rang me to keep me updated on the problems they were facing in the Green Zone. The area designated Green 13 on our maps was still proving impossible to reach. As far as we knew it was just a junction on a road – no more than a B road in the UK, although only if that B road was built of dirt. It was on Route Devon, about 2 kilometres further out than Taalander. Peripheral, in other words, but important.

However you looked at it, it had been hellish in my absence. Mac was leading the line brilliantly but he and the rest of the multiple were facing hardships, no question. That he or Fergie would give up their rare opportunities to phone home to phone me was testament to the bond we all had.

Sam's birthday came round while I was at home. We all went to Pizza Express with family and friends. I had to pull out all the stops to look as though I wanted to be there. I really tried. It took everything I had.

At another party a few days later I realised that I was spent. I had nothing left to give. We were in a beautiful village in Somerset on a boiling hot summer's day, and I remember sitting on a kids' climbing frame watching the boys play with their friends, desperately trying to find some joy in the sight but feeling nothing at all. After ten days our friends knew better than to approach me. One guy, whom I didn't know, came up. He was dad to one of the other boys. More importantly, he was a Navy pilot.

'You don't want to be here, do you?' he said.

'Nah.'

'You think you don't deserve happiness while your men are suffering?'

'Spot on.'

'Well, I'm not going to lie. It never gets any better.'

'Cheers.'

'But you're not alone. There's plenty of us who've been through it. Plenty of us you can talk to.'

Then he added, 'From what I see on the news you guys are suffering. Do yourself a favour. Take this opportunity to recharge the batteries. You'll need it when you go back.'

Wise words, the wisest I'd heard in a good while. But I couldn't do it. The only way I could find any solace was in booze. I'd been starved of alcohol for so long that it had a sledgehammer effect on me, but I liked it. I welcomed it. I drank till I didn't feel the shame of a deserter any more.

I found myself willing the days away. Then an odd thing happened. The closer my return date came, the more anxious I became. I still struggled to connect with Carly and the boys, but not because I was thinking about my men. I was thinking about my own mortality. In the space of a fortnight I'd gone from desperate to get home, to desperate to get back, to being scared shitless at the prospect of returning.

I think I'm going mad.

Come D-Day, however, and I was settled. I knew what I needed – what I *wanted* – to do. I had to get back to Daqhiqh. I wasn't scared, I wasn't ashamed, I was a marine. And I had a job to do.

My dad drove me to RAF Brize Norton in Oxfordshire. I wish it could have been a more pleasurable experience for him. I remember trying to articulate what was going through my head – with him a chief inspector in the Met, there was a good chance he would understand. The thoughts I managed to spit out were honest, but I'm not sure they were coherent.

I just needed to get back . . . *home.*

* * *

Camp Bastion never looked so appealing. I picked up the box containing my uniform, grenades, ammo, etc. and nearly threw up at the stench of some of it. To say it had seen better days was an understatement. The fella in the store – doing the job I used to do – asked me if I wanted new supplies of anything. I looked at the desert camouflage rags, the well-worn gloves, the dented helmet and distressed boots, and thought, *They've got me this far – they'll do me all right*. I can't explain it with any logic. I was operating on pure instinct. Every bit of kit with my name on had played its part in keeping me alive when plenty of my mates hadn't been so lucky. Who was to say it was a coincidence? Stench or no stench, I couldn't risk changing even a pair of socks.

Buoyed by superstition, I went next to the shop and loaded up on enough cigarettes for the next few months, then went for a mini debrief. They showed me into their ops room. It was like something out of *Star Trek*. Huge screens, data flying everywhere, maps alight with dots and moving icons.

They showed me Daqhiqh. It was red with action.

'What the hell's going on?'

'The same as every day you've been gone. The same as every day you've been there.'

August, it seemed, was going to be as kinetic as July.

But I was soon given bigger things to worry about. Green 13 had been the most active district in the region and there were no signs of anything changing soon. In the short time I'd been away there had been several nine-liners sent from my boys' patrol or M'lord's or Al Blackman's or Tom Phillips's near by. More worryingly, we had proof from locals that every compound in the vicinity had been receiving letters by post saying, 'Co-operate with the Americans and you will die.'

There was no doubt: the whole area was under Taliban control.

Not just Daqhiqh, either. I arrived back at my CP to learn that one of Taalander's men – Marine James Wright, whom I'd met and liked – had lost his life. It was just his misfortune. He'd been out on patrol, they'd seen a firefight and made it back to camp. The lads were either repairing their kit or resting. Jim had been in his tent when a grenade came over the compound wall and landed square on him.

UGLs –underslung grenade launchers – are serious weapons in the right hands. They can be fired from up to 200 metres away and hit with the ferocity of an IED. The truth is, we'd suffered attacks from them more times than anyone. But Daqhiqh was the size of two football pitches. The odds of landing a grenade on anything of note from a distance was remote, and so it proved. We lost bits of tree, bits of wall, bits of storage room. Our biggest casualty was the HLS – hence the engineers having to come back to fix it. Had the Taliban gained an inkling of our layout it would have been worse. But they were in the dark, and that was how I intended to keep it.

Jim wasn't the only casualty. Shortly after my return we received notification of a 'man-away' from a Scottish section of L Company. There had been a couple of incidents over the years of men going missing during a battle or an evacuation. But Marine policy is always to go back. As soon as HQ realised there was a problem we were all called into action.

Canals and waterways had to be searched, road blocks established. Since we were situated on one of the major routes we stepped out and set up a block. We searched cars, trucks, even tractors. No bale of hay went by unscrutinised. This lasted a couple of days. Then we got word that a body had been found.

Crucified.

It was reported in the international media, but the full truth was held back. Only those of us on the ground got wind of the true horror of that young Scot's death. I can't say it filled me with anything other than a desire – no, a passion – to see the bastards responsible die. Perhaps I'd have sought justice once. But in August 2011, after everything I'd seen, justice and death had become one and the same to me.

I wasn't alone. For the next few days every patrol in the region had an added spice to it. If a moped went by that we didn't like the look of, instead of flagging it down and tutting if it didn't stop, my guys were rifle-butting the driver's helmets the second they were in reach. If you think that's wrong, consider this: nine out of ten drivers we did it to flagged up red on the biometric scanners. I put it to you that had we been able to roll out that kind of initiative to our firefights then certain incidents, certain casualties, even certain fatalities could have been avoided.

I wish I could say the arrests gave us any pleasure. The reality is that each man in Daqhiqh knew that for every insurgent we arrested, processed and despatched back to Camp Bastion, most of them would reappear on the streets a few weeks later. What was the point of risking our lives apprehending Mohamed Mohamed one day, to watch him blow up a convoy a fortnight later?

The lads were beginning to whisper. Once that happens in a camp, then you're on the slippery slope. Authority in war is key. But what could I say? I knew that authorities above our new Sunray weren't on the same page as us. I knew because of the constant questioning of the reports I filed. I knew because of the constant denial of the assistance I requested. I knew because it didn't matter what we did to the Taliban, they were confident that they'd stay one step ahead of us because they had no rules. And we did. Rules for everything. As commander of the multiple it was my job to head off any such grumblings among my lads. But what if I believed them myself?

I'm not sure how long I can keep doing this . . .

* * *

During my R&R, our new Sunray at Shazaad, had been liaising with the captain of the Afghan National Army (ANA) contingent based to the north of us. Now, the army could loosely – and I mean loosely – be described as professional. Compared with the Afghan National Police, however, they were gods (the police were mercenaries, scum – pick an insult and if they hadn't earned it already they soon would). Since Ollie had gone, the remains of his OMLT (operational mentoring and liaison team) had been mentoring the shit out of the military, while the SFSG's work with the Afghan forces was having results. But there was still a morality gap between us all. What we considered out of bounds they considered normal. The temptation was, of course, to dismiss their views as those of the primitive state. But as time went on . . .

By the time I returned the main parties had agreed for us jointly to host a shura – which seemed sensible enough. They'd also agreed that we would march north and conduct joint patrols with the ANA – which was not so well received by me or the lads. It felt bad tarring them all with the same brush, but the ANA guys we'd met didn't exactly fill us with confidence. They were of the shoot-first-ask-questions-later school. And they didn't particularly mind who they shot.

The shura went surprisingly well. The locals listened to us, and when we invited suggestions for co-operative operations they had a list. Their biggest bugbear was water supply. Any problem up towards the north of Helmand had a knock-on effect, often resulting in the water being turned off. Without a regular flow the irrigation to their non-opium crops would be affected.

So we said, 'We've got all these engineers, maybe we could help.'

The engineers came up with a plan to enlarge culverts under the road, to improve the flow of water. At the same time they worked to educate the locals – and engage them in the graft. For three weeks specialists from Bastion and dozens of young men from the area worked together to unblock streams and create a new, more effective network. The plan was twofold: one, to engender goodwill among the locals; and, two, to decrease the danger towards us. If all the young men in the area were working, they couldn't be shooting at us.

Even in the darkest situations you find the humour. 42 Commando had been posted to Afghan to 'build bridges', and there we were, quite literally, doing that. All we needed next was to win some genuine hearts and minds . . .

Whatever our intentions, the threat was never far away. The shura itself had been packed with many of these young men, stationed there to intimidate the locals, I'm sure. Our biggest worry, however, was the Afghan Army. A lot of the infrastructure being plumbed in needed equipment to be shipped up to us. Much of it had to be stored overnight at Daqhiqh. That meant a ton of Afghan military and Afghan police staying with us. Not a thought to give you a good night's sleep – not that we ever had that luxury. We didn't know them, we didn't trust them, we didn't even speak the lingo. And they outnumbered us two or three to one. There were reports buzzing around of the insurgency infiltrating the armed forces. What if these strangers were a Trojan Horse? We could all be killed in our beds. It was a security nightmare.

In a weird way, the only proof we had that there weren't moles in the camp was when the military escorting the supplies up from Shazaad were attacked. We knew from Mohamed Mohamed that the Taliban wouldn't usually target their own. But we also knew their respect for human life was markedly different from our own Western ideals.

On the day of the final supply delivery the convoy was between Omar and us when it struck an IED and immediately came under fire from watching insurgents hidden in the tree line. We were the closest CP. I scrambled a QRF (quick reaction force) together and we hightailed it down Cornwall as fast as the Vallon man could clear a route. We were within sight of the convoy when the shooting started coming in our direction.

'I need eyes on the shooters,' I screamed at the men ahead of me.

'Fuck's sake!' Matt came back. 'I think it's the army shooting.'

Fergie knew my doubts about the ANA. He was straight in my ear. 'You think they've turned?'

'Nah,' I said. 'I think they don't know what the hell they're doing.'

We were on the radio for what seemed like minutes trying to get the message across that we were there to help. Then the Afghan police started taking pot shots at us as well. It was ridiculous, and was only going to get worse. For them, at least.

We managed to secure the area. In pure numbers we dwarfed whatever force the Taliban had mustered in the trees. While my lads provided cover and basic medical aid, our new medic launched herself on one of the seriously injured ANA guys – 'herself' being the operative word.

The man, who had a hole in his side, immediately started spasming. Another soldier blocked the medic's way and shouted something.

'Max,' I said, 'get over here.'

It turned out the Afghan victim was refusing care from a female.

'But he's going to die without her,' Max explained, to no avail. The soldiers pointed to my men and said, 'We'll only be treated by them.'

Don't get me wrong, I'd trust my multiple to patch me up any day of the week. Tourniquets, emergency care, it's all in the training. But anything beyond – anything like extensive trauma injuries – requires specialist surgical skills. For that, if you've got any sense, you get the professionals. In the end two of us had to administer the medical care with our medic pulling all the strings like a puppet master.

Somehow it worked, and we stabilised the casualty. But any satisfaction I got from watching our team pull lives back from the brink was overwhelmed by the feeling – not for the first time – that these people didn't want to be saved.

You'd rather die than be mended by a woman? Someone explain to me how that helps anyone. Or any god.

You might think that trust is a universal concept. I beg to differ. Even though we'd risked our own lives to save theirs, I never thought it would count for anything with the Afghan soldiers. Back at the CP I still couldn't relax with our visitors. In the end, nothing happened. Not directly, anyway. But after the convoys stopped lodging with us, the grenades that were lobbed our way on an almost daily basis suddenly became a lot more targeted. Whereas they had used to hit the walls fairly harmlessly or cascade down from the trees in the orchard, now they were all landing within spitting distance of the ops room, my tent, the canteen, the ammo hut. It was almost as if the Taliban had acquired inside information about Daqhiqh.

'That's it,' I instructed everyone. 'Not one more Afghan sets foot inside these walls.'

I looked at our interpreters.

'No offence, Max, John.'

Max laughed. 'You'll get no complaint from us. You should have made that call ages ago.'

* * *

For as long as I live, the whole 'I'd rather die than be touched by a woman' thing will never make sense to me. At least in the case of the wounded Afghan soldier he had been making the decision for himself. That I could just about accept. When it was someone deciding the fate of a person in their care I wanted to do unspeakable things to them.

There was a kerfuffle at the gate one day which turned out to be the arrival of a man with a wheelbarrow. He got the full weapons-on-standby welcome until we realised that the cargo he was pushing was a young boy. Very young and very, very sick. I actually thought he was dead. The smell of rotting flesh was nauseating from metres away. The boy had been caught up in some kind of explosion. The man said from one of our mortars; I felt it looked more like shrapnel from an IED. For that reason I couldn't get the kid out by casevac. But we had the next best thing.

'Leave the boy here,' I said. 'We'll do what we can.'

Fergie said, 'Well done for not letting the dad in. I wouldn't put it past these people to injure their own kids to get eyes in here.'

'Exactly what I thought. How sick are we for even thinking that?'

'You can only play the hand you're dealt.'

We were both right.

Our medic cleaned the wound and applied what treatments she could. Then we put the boy back in the barrow and handed him over to his father

'Bring him back tomorrow,' I said. 'He needs regular treatment.'

Over the next few days we repeated the process. Gradually I saw an improvement in the lad. The father was pleased as well. On day 5 he was so smiley and chatty that my man on the gate forgot to make him wait outside.

Big error.

The medic was already getting ready to receive her patient when the dad came running over, screaming unintelligible noises and gesticulating at the woman. Before we could do anything he scooped up the wheelbarrow handles and ran his son back out of the CP. Absolute madness, if you ask me. And fucking selfish as well.

'What do you reckon the kid's chances are?' I asked the medic.

She was pulling her hair out. 'If he kept coming here, fifty-fifty, maybe sixty-forty. Out there . . .?' Her voice trailed off.

I was angry. Not for the first time, I felt impotent. Three days later I'd had enough.

'I'm going to get that kid.'

I made a point of engineering our patrol that day so that it finished off by the dad's compound. I knocked on the door and demanded to to be let inside. The atmosphere wasn't exactly welcoming. Not threatening, but not happy either.

I knew immediately the boy was dead.

I looked in the father's eyes and said, 'You killed him.'

He didn't need to speak English to get the message.

Barely two weeks later there was another case, worse I'd say. The Afghan police had set up a road block on Route Cornwall. A car hadn't stopped so they'd shot at it. The driver wasn't an insurgent – he was just late for prayers. So late he thought it worth his wife being shot and his daughter injured when the car crashed.

As the closest CP we went straight out to help. The car was a write-off. The mother and daughter weren't much better. We all dived in to help but the driver took one look at our medic and it was the usual story.

'She can't touch us!'

I was shouting at John, 'Tell him his family are going to die unless he lets us help.'

John told him, but it didn't matter. The man was too distressed to listen. He had some sort of rag which he kept hugging. What did help was John starting to recite passages from the Holy Book. It calmed the man down, and for a minute I thought he was going to let us tend to his daughter at least.

But no.

I watched those two poor people bleed out before my eyes. If I'd had my way there would have only been one casualty, and it wouldn't have been the women. That man – that fucking horrible excuse for a father and husband – chose to rub some shitty cloth on his wife while she died rather than allow another woman to save their lives.

Remind me why we're trying to save these people.

* * *

When it came to reporting the convoy incident I explained the facts as I recalled them. Not for the first time, I got the distinct impression that the severity of the ambush wasn't being considered. When I saw a copy of the official report it wasn't exactly airbrushed but it wouldn't make anyone reading feel that thirty-plus men and women had been exposed to a life-or-death situation.

It was the same story every time I made my daily updates to Shazaad. I'd list the number of grenades landing in our compound, the number of bullet strikes picked up by the sonar scanner, the sheer aggression we'd faced that day out on patrol, and I'd get the sort of reply that made me feel they didn't believe me. I knew that wasn't true. We had cameras on our helmets, we had computer read-outs, we had data from every weapon discharged. So it wasn't that they didn't believe what my multiple was going through.

It was that they didn't *want* to believe it.

In hindsight, I recognise that, to the top brass, the picture of Afghanistan in August 2011 was of a country 'saved' by the ISAF coalition. It was a lion that had been tamed by visiting experts. It was, essentially, a war that had been won. And my daily reports of wide-scale local aggression did not fit that narrative even slightly.

Later in the month whispers of our withdrawal from the region started to come through. Not just J Company's exit – the whole international force. Operation Liberate Afghanistan from the Taliban was being wrapped up. Job done. Mission accomplished.

So why didn't it feel like that to me?

Every single day since June we'd risked our lives for a cause that shifted in the wind. We'd do it again and again until we were told to stop. It would just have been nice to think that we were being useful.

* * *

Coming back after R&R I realised a few home truths. The biggest was how shit my men looked. I knew if I picked up a mirror I'd look no better. We were the ghosts that I'd seen haunting Camp Bastion five months earlier. But what could I do about it?

Very little, in reality, but I did what I could. I tinkered with the patrol rota so that, where possible, no one would go out for more than two days in a row. Myself included. Two days out, one day in on domestic duty, be it in the sangars or the ops room, or working on some other task. It didn't mean we got any more sleep but it felt like it. Not being on hyper alert for eight hours in a row was the closest we got to forty winks.

Nothing replaces the real thing, though. August and September were littered with fist fights among the lads, petty arguments over meaningless shit, and regular visits to me saying, 'I'm not going on patrol if So-and-So is.' It was all ridiculous stuff, but that's what happens when you are living on a powder keg. There wasn't one individual I wouldn't trust with my life. To see them at each other's throats, however temporarily, was all the proof I needed that something was seriously wrong.

I did what I could to resolve matters. What did the trick more than anything, though, was action. After another week of being on the receiving end of firefights on patrol, I decided that we'd take the initiative. Take the fight to the insurgents. We just had to work out how to combat our two main enemies.

The Taliban – and our own rules of engagement.

* * *

Just as the insurgents seemed to know exactly for how long to hide when a Tornado aircraft was in the vicinity, they had an unerringly accurate ability to shoot at us from mopeds when they knew we weren't in a position to deploy our heavier artillery. Either they would stand outside a civilian building or between us and another patrol, or they would run into a mosque – all out-of-bounds targets. Their tactics were as clever as they were frustrating. The fact they were able to spend entire days monitoring our movements before launching their own ambushes didn't help.

I knew for a fact that the genial old gent in the compound opposite our CP was in cahoots with the Taliban. At 7.30 a.m., without fail, he'd appear outside his wall sitting on a chair, for all the world taking in the early-morning sun. Of course, if we happened to send out a patrol during his time sitting out there, it was mere coincidence that he'd disappear inside his compound and we'd hear on the ICOM: 'The Americans are leaving.'

He wasn't the only one. I spoke to the owners of every single compound in our district and each man, each respected elder of the region, assured me on their children's lives that they would never co-operate with the Taliban. And yet, I began to notice an awful lot of bonfires being lit that August. No sooner would my patrol have passed a compound than a distinctive cloud of grey smoke would billow above the compound walls. Every building we passed lit its own fire, no matter what time of day we were there. At first I put it down to coincidence; then, to dinner time – people were obviously cooking.

Eventually I had to admit the facts. Every owner of every compound was in the pocket of the insurgency. We couldn't go into a compound without noticing a bonfire prepped and ready to be lit the second we departed.

Via Max and John, I asked Afghan after Afghan why they were siding with men who would kill them as soon as look at them. Eventually we found a man brave enough to answer. Taking us behind a wall where no prying eyes could see, he said, 'No one chooses to help them.' He looked around anxiously. 'You are good men. You have powerful weapons. But you won't kick down our doors in the middle of the night, steal our children and kill our wives if we don't co-operate. The

Taliban will. And they do. No one wants to help them. But we are more scared of them than of you.'

It was actually a member of the Afghan Army who put it into perspective: 'As a people we don't respect a man just because he has the biggest stick. We respect a man who will use it.'

The truth hurts. All ISAF troops had sticks bigger than the Taliban's. But none of us, not even the Estonians, were prepared to use them. And both the locals and, more importantly, the insurgents knew that. I was glad I didn't know the Afghan word for 'toothless' because I suspected I'd have heard it said of us more than once.

I was actually embarrassed. I thought, *We have to show our strength.*

According to Card Alpha, launching an ambush against the Taliban was illegal. Off limits. Totally outside our rules of engagement. Which is why I would never authorise such a tactic. And yet . . .

A 'standing patrol' is a group of men stationed on watch. They can be in plain sight but it makes more sense for the patrol to be shrouded. Hidden, even. Their role is to monitor the surroundings and, if appropriate, to respond. If that means leaping out on unsuspecting insurgents, so be it.

But they are not an ambush. Because that is illegal.

I didn't really have the numbers to maintain standing patrols. Luckily Tom Phillips, H, M'lord and Al Blackman all offered to chip in men, as and when I needed them. That proved to be sooner rather than later.

Based on all our patrols, the patterns of attacks and where the mopeds seemed to zip off to after an ambush, I had a pretty good idea that a mosque to the south-east of our CP was a place of interest. One morning – hours before the old guy across the road took up station on his chair – a bunch of my lads, led by Mac, climbed over the wall and headed off east towards the mosque 2 kilometres away. At the same time Tom Phillips, his guy Sibsy and a couple of others sneaked in. At 7.30, when I knew the spotter outside would be in place, we set off as though on a normal patrol, me, Tom and his guys.

My genius plan was for our patrol to take the direct route to the mosque and draw fire from the usual insurgent pests. I'd worked out the most likely place for a 'shoot-and-scoot' attack from one of the moped menaces. By coincidence, it was near where my men, the standing patrol, were lying in wait in a field – not in ambush, obviously, because that would be illegal.

I've never been so excited about the prospect of being shot at. I really thought this would be the day we snared a couple of Taliban.

We were still in sight of Daqhiqh when the ICOM started. The old man hadn't let me down. The further we walked the more call signs came on line. They all had weird and wacky names. 'Pumpkin' was the probably the best one that day. The radio chatter correlated with the number of young men brushing past us on mopeds. I tried to take in their faces but they may as well have worn masks. They all looked identical.

It was a slow walk to the north side of the mosque. We still had the threat of IEDs to contend with. Mac's team had eyes on the east.

'Is it clear?' I asked him.

'There's a lot of activity. Loads of young men hovering around the building.'

'That's promising,' I said. 'It's the wrong time for a call to prayer.'

I wanted to know if any of the men were armed.

'Negative.'

According to the GPS we were one building away from seeing the suspicious activity with our own eyes. A few more steps, one corner, and we had to be prepared for anything.

'Standing to, guys,' I said. 'Let's do this.'

I was just about to lead the men out when a bullet suddenly hit the wall inches away from my head. Others were close behind. We all dived into kneel-and-shoot pose. Mac heard the mayhem. He was shouting over the radio, 'Everyone outside the mosque has found weapons and they're heading in your direction.'

'Can you engage?' I said.

I waited for him to respond but he didn't answer. The next thing I heard was a raw explosion from the other side of the wall.

'Mac?'

Another explosion followed. Then the sound of machine guns.

When Mac got back in contact he reported two grenades had been thrown at them from the rear. They also had three assailants shooting at them no more than five metres away. The non-ambush had met the real thing.

'So much for the element of surprise!'

There was nothing for it. We had to retreat. Somehow we made it back to Daqhiqh to take stock of the situation. Tom Phillips couldn't believe how the insurgents had seen through our subterfuge.

'It doesn't matter what we do,' I sighed, 'they're always one step ahead.'

'I'd like to see them stay a step ahead of an Apache,' Tom said. He was as frustrated as I was.

'Me too. But that's never going to happen.'

And that, we had to admit, was a harder pill to swallow than being beaten into a retreat. Knowing you have the tools to finish a job – in this case, helicopter gunships – but aren't allowed to use them sucks.

At least we'd proved, with some certainty, that the mosque was a place of interest. HQ agreed. Two days later we took in a troop mentoring some local Afghan Army forces. These were locals I didn't mind staying over at the CP. I put it to them that we should hit the mosque en masse.

This time there was no standing patrol, just sheer numbers. The Afghan Army took the initiative and I couldn't have been happier. Where we were tied up in red tape they treated the insurgents the same way the insurgents treated us. The second we encountered a suspicious-looking young male near the mosque, he was grabbed before he could retrieve a gun from behind a wall. In seconds his bare feet were bound and he was tied to a tree. Then the Afghans began whacking the soles of his feet with a cane. As they did so, they yelled out to the local people standing around us, staring.

'What are they saying, Max?' I asked.

'They're saying, "This is what happens to Taliban scum. Stay away from the insurgents or end up like this."'

I couldn't help smiling. This was better than watching crops burn. 'Is it too late to join the Afghan Army?'

While this public humiliation was taking place, the main body of men stormed the mosque. The Afghans' commander called me over. I was reluctant to enter the building, not being a Muslim, but he wouldn't hear of it.

'You're about as deserving as anyone who's set foot in here,' he said. 'Even the Imam's a fake.'

As happy as I was at that stage to see any Afghan in handcuffs, the idea of arresting a religious leader could result in an awful lot of paperwork if not handled correctly. Refreshingly, that was the last thing on the commander's mind.

'Are you sure about him?' I said.

The leader nodded. 'Tell me what you see over there.' He pointed down the hall into the main chamber.

I'd been inside London mosques with the police. As in those, here I identified prayer mats and, on a lectern at the far end, a copy of the Koran.

'Look again,' the Afghan commander said. 'It's not the Koran.'

'What is it then?'

'Some old shit. The point is, the Imam can't read. None of his flock can read. I bet the only thing he's spouting at prayer times is political hatred.'

As if that wasn't staggering enough, we unearthed enough military hardware in the mosque to keep the insurgents firing at my men for weeks. It was a good job well done. You might have thought that I might be envious that the Afghan Army took the lion's share of the credit, but they deserved it. There was none of the smug silence that people like Mohamed Mohamed had shown me. The Afghan Army meant business. What's more, they knew how to connect to the locals – because they were locals too.

As I watched them break prisoner after prisoner I found myself torn emotionally. As a British Royal Marine I knew I couldn't be party to that kind of intimidation.

But as a soldier, robbed of sleep, almost constantly under threat, abandoned – or so I felt – by my political leaders, I was jealous. I knew that if I turned in the men the Afghan Army had arrested they'd be processed at Bastion and back out on the streets within a fortnight – probably to take pot shots at my men or to plant IEDs. I can't lie: the Afghan Army way was a breath of fresh air. There wasn't one of my men watching who didn't think, *If we were allowed to act like that this war would already be over – and our friends like Sam and Ollie would still be alive.*

CHAPTER NINETEEN

GO FIRM

By the end of August I'd been in Afghanistan nearly half a year. I swear I could stay a lifetime and still never understand the people.

One day H's Kamiabi patrol were caught out in an ambush. They'd been cornered like rats while bullets rained down from a nearby compound. It was deadly stuff, although at least they knew where the attack was coming from.

In other words, they had a target with a bullseye on it to hand over to air support.

I can only imagine the buzz among H's men as they waited for the Predator drone to arrive. Knowing that all they had to do was keep the Taliban shooting, then wait for the fireworks. It never gets old. The only thing that would have made it better was being able to see the looks on the Afghan faces in that split second when they realised they were about to be blown to smithereens.

The 200-pound bomb did exactly what it was intended to. Each insurgent was wiped off the face of the earth. Unfortunately, so was most of the compound, including the family that lived there. The only survivor was the father. He was casevacked to Bastion to have his shattered leg amputated.

As a father myself, I felt for him. As a man I was appalled that innocent people were being caught up in this ridiculous war. But, as a marine on the wrong end of six months of compound owners like him letting Taliban scum use their properties to try to kill me and my friends, his personal tragedy barely registered. Play with fire and you get burned. Harsh perhaps, but that's what I thought.

That is, until I was told I'd be doing a welfare check on him.

As per ISAF rules, once he was out of hospital the man had been given financial compensation for his loss. He had used it to buy another farm, which happened to be within our AOR (area of responsibility), hence my being tasked with this hideous job. Being betrayed by the locals we'd sworn to protect was one thing. Being asked to walk up to a bloke whose entire livelihood and family – and leg – had been wiped out by people on my side of the fence was something else entirely.

What – am I just going to say, 'Sorry, mate', pat him on the back and that'll be it?

As we approached the new compound I went over and over in my head what I was going to say. Nothing sounded right. I felt more nervous than if I had been facing a firing squad. At least with guns I could respond. Whatever this man said I would just have to listen to and suck up.

We reached the gate and knocked. There was a strange scraping noise the other side, then the door flew open to reveal a farmer with a wooden leg.

We've got the right place at least . . .

I braced myself for the onslaught, but the moment the guy recognised our uniforms he welcomed us into his compound with open arms.

'Come in, come in,' he said. 'You must be hot. Let me get you a drink.'

Well, this is weird.

One of the worst things you can do to an Afghan is refuse his hospitality. Even if you are convinced you are going to be poisoned. I couldn't take my eyes off the bloke. I didn't want to be hostile but I didn't dare trust him, either. When he offered me tea, I only took a sip of it, and once he had done so. When he produced some sort of cake, I made sure I bit into it after him. Obviously, I couldn't rule out the chance of a 'suicide chef', for a man without hope might easily take his own life as well as mine. But something about his persona said he wasn't in any hurry to die.

'John,' I said to our interpreter, 'let's get this over with. Ask him what we can do.'

The man replied, 'You have done enough!' Then he hugged us all.

Confused, I began reciting my rehearsed speech. The man barely listened. In fact he stopped me before I even got to the apology bit.

'My friend,' he said, 'I didn't really like my wife or children. You did me a favour. With your American dollars I have bought a better farm, I have more cattle than I ever dreamed of and I will be able to afford to buy two wives who will give me more worthy children.'

As the translated words came out of John's mouth I thought that he had to be lying. The look on the farmer's stupid happy face, though, backed him up.

I thought, *This is beyond insanity*.

'I can't do this,' I said. 'We have to go.'

I actually found more comfort on the way home when a gaggle of shooters engaged us in a firefight. At least that made sense to me. Everything else? I don't think I'll ever understand.

* * *

Watching the Afghan forces at work gave me hope that the populace could be saved. Just not in the way that we were going about it. The Afghan Army knew the people we were working with. They knew the culture. They belonged to it. To make an impression on the inhabitants of Helmand Province you needed to think like them and act like them.

'You can't fight fire with sweetmeats,' one of the Afghans explained. 'You have to use fire or get burned yourself.'

I knew our kid-gloves tactic wasn't working. If I saw Mohamed Mohamed once, I saw him half a dozen times. On each occasion that he was captured he was arrested and sent to Bastion. The joke was that he knew he'd be back.

Luckily for him he was unarmed each time we arrested him.

'You won't be smiling if I ever catch you with a weapon,' I said. 'Then you'll see what I'm allowed to do. Then you'll see justice.'

Of course, the insurgents were well aware that if we saw that they were armed, then we could stop and arrest them. Shoot them if they didn't co-operate. Yet they always seemed to have a gun to hand to shoot at us when we least expected it. How were they doing it? We got an idea during one patrol when Mac found something hanging from a tree. It wasn't a body. It was a loaded AK-47. The rifle wasn't there by accident. It could be reached easily from the road.

It explained the 'shoot and scoot' practice – when a moped carrying two young men could race past us one minute and then those same men could be blasting at us with automatic weapons a minute later. They'd drift by, casual as you'd like, produce a weapon from a hole in the ground or behind a particular bush, take a few pot shots, then wheel over to the next hidey-hole. It was cunning. Unless we were actually to shoot them we would never find them with weapons.

And what were we doing in return? Compared with hiding serious military hardware in trees, something passive, you could have bet money on that. And the insurgents knew it. One of the initiatives we rolled out was to post letters through every compound door asking for help from the locals in hunting down the Taliban terrorists. We offered the full protection of the British war machine.

And the insurgents just pinned these letters on local men's backs and sent them back.

That's when they were being respectful. On one patrol we found a hundred or so paper aeroplanes littering a narrow track. They were all made from our charming little peace proposals.

'They're laughing at us,' I said.

No one could disagree. But what could we expect? We were applying Western standards to non-Western culture. We expected Afghans to react in the way that we knew citizens of Canterbury or Hamburg or

Bruges might respond. I don't think that our masters – the analysts and planners – paid any heed to what pushed the buttons of this very different breed of people.

* * *

Achieving justice, or making our mark on the enemy who had terrorised us for so long, was becoming more important to all of us with every passing day. Someone needed to pay. We weren't even that fussed who it was. We'd take any win by then. A guy presented himself at the CP one day claiming compensation for a bullet wound for which he said we were responsible. I felt he was probably right. But part of me was thinking, *I'm glad you got shot. I bet you deserved it, as well.*

One day there was an 'ops box' command from Shazaad. The American Special Forces were initiating a raid so we were ordered to avoid a certain area for twenty hours. The assault, when it came, was of biblical proportions. Two attack helicopters have the firepower to level a building. The combination of Tankbuster and Spectre Gunship planes levelled a huge area. Then two helicopters dropped a squadron of SF guys into the zone to hoover up the pieces. There was bombing, machine-gun fire, and fireworks to rival the Fourth of July. For ninety minutes we had the best seat in the house, watching and listening. Then it was all over. The helicopters returned, the SF went home – and the dead stayed dead.

The next day we were commissioned with a recce to confirm the numbers killed. It was as impressive as it was horrific. Where six compounds used to stand there was just rubble. Bodies and limbs were strewn everywhere. For the first time I actually saw something like fear in the eyes of the locals.

'Why did you do this?' they kept asking.

'It wasn't us.'

But, I thought, *I bloody wish it had been us.*

Our camp was attacked several times that night. It seemed fair, somehow. And it was expected. Maybe it was retaliation, maybe it wasn't. Maybe the insurgents really did believe that we were responsible for the huge onslaught. We were attacked most nights regardless. It was difficult ever to pinpoint a reason.

* * *

I don't remember what day of the week it was. Maybe Monday, maybe Wednesday. I didn't hear my alarm clock, but I did hear the shouts of my men on the perimeter. There were holes in the mud. Someone had been digging underneath the wall. By sheer chance an outdoor patrol had spotted it. When they traced it inside we realised the hole had almost broken through.

'Shit. Another few inches and they would have been in. Why do you think they stopped?' No one knew. The best we could come up with was 'luck'.

A few days later it happened again, but on the other side of the compound. This time they didn't get as far. It was obviously laborious work and they'd been interrupted. I wasn't sure we'd be so fortunate a third time.

The men were agitated, even jumpy. Considering how wired we were, anyway, through lack of sleep, this only magnified matters. We were all concerned about having our throats slit in our beds.

'Just as well we never get to sleep then, isn't it?' Robbie said.

He had a point. Even so, despite getting barely three hours of shuteye in every twenty-four, I found myself taking my pistol to bed. I put it under my pillow. It wasn't enough to be able to roll out of my trench and into the ops room or the sangar. I wanted to be able to take an insurgent out with me. It was lucky I couldn't hear my alarm clock, because I'd most definitely have taken that out as well.

The tension within the team was already strong, overwhelming even. Discovering those tunnels so near completion tipped us over the edge. Without ever discussing it as a group, we all realised that we would rather die than risk capture by the savages that were the Taliban. As a result, we hatched a plan to place explosives all around the CP. In a critical emergency we'd activate one bomb, which would trigger a chain reaction, bringing the entire compound in on itself and taking with it anyone inside Daqhiqh.

We called it the last line of defence. What it really was – and what everyone acknowledged – was a giant suicide bomb. We all preferred to die at our own hands than be tortured, maimed and strung up as trophies.

* * *

The decisions you make in 50-degree heat and 70 per cent humidity, when you're dead on your feet and feeling increasingly powerless. It didn't help that Sunray couldn't prise any further reinforcements from Bastion. He sounded as frustrated as I was. It was almost as though the new command didn't believe we had a war on our hands. Perhaps, with 42 Commando HQ moving across to Sagin, it was because we were now under 45 Commando's HQ.

But plenty of people knew exactly what we were facing on the ground. One day I got a message from a camp further in towards Shazaad. As far as I knew, they hadn't seen any action at all in six months.

And that, it turned out, was the point.

'I've got a couple of signallers here, Rob,' the commander of the CP said. 'They really want to get their hands dirty. Can they join you for a couple of days?'

Honestly, at that point I would have taken anyone apart from our former medic. The more bodies the better. Just a couple would allow two of my guys to close their eyes for more than forty winks.

It began to happen a lot. Men who hadn't seen any kinetic action were signing up to join us for a few days. They'd arrive, we'd patrol, get shot at and respond. Then we'd come home, write reports and do it all again the following day. Forty-eight hours later the visitors would return to their CP with their still fresh uniforms and their stories of derring-do. 'War Tourists' I called them. I meant it derogatorily, but I think they may have saved our sanity, if not our lives. For every 'bullet backpacker' we got, my guys scrambled an average of one hour's extra kip. When you're being shot at or bombed every single day, the currency of sleep tops the exchange rate.

People who drive on motorways when they're exhausted experience the phenomenon of micro-sleeps. They don't know how they reached their destination. Or they suddenly realise they're bouncing over the bumps of the hard shoulder. My men went through that every waking minute. 'Waking' being the operative word. I realised the hollowed-out men I had seen all those months ago at Camp Bastion weren't ghosts. They were zombies. They were the undead. Men who'd forgotten how to sleep. That's what it felt like, anyway.

* * *

At some point during late August we lost sight of our mission. Hearts and minds were in short supply among the locals we encountered. How could we hope to win what we couldn't find? With just over a month of the tour left to complete we were focused on a policy of 'kill or capture'. The emphasis was not on 'capture'.

I decided to take the men to the place where we'd have the best opportunity. Green 13 had caused us all sorts of problems in the past. It was where we had finally realised, once and for all, that we were the rodents in this grown-up game of cat and mouse. It's where I knew that, if any killing was going to happen, it would be there.

Bearing in mind what happened to us every time we ventured that way, it would take some planning, some skill and some luck not to be on the receiving end again. I spoke to Tom Phillips and we brokered a joint initiative to move up there together. But first, I said, I want to get some eyes on the place.

'Are you sure? You've been ambushed every time you've gone anywhere near.'

'I have a cunning plan . . .'

Early one morning, eight of us used the little stream in the compound to swim out, just as we'd done in Toki. We still had to cross Route Cornwall, though. As we stood poised to rush across, the remaining lads in the CP set off smoke grenades and fired several rifle rounds. The distraction worked. We bolted across Cornwall, dived into the canal and waited to hear what the ICOM had to say.

Plenty about the smoke grenades – but nothing about nine marines trying to be invisible.

'Perfect.'

We made our way carefully. It was slow going. Some of the rat runs that afforded the best cover weren't the most direct. It was worth following them, though. Concealment was the key. Barely a metre of track passed without our being reminded of what had happened on previous visits. There were crops still bent from our trampling through. Walls scarred with bullet holes. Patches of flattened grass where we'd dived for cover.

All the subterfuge paid off. We made it to within a building's depth of the infamous junction. Turning left or right would bring us directly onto the road.

'What's it going to be, Rob?' Fergie asked. 'Left or right?'

'Neither,' I said.

'Are we staying here?'

'No. We're going *up*.'

We always have collapsible ladders on us, but the building protecting us had New York-style fire escapes running up the wall. Two minutes later we were all lying prone on the flat roof, barely able to contain our laughter. How the fuck had we managed to get so close? In the past we'd been shot at just for thinking about Green 13. It made no sense.

We waited for ten minutes. When I was convinced our high-level sortie had gone undetected – the ICOM was the litmus test, as always – I inched on my belly towards the ridge of the roof, which, according to my maps, should overlook the crossroads. Fergie and Matt were right behind me.

The picture I saw below was pretty much as the intel had shown. A bustling junction on Route Devon, barely 2 kilometres from Taalander, full of mopeds and other small vehicles zipping up and down and across the junction, this way and that. Devon itself was lined with not exactly shops but booths or lock-ups. Whatever they were, dozens of young men were sitting on chairs outside them drinking Coca-Cola and smoking. Like any other men enjoying a sunny day without a care in the world.

'You could almost think these bastards didn't want to kill us,' I said.

'What do you think they'd do if they knew we were here?'

'I don't know, Fergie. Shall we find out?'

'Are you crazy?'

'Maybe.'

I decided to sit up. The lads with me did the same. It felt weirdly naughty, as though we were mischievous schoolboys up to no good. In a way we were. Given everything we knew about the insurgents, about the ruthlessness of their tactics, about their expertise in navigating the warren of streets in the vicinity, it bordered on madness to get their attention.

Put it this way: I wouldn't have done it in March, April, May, June or July. But, after five weeks of being shot at, bombed or cornered close to IEDs nearly *every single day*, you start thinking differently. Seriously differently.

When the men below failed to notice us I decided to up the ante. Again, you won't find this in any training manual. But we were there for a recce. I wanted to see what we were dealing with.

'Morning, boys,' I called down. 'Lovely day for it, isn't it?'

In the street below us a couple of lads sipping coffee looked at each other. It was beautiful to watch. Above the din of the mopeds and the general chat and laughter they'd heard something. They couldn't put their finger on it. What was it?

You could actually see the penny drop.

English!

A ripple like an electric current went through the groups of men relaxing with their Cokes or cups of coffee. It was like watching dominoes fall. One by one they all got the message that something was wrong. They looked left, they looked right.

And then they looked up.

The expression on their faces when they saw eight British Royal Marines waving down at them was priceless. A second later it was as though a powder keg had gone off. They leapt out of their chairs. Some ran inside the buildings. Some into the road. Mopeds were flagged down and cars were stopped.

'I think that's our cue to leave,' I said.

We scrambled down the ladders and dashed back along as close to the exact route we'd followed on the way in. The odds of its having been contaminated by IEDs when none of the insurgents knew we were there were slim. Amazingly, we made it back unscathed. There wasn't even a firefight. In fact, the loudest noise for the entire journey was the ICOM having a fit. One particular call sign was broadcasting virtually non-stop.

'Someone's not happy,' John laughed. 'Those boys are all getting it in the neck.'

That night our CP was targeted with grenades, machine-gun fire and any other shit the Taliban could muster. It didn't matter. Inside those mud walls we felt untouchable.

Amazing what sleep deprivation can make you do.

The next day I started hatching a plan to go back to Green 13 in force. HQ agreed to have air support on standby and feed Shazaad's intel directly to us. Tom Phillips would lead a patrol from Taalander.

'Maybe a bit less kamikaze stuff this time, though?' HQ added.

We moved out in exactly the same manner that had proved successful before. We got across the canal and sneaked our way to the last compound between us and Green 13. To the north-west of us Tom Phillips was doing much the same thing. There was no ICOM chat and we saw no bonfires lit en route. Yet for all our stealth, to achieve anything we had to cross Devon. And we knew exactly what would happen when we did.

The shooting began the moment Robbie set foot outside the compound wall.

Click-click-click.

Click-click-click.

But he was ready. We all were. We knew exactly where the shooters were because the PGSS camera had picked them out. Robbie dropped to a kneeling position, cool as a cucumber, fixed the direction of fire and responded in kind. Moments later he was joined by Matt, me and the rest of the snake's tail, all raking fire at our enemy.

Now it was the attackers' turn to be caught out. The wall they were hiding behind was solid but our wall of lead was already making inroads. A few more minutes and it would be more holey than a Swiss cheese.

I radioed the camera operator at Shazaad.

'Status?'

'They're moving.'

I almost got him to repeat it. After six months of being shot at, being made the target in this lethal game of cat and mouse, we'd never once got the locals on the run. Until now. I hoped I could remember what to do.

We were to the north of the insurgents. Wherever they went it had to be south. A couple of minutes went by, then Shazaad came back on line. 'They're in compound 155.'

I checked my map. We were outside 157.

I gave the order to advance. It was slow. We had to be prepared for other shooters to pop up. Judging by the ICOM that was a possibility, although it wasn't happening yet. In any case, I had every faith that our eyes in the sky would give us the nod.

Although I was exhilarated to have the back-up I found myself wondering, *Where was all this support during the last six months?*

Knowing your target's location and getting to it are two very different things. They fired, we returned fire, they shifted position, we followed, and the process continued. The longer it went on the more confident I felt in getting a result. Since a flat roof had been useful on our last visit I decided to go up high once again and try to smoke them out. Four of us climbed up on to a roof. We could make out the movement the other side of the wall and fired on sight. The problem was, they could also see us. For a few minutes it was like a proper cowboys-and-Indians rifle shootout. What's more, we were winning it.

'They're getting thrashed,' Fergie said. 'I don't know why they don't use their RPGs.'

The words had barely left his mouth when a grenade flew over our heads and into the building next to us.

If their aim was anything to go by, we had them rattled. They ran to another compound, then another. Thanks to the running commentary from our man on the camera at Shazaad we were never more than a minute behind. Each time they deluged the ICOM with pleas for back-up.

'The Americans have us cornered. We need the Big Thing. Send the Big Thing.'

They were scared. They were panicked. If they knew Tom Phillips was a hundred metres from joining in they'd have been terrified.

And if they heard the news I was just getting from Shazaad they'd have packed up and gone home.

'Guess what, boys,' I said.

A couple of the lads humoured me. 'What?'

'There's an Ugly on station.'

Instinctively eight heads swivelled up and round. They knew that was the call sign for an Apache. But the sky was empty. Nothing to see.

'Are you sure?' Matt said.

He was joking. You don't see those buggers unless they want to be seen. And if we couldn't spot them hovering on the horizon 4 kilometres away, what chance did four or five renegades have crouching behind a wall?

The pieces were falling nicely into place. Even so, I knew from experience that things in Helmand could go tits-up in no time at all. If back-up did arrive we might even take casualties.

'We have to end this before they get themselves organised.'

'What are you thinking?' Matt asked.

'I'm thinking we do this the old-fashioned way. We go in hard and fast. We've got them pinned back and outnumbered.'

I outlined my plan for a two-pronged assault. A buzz went around the group. This was already our best day ever in Afghanistan. After all the shit we'd taken in Daqhiqh, if we got to take a few scalps as well we could all go home with our heads high.

I ran the plan past Tom. He said he was almost in place to provide cover. Then I went to Shazaad. Unfortunately Sunray had different ideas.

'Negative,' he said. 'Go firm.'

'Go firm' means remain where you are. There was only one reason: they were bringing the Apache into play.

'With respect, sir,' I said, 'I think we can end this one on the ground.'

'Negative,' he repeated. 'Go firm. Repeat: go firm.'

What choice did I have?

Breaking the news to the lads was difficult. The only sweetener I could offer was knowing that someone would have to go in and clear up after the helicopter had done its job.

'If we're lucky we might find some survivors.'

I was patched into the chopper's comms. Their optics were out of this world. We couldn't see or hear them, but their weapons guy had three insurgents in his crosshairs. There was a tense few seconds while they verified their orders.

'Kill or capture' was off the table. This was 'kill' all the way.

I heard the all-clear come through from Sunray. I turned to the lads.

'Here we go.'

A couple of seconds later a section of wall 25 metres south-west of our position disintegrated. With it the lives of three insurgents. They wouldn't have had a clue. We saw the blast before we heard it – and we were expecting it. It was swiftly followed up by a torrent of anti-tank machine-gun fire. There was no mistaking that noise. I think it could have been heard in Shazaad.

I know it was the sensible option to bring in the Apache. But I wasn't interested in sensible. The eight men around me had been hung out to dry for the last few months, treated as target practice by a Taliban we weren't really allowed to engage. We were deprived of sleep, of clean clothes, of back-up. And now, the only time we hadn't been hunted down like dogs, when we'd had the chance to put down a bit of a marker for the honour of Daqhiqh, it had been denied us.

As I said, I wasn't thinking sensibly. How could a sensible person think that giving his men the opportunity to kill other human beings was a treat? But I did. That's what six months in Afghan had turned me into.

At least we still had the BDA (battle damage assessment).

When the dust settled and the plumes of smoke dissipated I got the boys ready to break cover. The BDA needed to be conducted as soon as possible. People had been known to survive some horrific Apache onslaughts.

I gave Sunray our position and said we were geared to go.

'Tom's closer,' he said. 'His men are doing it.'

You are shitting me? After all this? This was our operation.

I am still amazed that I held off saying it. But the thoughts were loud enough. My lads were as gutted as me. And, when we listened in to the commentary from Tom's advancing party our mood got worse. The Apache had killed only two insurgents. A third was making a run for it – and was armed.

The rules could not be clearer. Not just rules – the *logic*. HQ had given the order for those three insurgents to be wiped off the face of the earth. They'd sent their most efficient death machine – an Apache helicopter – to make it happen. For anyone who had miraculously survived, his death warrant had already been signed.

I confess, when we heard Tom's man, Tom 'Smudge' Gilbert, getting the rounds down, I had mixed feelings. Part of me wanted to punch the air, safe in the knowledge that the world was now short of one Taliban ambush group.

Another part was pissed off that it wasn't me pulling the trigger. Or Fergie, or Robbie, or Matt, or any of the others.

We were owed this.

I could only hope our time would come.

* * *

When we finally moved over to the scene of destruction, it was to find one corpse without its face, another shredded and a third riddled with bullet holes. We collected DNA and then, as the locals began to appear again, tried to establish identities. The man without a face proved tricky but one of the others, a surprisingly tall man by Afghan standards, drew a less than concerned response from a couple of people.

'He wasn't from here,' one said. 'He was a pig. I'm glad he's dead.'

If I hadn't recently heard a farmer use similar words to describe his own murdered family I might have been more impressed.

Despite our ultimately frustrating day, back at Daqhiqh there was something of a party mood in the air, encouraged by Ugly doing a fly-by low enough for the pilot to give us a wave. The fact that we were celebrating three deaths tells you a lot about what we had become as people. The fact that we'd have been even happier if we'd pulled the triggers ourselves tells you a great deal more. We were beyond the point of seeing the Taliban as people any more. They were the enemy. Plain and simple.

And the sooner they were all dead, the better.

CHAPTER TWENTY

STEER OFF

In late August we had another visit from the CO and RSM. They came armed with cigarettes and welfare packages, but also with the news that we would be reassigned to 45 Commando RM operational command, as 42 HQ were relocating to Sagin with the US forces. This was significant as 45 were used to a different AO and had been able to employ successfully a hearts-and-minds policy; they were far less supportive of 'use of force' to which we had become accustomed. In my opinion this was when the frustrations reached boiling point.

War tourist applications went through the roof after our Green 13 'victory'. One I didn't expect was from our Sunray. I wasn't sure if I was more grateful that he'd at last see how reduced to the bare bones we were, or that he'd be travelling with his own multiple of men. It turned out to be the latter. Those extra bodies on sentry and patrol meant that over the next few days my entire multiple could get at least one full night's sleep – in every case the first since their R&R had ended. We had all the arms and armour in the world at our disposal but the one thing we craved – something that cost nothing – we were made to feel privileged to get.

I think the OC saw this. I also think it hurt and frustrated him that he could do nothing about it.

'Not even when you know that I sometimes have to work with eleven functional men?' I said, in a moment of frank discussion. 'Not even when that sometimes means leaving only three people to guard this CP while we're out on patrol? Not even when it means that if something happens during a patrol we're fucked because there's no back-up?'

'Not even,' he admitted.

The fact that we were too stretched to make any decent fist of 'rebuilding'; or of pursuing the policy of 'hearts and minds' with any gusto, didn't faze him. That's when I knew things must be bad, and when I realised that he was as frustrated as I was. The men he had at his disposal were spread just as thinly everywhere else. It was our misfortune that Daqhiqh was so much more active than the rest of the battle group. He soon saw it for himself. His chopper was shot at while it was trying to put down on a nearby HLS, which surprised none of us in the CP. Each night of his visit there were small-arms attacks and IEDs planted along our stretch of Cornwall. According to the ICOM chatter the Taliban were well aware he was there. They'd already claimed one Sunray and were pulling out the stops to nail another. He and his men managed to get in and out with their lives, but he was left in no doubt about what we were facing twenty-four hours a day, seven days a week.

'I just wish there were more I could do,' he said. So did I.

With no sign of back-up from Bastion or beyond, September saw us coping as best we could. I lived in daily fear that the insurgents would discover just how paper-thin our resources were. To give the men the slightest chance of rest, we took to putting 'fake' marines inside the super-sangars. To anyone beyond the perimeter it looked like two or three men permanently on look-out. To anyone closer it looked like what it was: one tired bloke plus the silhouettes of a few hastily thrown-together uniforms on sticks.

I also began running 'dummy' patrols. I'd lead a team of eight out in the morning then head back at lunchtime. We'd change our uniforms as much as possible, add the odd bit of distinctive kit plus one or two new faces, then head out again – for all the world, especially to the Taliban spotters, like a second patrol.

I think all this was a sign of desperation, a desperation that began to show itself everywhere. After the horror that was Toki I'd started attaching all sorts of value to various inanimate objects. I wasn't just hugging my pistol in those rare moments when I got to sleep, but I couldn't patrol without the exact same pair of gloves or boots that I always wore. The more you cheat death the more you find yourself looking for a reason. I don't believe in God, so that left my lucky uniform, my lucky rifle, my lucky pants – basically whatever I was wearing or carrying the last time I dodged a bullet. Or a grenade. Or an IED. The more contacts I survived, the more weight I ascribed to my superstitions. Crazy, really, but no more crazy than half the other stuff we were getting up to.

September continued in the same vein as August: namely, shootings or bombings. We were in survival mode, plain and simple.

I remembered how keen I'd been to escape early for my R&R in July. My emotions had said I needed to be with my troops. My instincts said I needed to get out. And fast.

It would have been a different story if we hadn't felt so damn exposed. The more times you jump out in front of the train the more chance you have of being hit. It felt like we were jumping out every damn day. If the Green 13 episode had proved one thing, it was that if we went out with the full weight of resources at our disposal – and a clear plan to eliminate the opposition – then a handful of amateur killers were no match for us. You might even argue that during our six-month tour we could, with the right back-up, have torn through the Taliban's ranks. But we didn't. The order to provide us with that level of support was never given, and 42 Commando took heavy casualties as a result – many of which could, in my opinion, have been avoided.

A case in point: Green 13 had been a cesspit. It was by no means the only one. Over a period of weeks we worked out that another region, Green 23, seemed just as well defended. Whenever we got close, the level of attack would increase. Obviously, it became an area of massive interest.

To me, anyway. To Sunray as well. Above him? Not so much.

My logic was simple. *We broke 13, we can break 23 as well.* I would keep patrolling that way until I either cracked it or we got cracked. Day after day we were beaten back. This particular day looked like being like all the previous ones. I'd got tired of retreating so we'd pushed aggressively through the danger spots. We got close to the compounds that were giving us trouble when suddenly shooting came at us from both sides. It was a classic ambush – not even a pretence at a standing patrol. Totally illegal by our rules. Totally acceptable by theirs. Totally effective whichever way you looked at it.

We took cover and returned fire. I radioed a sitrep to Shazaad. It was war by numbers. We'd had so much practice we could have done it in our sleep – if we had ever had any. What usually happened at that point is that Sunray or his 2ic would have told us they were monitoring the situation. On this occasion he said something else.

'You have air support near by. Go firm.'

Well, that was unexpected.

I ran the info down the line. The lads were as shocked as I was. Grateful, though. We had enough ammo for now. It wouldn't last. At some point we would need to be retreat. We didn't want to be doing that having to count our rounds.

It turned out that aerial surveillance had clear pictures of us, of the ambush – and of another group of men assembling in a nearby compound with what looked like some serious artillery. In total there were about fifteen men within a tiny area. Throw in the weaponry and an airstrike could take out a significant chunk of Taliban personnel and resources.

There was a natural lull in the shooting. At the same time the OC gave his final prep to the pilot.

'Here we go, lads,' I said. 'Get ready for the main event.'

We all stared at the compound, waiting for it to disappear. Any second now. Any second now. Any. Second . . .

'*Shit!*'

'What is it?' Fergie asked.

'It's the air strike,' I said. 'It's not coming.'

'What the fuck's Sunray playing at?'

'It wasn't him. He was overruled.'

I heard it with my own ears. One minute the OC was giving the go-ahead to remove fifteen bad guys and a shitload of guns from the playing field, the next he was told to stand the chopper down. An analyst at Bastion had decided that the compound was too near crucial 'infrastructure'. They didn't want the collateral damage.

'I'm sorry, Eleven Lima,' Sunray said. 'They said we're meant to be rebuilding the region not blowing it up.'

'Tell them from me it's a damn sight easier to rebuild something when you're not being shot at.'

It was a kick in the teeth. I felt abandoned. All the lads did. There had been a gilt-edged opportunity right in front of us to make tomorrow a safer day for everyone in 42 Commando and beyond, and we hadn't taken it. The lives of murderers were considered more valuable than ours. That's how it felt.

The march back to Daqhiqh was glum. As far as we were concerned the only people with a true picture of what was going on in Helmand were those of us on the ground. We had radios but no one was listening. We were fighting for our lives, literally, on a daily basis, but the planners at Camp Bastion were treating the operation like a theoretical exercise. They seemed to have no will to win.

* * *

lways hope tomorrow will be better. Even Bill Murray in *undhog Day* did. Every day he woke up in Punxsutawney, listening to that same song by Sonny & Cher, he thought he could change things. It was only when he realised he couldn't that he did. Our H was a long way off working that out.

The day after air support was called off we could have sat around Daqhiqh moping but I guarantee that would have invited a storm of grenades and small-arms fire in our direction. The only reason our camp had not been overrun, I firmly believed – and still do – is because the Taliban thought we had far higher staff levels than we did. If they'd got an inkling that sometimes just two or three fit men were manning all the defences while the rest of us were out, there's no way they wouldn't have come against us mob-handed. If they had known how tired we were they might have had a go as well. The way to dispel any hint of weakness was to keep the patrols going. Even when we knew HQ couldn't give a damn what we discovered.

I decided to push back towards the same territory. Knowing that fifteen pairs of eyes that should have been closed for ever might be staring at us, plotting our downfall, didn't exactly fill the lads with confidence. We're marines, though: we do what we're told.

If we were going to make inroads, I knew, it would have to be with our own skills and our own wits. If that meant taking out fifteen terrorists one at a time, so be it. We had a couple of weeks left of the tour to do it. By a stroke of luck, this was the day a local decided to help. He was furtive as fuck, desperate not to be seen talking to us, but he revealed that a senior insurgent would be planting an IED on Cornwall early the following morning. He was telling us not because he liked us but because his family used that route – and so did he. Whether he was the first Afghan I met that actually cared about his children or whether it was the threat to his business that concerned him more, I couldn't say. The intel was all that mattered.

The spot he mentioned was about 1,000 metres south of us and therefore about the same distance north of Omar – in other words, the most difficult place for the two CPs to monitor. That wasn't to say we couldn't. I tasked our surveillance cameras to pick up that section of Route Cornwall and got on to Shazaad to request that they focus on the same length of track.

Even at the crack of dawn on a normal day there would always be a fair few shifty-looking people, mostly zooming around the province on their mopeds. Suspicious is suspicious, though. About an hour before sunrise we hit pay dirt. A young man stopped his moped and, brazen as you like, began burrowing into the track.

'That's it,' I said. 'He's laying the IED.'

Based on how quickly we'd been set upon in the past, I knew he could get the device in the ground and operational within ten minutes. Which gave us a maximum of that long to reach him. We could do it, but not safely. Luckily we didn't have to. HQ were bringing the remote missile system online.

I know that decision would not have been an easy one to get made. Just getting a cup of tea at Bastion took three signatures and a blood sample. A request to bomb a Taliban member had to go up and down numerous authorisation channels before being green lit.

My men were gathered at the gate, ready to go the moment we heard the explosion. In my ear I had a running commentary from my ops room and those at Shazaad and Bastion.

'The target is still there.'

'Missile is armed.'

'The target is still there.'

'Missile is ready.'

'The target is still there.'

'Missile is live.'

I couldn't help grinning. 'It's in the air, lads.'

'The missile is in the air.'

'The target is still there.'

'The missile is in the air.'

'The target is still there.'

Come on, come on, any second now . . .

The prospect of one fewer insurgent had us all buzzing. Forget lack of sleep: I'd never felt so alert.

'The missile is in the air.'

'The target is still there.'

Then:

'Steer off! Steer off!'

'What the . . . ?' I couldn't believe what I was hearing. 'No, no, no – not again!'

A second later we heard the explosion.

'Report?' asked HQ.

'In the canal,' the missile pilot said.

'Eleven Lima,' Sunray said, 'time to move.'

We flew out of that compound. Even as we ran the lads were saying, 'Rob, what the fuck happened?'

The details were still filtering through over the radio, but I got the gen.

'The guy was planting the IED on a power line,' I said, not easy running at full speed. 'It's their new trick. They know it makes it harder for the Vallons to pick them up.'

Our usual Vallon man, Robbie, had sat this one out. His replacement was a good lad from Kamiabi sent by H to bolster our numbers, Jolly by name, jolly by nature.

'Tell me about it,' Jolly said.

'So what?' – Fergie, obviously.

'Apparently HQ don't want to be blowing up power lines.'

'Who gives a fuck?' Fergie shouted. 'We've got generators.'

Each man of us seconded that opinion.

'On the bright side,' I said, 'if we're lucky there's an injured insurgent waiting to be finished off when we get there.'

That put a spring in everyone's step.

Two hundred metres short of the GPS co-ordinates, I slowed everyone down. The prospect of a wounded Taliban provided a decent fillip for the lads, but he would still be very dangerous. Not only would he be carrying some kind of assault rifle, he'd have grenades and might possibly have planted more IEDs. Time for our A game.

Another 100 metres further and we could make out the crater left by the missile. A good section of the dusty track that provided the main thoroughfare for this part of the region was missing, along with a sizeable chunk of the canal bank. There was no obvious sign of a body. This wasn't turning out how I'd hoped.

But it could always get worse.

About 10 metres from the bomb site, scanning the whole area as you do, I happened to be looking forwards. In fact, I happened to be looking directly where Jolly was about to tread.

'Go firm! Now!'

We'd all have won the game of musical statues at one of my little Sam's birthday parties. Everyone dropped to one knee and froze.

'Jolly!' I yelled. 'In front of you. That mound.'

'Shit.'

Half a metre ahead of him was a rustic pile of stones. The track was rough and ready, but an obstruction like this was unusual, given the amount of traffic. Gingerly, we lifted the rocks away and, sure enough, there was a cable embedded underneath. We traced it across the canal and discovered a hidey-hole in the bush where the insurgent had been planning to sit until a suitable target passed. Tracing it in the other direction, we discovered the IED itself. At no point in between did we detect a corpse, or even any blood.

'For fuck's sake!' Matt said. 'What a waste!' He meant the missile.

Damn right. What was the point of being here? Hundreds of thousands of pounds of military hardware had been thrown away rather than take out a man hell-bent on killing *us*. Maybe not me personally, maybe not my men. But he wasn't planning to sit in the trees with a bomb at his command for the sake of it.

I couldn't have felt lower. Or so I thought. Then, one of the lads called out from the canal.

'Rob,' he said, 'check this out.'

I was hoping he'd found a body. I couldn't wait to see it. What he'd actually discovered was a metre of tubing shredded almost beyond recognition.

'The power line,' I said. 'So much for that great idea.'

I used to joke about Daqhiqh being Groundhog Day because every day was the same. We'd stick our heads above the parapet and be shot at for fun. We'd survive, there were no headlines, HQ carried on ignoring us. Same old, same old.

This was different. This was a carbon copy of the command cock-up, in my opinion, forty-eight hours earlier. Two decisions that could – and almost certainly would – at some point cost ISAF lives to the benefit of the enemy we had been charged to eradicate.

Seriously, what was the point? And for the cherry on top of the icing on the cake? We were then tasked with babysitting an IED until the bomb squad arrived.

'Let's just blow it up and go home,' someone said. The 'Rob' in me agreed. The 'sergeant' in me almost did. It was a close call. There was no logic. We could have removed a known killer from the board. Instead he was free to roam and maim and destroy. Maybe we'd get lucky and arrest him on a biometric flag later. So what? Based on Mohamed Mohamed and dozens more like him, he'd be back out on the dusty tracks that served as streets within a couple of weeks.

No, I realised, *this isn't working. Whatever Herrick 14 was set up to do is broken. It's built wrong. Forget hearts and minds. Forget capture or kill. The only way to win this war – if you can still call such a one-sided contest that – is to kill. Kill before you are killed. It's that simple.*

Why the hell the people in charge couldn't see that, I still cannot tell you.

I just prayed they wouldn't shaft us any more when we tried to do the job that needed doing.

CHAPTER TWENTY-ONE

PASSED ON

Sunray was frustrated. My men were frustrated. The other CP commanders were frustrated. How many more times was the enemy's safety – their comfort, even – going to be prioritised over ours? H, Al, M'lord and the others all agreed: it wasn't worth putting our lives on the line if we weren't getting back-up.

And yet we continued to put our lives on the line. Every day we patrolled and we patrolled and we patrolled. We got in firefights, we discovered IEDs, we returned home shattered and torn, ready to drop. What choice did we have? If we didn't stay on the offensive we'd look a weaker target. We weren't doing it to be the Big I Am colonialists, looking to tame this wild terrain.

We were doing it to survive.

When an insurgent managed to get inside Kamiabi I knew we were doing the right thing. It was killing us. Luckily a couple of things began to go in our favour. For a start the weather began to cool noticeably. Instead of patrolling in 55-degree heat with 70 per cent humidity, we had 40 degrees with 50 per cent humidity. Still unbearable but less deadly. The other piece of good fortune was the next phase of the agricultural season. In September the irrigation system in the Green

Zone was cranked up, flooding a lot of the fields. I'm no farmer, but apparently this was essential for the crops. What I do know is that it was bloody good for us as well. IEDs can't function in water so for the next few weeks we just moved, as far as possible, through the watery fields. Of course, water isn't much protection against Kalashnikovs, but the absence of IEDs meant one thing less to worry about.

It says a lot for our successful hearts-and-minds policy that the Afghan growing season carried on regardless all the time we were there. But, like the lull we had experienced in April while the insurgents were harvesting, it says more about our impact on the region that particular dates on the calendar had a greater influence on our safety than anything we could do ourselves.

Which is not to say the trouble stopped. We were lucky enough to have two vehicles with us at Daqhiqh which meant that we weren't reliant on the supply schedule. It was a mixed blessing. Shazaad quickly used our trips to drop off kit to the other CPs. One day, as one of the vehicles was coming up along Route Devon, it was targeted by an IED. I took as many men as I dared over to the scene – and found Jolly, Sam and Duncs grinning like loons and posing for pictures by the wreckage. But it could have been nasty. Either way it was bad news for the camp because we had lost 50 per cent of our vehicles. But in survival mode you see every narrow escape as a miracle. And miracles need to be celebrated.

On 15 September there was more traditional action. A single moped was causing chaos all around the area, attacking each CP's patrol. M'lord's Taalander came under fire to begin with. The first they knew was when this bike with a couple of straggly youths on sailed past, unarmed as usual – and then miraculously produced weapons from the air and began shooting. Before they could be tapped, they hopped back on the moped, again gunless, and sped off towards H and Kamiabi. They were the next targets. And so it continued. Just by using the three main routes plus a few little rat runs, these two blokes managed to create havoc.

Initially I'd taken the patrol west and then we'd crossed back over the canal and, after small-arms contact on Route Cornwall, had disengaged and started heading north, back up towards Daqhiqh. That's when I heard the big fuss going on to the west of us.

I thought, *Sod it. We've just had to retreat from there.*

I got on the radio and broadcast our position to all the commanders, then said, 'We'll march back and join the fray as soon as we can.'

By then all the CPs had decided to work a bit more with each other. We didn't want any slip-ups during the last few weeks of our tour.

Al Blackman came back to me immediately.

'Eleven Lima, mate, your boys have been out all morning. You head back, we'll go over and assist.'

It made practical sense. Not only were the Omar lot fresher and nearer than us, but having two units on the ground in close proximity increased the chances of casualties from friendly fire.

'Okay,' I said, 'we'll monitor from inside the CP and be ready to respond if necessary.'

And that was that.

If I'm honest, none of the lads was too keen to go back out again after the three gruelling hours they had already spent on patrol. Not that we weren't interested. After shedding the armour and most of my weapons – I hung on to my pistol for dear life – I went straight into the ops room to monitor the unfolding situation. I wasn't alone. We all had a sense that the current operation was going to be another Green 13. HQ had a target, we had multiple patrols on the ground. It was only a matter of time before we got another couple of notches on our dead post.

I can't say any of us was too bothered not to be involved. There was always the chance it would turn out to be another cock-block performance from HQ and the 'kill' order would be overridden. For that reason we weren't listening that attentively. But we sat up all right when we heard the words: 'Call sign Ugly.'

The news produced mixed feelings. Number one: something was very likely going to happen in our favour. Number two: we needed to be on standby in case we were called upon to assist in the clear-up.

We'd barely been back at Daqhiqh an hour, and now we had to be prepared to go out again.

I began listening intently to the reports coming in over the radio. The two insurgents were coming east. Al, travelling north, would soon be in the perfect location to cut them off. Before he could do anything, though, we heard the distinctive sound of the helicopter's missile releasing.

'Ugly has engaged.'

Everyone in the compound heard the explosion, the sound rippling over the wall. As we all assembled by the gate, still pulling on our kit, we could make out the 'rat-a-tat' eruption of the Apache's machine guns. Over the wall we could see the smoke where the missile had hit.

'Call sign Omar are conducting BDA,' Shazaad said. 'You can stand down, Rob.'

Even as we began shrugging off our kit again, I still kept the comms link open. Nothing stood out. It was absolutely normal radio traffic. The kind I would send without hesitation or embarrassment. Al and his men were approaching the BDA site.

'There is one corpse,' Al said.

By now I was back in the ops room. The comms were on loudspeaker so everyone could hear. It was like listening to a football match that didn't involve your team. The commentary wasn't exactly the centre of our attention but we all wanted to hear the result.

Al gave a description of the state of the corpse and that of the moped. We knew there had been two shooters. Where was the other one?

'Blown to kingdom come, hopefully,' someone said.

That turned out not to be the case. There was a fair amount of chat going on in our room when I became aware that Al was talking to his men and to HQ. The voice from Bastion said, 'Do we need to recover him?'

'Wait a minute,' Fergie said. 'The cunt's not still alive?'

Suddenly we were all ears. The second insurgent, it appeared, had somehow survived the onslaught. HQ was asking if Al needed a Mastiff party sent out.

'That's fucking ridiculous!' Fergie again.

'I know,' I agreed. What would it entail? Four vehicles, minimum, that's sixteen men, and half a million pounds' worth of hardware negotiating a route along a road routinely wired with mines. The risk to our troops was too great. That much was obvious to anyone. 'They need to finish him off. You can't be getting Mastiffs out for these murderers. They've probably IED'd the road on the way there.'

'Yeah, damn right,' murmured everyone else.

The chat from Al's patrol was only part of what we were hearing. Radio operators from all over the Green Zone were giving co-ordinates for and updates on the various active patrols. Who was doing what and where? There was a lot of intel cascading down the channels. Al's situation was just one strand.

His, however, was the one that all those of us in the Daqhiqh ops room were interested in. The more we listened the more certain I became that HQ might have been *saying* all the right things – for example: 'Do you need this? Do you need that?' – but to my ears the message was not so clear.

The HQ spokesman was asking whether they needed to send a convoy of Mastiffs, but I picked up an understandable reluctance to actually despatch a convoy.

That's what I heard. That's what my men heard. I'm pretty sure Al would say he heard the same thing. Two minutes later the message went out again from HQ.

'Do we need to send a recovery team? Or is he dead?'

There was some chatter, and then the sound of Al's voice.

'I hate to say it, administering first aid to this individual, he's, er, passed on from this, er, world.' Followed by the sound of a gunshot.

I can't say any of us punched the air or hugged or even high-fived. As far as we were concerned the correct procedure had led to the correct result. A great result. HQ had wanted the moped scum obliterated, and that had duly happened. The Apache hadn't been able to finish the job but Omar CP had. It was no different, no better, no worse, no more spectacular than Smudge's polishing off of the insurgent at Green 13. Hats off to Al Blackman for firing the lethal shot. Another win – another *rare* win – for the ISAF team. They'd done what needed to be done. They'd done exactly what I or any of my men would have done in the same situation. They'd done their job.

They'd also, to my mind, possibly offered a stay of execution to the Mastiff boys. Any legitimate casevac would have risked a lot of lives in the air and on the ground. Okay, Mastiffs generally withstood the blast of a roadside bomb, but you needed only one exception to prove that it had been wrong to take the risk. And this venture was not worth anyone's risk. We were all agreed on that.

We all sighed with relief when Al announced that he and his men were heading back to Omar. Tom Phillips's mob moved in to carry out the site exploitation. It was, as far as we were concerned, situation normal.

* * *

The next day we patrolled out and got shot at. The same the day after that. Normally my men would have take it all in their stride. But these weren't my men.

After seven long months our tour was coming to an end. In the same manner we'd arrived we were leaving. A new company was replacing us – this time from the Army. I can tell you now, there was no way I was going to be as ungracious as the Paras had been when I arrived at Mulladad. I was grateful for the bodies. That is, until I saw them in action. We Marines get accused of having a high opinion of ourselves. And we do. It's based on the fact that our basic training lasts thirty-two weeks, while the army's takes only twelve. And it's not because we're slow learners. The Royal Marines train harder, run further and faster carrying heavier loads. We are, without wishing to get technical, the dog's bollocks. Only the Special Forces and – begrudgingly – the Paras come close.

And, boy, did it show.

As my marines began to disappear each was replaced, in theory, by a like-for-like soldier. That could not have been further from the truth. For a start they all looked like kids. They were eighteen, some of them, but would have been asked for ID in any pub in the UK. More importantly, they were *small*. One fella – a good lad, nice bloke – was given his anti-IED kit to carry and he couldn't lift it. He literally could not stand up let alone walk or, God forbid, run. An actual thirteen-year-old could not have done worse.

We managed to get around that. As their numbers increased, though, and ours decreased, finding anyone strong enough to do their shift grew more difficult. We got there in the end and managed to muster a patrol. When we came under fire, as I knew we would, I was impressed by how calmly the newbies reacted. I was less impressed by their next steps.

While my three lads automatically returned fire, the Army kids just watched.

'What are you waiting for?' I shouted. 'Get stuck in.'

They all nodded and began loading their weapons.

'You weren't *loaded*? What the . . . '

I had to bite my tongue. They were good lads, just badly drilled. What do you expect when you can pass the basic Army course in three months? There's a reason we Royal Marines are the best at what we do. All of us. My guys were as experienced as me. Most of them could have led the multiple. I'd never once had to remind them to load their weapons. It was something we'd done from Day 1. I certainly never had to tell them to return fire. They weren't kids. They were Marines. Commandos. Green Berets. If ever I doubted what that stood for, I saw it then, during those final days of my tour.

Not everyone who joined my multiple was a dead weight. My mate Pinky made a very welcome return. Travelling up and down Helmand with his colleagues capturing the battle groups' stories on camera had its highlights but, with his time in Afghan drawing to an end, he'd moved mountains to get a gig with us. His bosses had said 'yes' and obviously I had no complaints. I'd have taken my mum. I was that desperate for bodies I could rely on.

'You don't know what you're letting yourself in for,' I laughed.

'I've done all the training you have.'

'Yeah, keep telling yourself that.'

Despite struggling to fill a patrol, I still hadn't given up on trying to get one over on the Taliban. If Al Blackman was still scoring victories this late in the day, why couldn't we? I was going over the data from recent marches and analysing where we'd encountered contact – that is, been shot at. It was easy to see the patterns. A plan had formed in my mind: I would send out two patrols. One would be 'normal'. The other would be 'ghost'. The 'normal' patrol would take a route where we'd always suffered fire and would, in theory, take the insurgents' attention, while the ghost mob would take the latter out. I put the plan before the troops. Everyone approved; everyone was eager to go.

The next morning, literally minutes after Pinky arrived, I announced we were going. Pinky was keen to join us: 'I'll catch a few winks later,' he said. Our first patrol moved out. On paper it was a suicide mission. Six men do not a workable patrol make, but I was banking on the Taliban not smelling a rat. That was the decoy. Twenty minutes behind those lads was my mob, my half-dozen men, including Pinky. We were following in the shadows. In the trees, in the bushes. Out of sight.

Very early on we knew it was working. The ICOM chatter was all about the first patrol. Whether they knew it or not, they were being monitored every slow step of the way. When they reached the field where we were always targeted I warned, 'Slow down. Get prepared. Let us catch up.'

They moved in. They were halfway through the field when I saw activity beyond the far perimeter. Several mopeds were pulling to a halt. Men were disappearing behind the stone wall. From experience I knew they would be unearthing arms from various bushes, trees and hidey-holes. Then it happened.

Patrol 1 was 100 metres from the edge of the field when I saw an insurgent step out with a rifle. I wasn't the only one who spotted him. Fergie and Pinky were right by my side. Without a word we all raised our weapons. Without a word we all took aim. Without a word we fired.

Warning shots.

Three warning rounds echoed around the field. Patrol 1 dropped to their knees. My patrol followed suit. The Taliban man disappeared behind the wall. There was a burst of shouting, a squeal of rubber and suddenly they were all gone.

'Cheers, boss,' the leader of Patrol 1 said over the radio.

'You're welcome,' I replied.

But inside I was torn up. Why had I fired a warning shot? Why hadn't I ended the bastard? The whole point of the exercise was to fire a lethal shot. Why hadn't I? And why hadn't the others?

They were experiencing the same anguish.

'I wish I'd ended him,' Pinky said. 'I don't know why I didn't.'

'Because you're a fucking commando and not a piece of Afghan scum,' Fergie growled.

Pinky began to reply but Fergie cut him dead.

'I wish I'd finished him too. I fucking hate being British sometimes.'

'Aye,' we all agreed. 'You can be too nice.'

* * *

Patrols over the next few days went from the dangerous to the insane. Back at Daqhiqh we were on constant look-out for new holes in the wall. Two days in, Pinky was sweating adrenalin. It could have been blood. He'd had a tough tour, like many others, but nothing like this. He'd certainly never been shot at so many times.

'How the fuck have you been coping with this?' he said. 'It's unreal.'

I just shrugged. To this day I don't know how we got through it. Especially suffering as few casualties as we did taking the risks we took on the amount of sleep we had been getting.

Personally I couldn't sleep for worrying about locals digging under our defences and ending us where we lay. I didn't realise I wasn't the only one until Pinky's time with us drew to a close. 'Fourteen hours,' he said to me. Over the ten days he was with us, he'd had just fourteen hours of sleep, he explained. This was quite normal to the rest of us.

By the end of the month he had left, along with more of my own men. With less than a week left of my tour I began to wind down the offensive side of the patrols. As part of the new boys' acclimatisation, I led us all down to Omar, to Al Blackman's checkpoint. The Army boys over whom I was pulling my hair out, all had friends there, so it seemed the decent thing to do. While we were there I was in the ops room chatting with Al about this and that, as usual, when I became aware of a group of his lads and mine laughing around a laptop. I stuck my face in and realised they were uploading films from various marines' helmet cameras. We'd done the same thing in my multiple. There's a wicked film of our death run along the canal path back to Toki which sends chills up my spine whenever I see it. One of the lads put a big booming classical soundtrack to it. It sounds epic. My dad has a copy and shows it to everyone who sets foot in his house.

Even though I was seeing the same trees and fields as Omar, it was interesting to watch their perspective on everything. Suddenly a film clip started playing that got everyone's attention.

'When's this from?' I asked.

'The day we took down the insurgent,' one of the marines said, '15 September.'

As I craned my neck to see that tiny screen I realised how much I had missed during the radio broadcasts on that day. There had been plenty of snatches of dialogue that I did hear, though. Plenty of Al's orders to his men to wait for the Apache, to get ready in case the gunship didn't destroy its targets. Other radio chat that, if I'm honest, I felt uncomfortable listening to. As the Apache approached the insurgents in the field and then deployed, the men from Omar were all whooping and hollering and cheering, like American spectators at the Ryder Cup. I half expected someone to yell, 'Get in the hole!'

It was ugly. While everyone else laughed I couldn't join in. The film showed the patrol to be unprofessional at best. Considering what had happened to their brothers, Sam, Ollie and Kaz, you could understand why. But it didn't look good. Maybe because I was detached from the group I had that distance, allowing me to see what they could not.

Just when I thought I'd seen the worst, the film began to show the moments when Al and his boys had discovered that the Apache had failed in its kill mission. 'The cunt's still alive,' one of them said. There was general derision at the chopper's failure. Again, not the drilled responses you expect of the corps.

I watched as they were shown going over to the bodies. The images were obviously jumpy but I saw them discover the insurgent was alive. I heard them speak to HQ about their options and I saw a couple of the lads, Corporal Chris Watson and Marine Jack Hammond, begin to apply first aid. Al put a stop to that. The messages from HQ, even now, listening to the recording, were to my ears vague. The insurgent was then dragged around. He might have been roughed up. Then I saw Al Blackman draw his 9mm pistol and shoot the man in the chest.

None of it was *how* I would have done it. But the result was the same. If it had been I who discovered that Taliban youth half dead then I would have finished the job. No question. That's what the Apache had been deployed to do. That's what I would have done. I would have expected the same response from any of my men, as well. We were at war. This man had been trying to kill us all. He'd failed, and had got his comeuppance.

It was the way it was done that was ugly. Clearly, Al and his team were under pressure. We all were. You could see from the video they were starved of sleep, and the paranoia and hatred that kept them awake at night were palpable. Yet, despite their doing nothing wrong, I sensed that in the wrong hands that film could spell trouble.

'Lads,' I said, 'enjoy the movie but you need to delete it. It was a good kill, no one's arguing with that, but I tell you now a lot of people will be uncomfortable with the cheerleading. Do yourselves a favour and get rid.'

I gave that order with a clean conscience. There was no attempt at a cover-up, no intention on my part to hide anything. I just knew from my two weeks' R&R that explaining things to people who haven't been to Afghan is more trouble than it is worth. We'd suffered enough on this tour – Omar patrol more than anyone. There was no point making unnecessary trouble for ourselves.

There was a general groan, as though I'd grounded a bunch of teenagers. But, with me standing over them, I watched as the movie was deleted from the helmet hard drive and the laptop.

What happens in the Green Zone stays in the Green Zone . . .

I honestly thought no more about that day, or the film. I'd seen too many worse horrors for it to register. We did a few more acclimatisation patrols. On each one there were fewer of my men and more of the Army nods. We were disappearing as quickly as we'd arrived. As per tradition, the sergeant leaves the checkpoint after everyone else. First in, last out. A few of the lads wouldn't let me do it alone. Fergie and Mac both insisted on seeing out the last twitches of the tour by my side, the way we'd done everything. Finally, in early October, our time came.

I can't say I looked back as we were driven away from Daqhiqh. There were no wistful glances out of the rear window of the massive transporter. It was a time for looking forward. A time for new experiences. A time to get back to being a normal human.

CHAPTER TWENTY-TWO

MENTIONED IN DESPATCHES

If you want to lose weight, try the Daqhiqh diet. When I went to Afghanistan my weight was about thirteen stone (eighty-two and a half kilograms). When I came back it was nine and a half (only just over sixty kilos) Robbie was down eight stone (about fifty-one kilos). To say our clothes were hanging off us sounds too flattering. We weren't ghosts when we reached Camp Bastion. We were skeletons.

When I arrived I found the rest of my multiple still there. It had been only nine days since I'd packed the first off but I was chuffed to see them. They'd all been through the first stages of decompression, if you like, for the process of getting them ready for the real world was well under way. I should have got a week at least. Instead we were all packed on a plane as soon as I arrived.

By rights we'd have flown to Cyprus for twenty-four to forty-eight hours' acclimatisation. Again, that stage was skipped. At the time we were happy. In hindsight it was an error. Cyprus gives you that valuable stage of winding down, getting certain things out of your system. In the end we were dropped back at Brize Norton and waved off. I think we were handed a leaflet on how to spot the signs of PTSD before we left.

My dad picked me up. I remember that it was 5 October, and that I'd just missed Will's birthday. It was still quite warm in England, but not by any standards I knew. While Dad was in a T-shirt I was shivering. He drove me to Taunton with barely a word shared between us. He could see I was shattered, and didn't push it. I barely hugged my wife and kids when I got home. I just remember wanting my bed.

Looking back, I think I slept most of the seven days that I had off, before returning to duty. When I did manage to stagger out of the house I was like a bear with a sore head. I wasn't the only returning hero in Taunton – it's that kind of town – but for my family and friends I was the only one that counted.

About the only time I could relax was when we went to visit my mate Greg Andrews and his family. They'd just moved into a new house. I remember the carpets being horrific. While the women and children were busy Greg and I went into the garage. He was a good friend. More importantly, he was an ex-marine. He'd served. He knew. *Knew* knew.

'Are you all right?' he asked.

I nodded.

'Do you want to talk about it?'

I sighed. 'Where do you start?'

'Wherever you want.'

It was refreshing to be able to unload in front of someone who wouldn't judge me. Who could listen without being disgusted. Even when I said how angry I was at the way we'd been neutered on the battlefield by our command, he just nodded. He got it. The only thing that foxed him was when I said, 'I don't have a victory.'

'What do you mean?'

'The Falkland boys had a mission. Succeed or fail, it was obvious. They secured the Falklands, so they won. We went over, we did our job but, if I'm honest, I don't know if it made the slightest difference. As far as I can see there was no endgame.'

'You did your job,' Greg said. 'That's all they can ask.'

* * *

After seven days of pretending to be human I was summoned back to Bickleigh Barracks. It's standard procedure after a tour. You get a week at home, then a fortnight with your unit before another six weeks to unwind with your loved ones. Getting back to like-minded people, however, was much more appealing to me.

There's a lot to admire about the way the military machine just 'does' stuff. For example, after our tour there was a UK-wide 'kit sale'. They do it for any company that has taken casualties, but it means more when it's for your mates. The ephemera belonging to every marine who has died or been critically injured is put up for auction and various companies or divisions bid for it. On paper nothing up for grabs would deserve much more than the incinerator, unless you particularly collect socks and bullets and boots. But that's not the point. All money raised goes to the family of the marine. And so you get the fantastic spectacle of a each piece of a bergan's detritus going for two grand here, three grand there. It's a magical moment seeing the full military family come together.

As for my own family, I was struggling. Alone with Carly and the boys, I felt like a fat man holding my stomach in to impress a young lady. Only back at base did I feel like I could let it all out and just be myself, because everyone else had gone through something similar. Or so I thought. I met loads of blokes whose tours seemed like summer holidays compared with ours. It was actually only the chaps from my multiple or those from Taalander, Omar, Kamiabi who got it. We had two big parties in that fortnight. One was the Seniors' Mess, at which we all got plastered. The second, called the Officers' Mess, was meant to be even bigger. But actually once Tom, Al, H and I got talking at the bar I just burst into tears. I remember the moment. We were talking to a fella who'd been based in the UK doing repatriations. Essentially his job was to knock on the doors of strangers and inform them that a member of their family had been killed.

'There's nothing worse than that,' he said.

And that's what got me.

'Nothing worse?' I said. 'You try being the poor sod who has to watch them die and then load them onto a helicopter while you're being shot at. I'd swap with you any day of the week, mate.'

That was it. The waterworks started. Nothing he said could stop it. In fact, my tears triggered the others. We just stood there, weeping like loons, while the rest of the company got shit-faced on cheap lager.

Those first months back from Afghan! Looking back, it was a positive physical reaction. Bottling that sort of emotion up is a key factor in PTSD. I was lucky not to suffer that. But that's not to say that Afghanistan hadn't left its mark. Over the next couple of months we had various rehabilitation tests and meetings as part of the homecoming programme. One of them involved seeing a medic. Despite the drastic weight loss I passed virtually all the physicals. The only thing that let me down was my hearing. The bomb blast that had knocked me over while I was carrying two lots of armour had perforated an eardrum, leaving me with permanent hearing loss and tinnitus.

'It's all right,' I told the doc. 'I've been getting by fine. Ask my men.'

'I'm afraid it's not that simple,' he said. 'You don't actually meet basic fitness levels.'

'What are you talking about? It's just ears. This happened to me in May. That was five months ago. I've led men on life-or-death missions every day since. No one would say I was damaged.'

'That's not strictly true. I would say it. Because you are.'

'So,' I said, 'bottom line: what are you saying?'

'I'm saying that I have to recommend you come off active duty.'

'Shit. And do what? A desk job?'

'That's an option.'

It might have been – but not one for me. Over the next few weeks I considered my options and regretfully realised that my time with the Royal Marines was over.

For once I had no plan.

* * *

This should be where my story ends. My military career was over, my days of touring the most savage parts of the world on Her Majesty's service done and dusted. But, like everything to do with Herrick 14, even escaping wasn't straightforward. This wasn't the Falklands Conflict, remember. We never had a goal, so we never knew if we'd won or lost. We never even knew when we'd crossed the finish line. Maybe that's because we never did. The vague remit of Herrick 14 – the wishy-washy 'build hearts-and-minds' agenda – never stacked up when we were there. After returning to the UK, it remained an ongoing grey area. Not only was my story not over, it was about to take a very dark twist.

Being taken off active service, I considered myself hard done by. After everything I'd done for the Marines and in their name, to be junked over such a minor injury – which had not in any way stopped me from doing my job, or even hindered me in it – seemed offensive to me in the extreme. I felt seriously down.

Even when I was awarded the honour of being Mentioned in Despatches for my bravery during that mission in May 2011, I couldn't take pleasure in it. The citation read: 'He never bows to fatigue or danger and there is no doubt that his remarkable acts of selflessness saved a number of lives for which he deserves significant formal recognition'.

I suppose I was proud to receive it. I'd have been prouder to have been allowed to keep my job. For the next year or so I retrained as a physiotherapist with a view to joining Carly's business as a physical rehab specialist. I believe we made as good a fist of it as we could. The hours were the killer – sixty or seventy hours a week each wasn't unheard of. It was tough going. It put a strain on the marriage from which, ultimately, we wouldn't recover. And of course I missed the camaraderie among the lads, my fellow marines.

Work wasn't the only thing testing my relationship with Carly. She was becoming more and more concerned about my sleeping – or, rather, the lack of it. On returning to Blighty all I'd really wanted to do was close my eyes and not wake up for a month. Getting to sleep proved to be no problem. Staying that way was impossible. On my first night back I think I must have slept no more than three hours before I became aware that I was sitting bolt upright. I was shouting and was covered in sweat. And I had an Afghan killer in my sights.

Except it wasn't an Afghan. It wasn't a Taliban murderer there to slit my throat as I slept. It was Carly. She had the duvet pulled up to her chin and she looked terrified to be within my imaginary crosshairs.

'Are you all right?' she said. 'You were tossing and turning so much.' I could see from the look in her eyes that I'd been doing more than having a fitful night's kip. I tried to calm her, to tell her I was okay, that it was just hard to adjust to being in a comfy bed. Even as I did so, I couldn't get away from the realisation that I was just as scared.

The next night it happened again. And the night after. And the night after. Not always identically, but never a sleep passed without incident. Two things were always the same: Carly's horrified expression, and my body being covered in sweat. In fact, it wasn't sweat. It was slimy and it had a smell of sweet vinegar. I really thought something was wrong physically. At my next round of MOD medical tests a few months later – run by the charity Combat Stress – I was told the sweating was not a physical problem at all. It was mental.

How can slimy sweat be a product of the mind?

'You're having nightmares,' the doctor explained, 'which your brain is interpreting as real-life situations. It thinks you really are under attack so your body is responding for real. The sweat is an adrenal response to what your brain considers a genuine attack.'

Wow. I sound like a fruitcake.

That was the last thing the doc intended. He was quick to stress that my condition was a common 'brain injury' experienced particularly by those with hearing loss. The brain is used to hearing certain sounds, and when suddenly it doesn't it assumes it's under threat and goes into 'safe room' mode. Adrenalin levels rocket, alertness switches to 100 per cent. It's a primeval instinct, and one without which our species would not have survived this long.

'Okay, so I'm not mad?'

'No, not at all.' He added that it would recover with enough time away from theatre; or he could prescribe medication. Over the next few weeks a series of other experts came to the same conclusion.

'What about my hearing?'

'That won't improve.'

I've said it before, but it bears repeating. Civilians can never truly empathise with men and women who have served in battle. Not really. Carly had seen my worst side but still I couldn't talk to her about it. Not without her thinking me a loony. I needed to reach out to one of my own. By coincidence I ran into my mate Pinky, who'd served ten memorable days with me in Daqhiqh at the end of our tour. I didn't want to dump my problems on him. Not immediately.

'How's the real world going for you?' I asked.

'As well as it's going for you, I reckon. I haven't slept since we got back.'

'Nightmares?' I said.

'Yeah. But never about the men I killed.'

'What about, then?'

'Honestly? I can't help thinking about the ones I let live.'

'Are you thinking of the ambush?'

The day when he'd accompanied me out on the 'ghost' patrol to try to smoke out the insurgents still played on my mind.

'Yeah,' he said. 'I can't get over it. Why didn't we take the lethal shot? Who fires a fucking warning shot when a murderer is aiming at you?'

'I'm the same,' I said. 'What the hell were we thinking? How many people did that bastard go on to murder or maim because we let him live?'

'I know,' he said. 'If I could change one thing, I swear it would be that day.'

'Really? Not even the sleep? What was it: fourteen hours in ten days?'

'Rob, mate, I'd go a month without shuteye to get another chance at that bastard. With him in the ground I'd sleep easier, I know I would.'

* * *

Clinical problems are one thing. Friends of mine were about to suffer something a lot worse.

October 2012. We'd been back a year. I'd just finished with a client in the clinic at home and I checked my phone. There must have been a dozen messages, all saying much the same thing:

'Have you heard?'

'Do you know who it is?'

'Call me back.'

Most of the guys were on other calls when I tried to get back to them. Corporal Sibsy was the first to pick up. He only lived round the corner from my house. It would have been easier to have walked over there.

'What's going on, mate?'

'What rock have you been hiding under? Seven marines have been arrested.'

'Shit.'

'Gets worse – they're all from Four-Two. Seven of *us*. Can you believe it?'

'Do you know what the charge is?'

'Haven't got a clue, mate. They could be coming for any of us. What do *you* know?'

'Sibsy, mate, I know I'm not sleeping and I know I can hear fuck all. That's about it.'

I called all the lads from my multiple to check that they were still at liberty. All present and correct. Then I managed to get hold of Steve McCulley. It took a few goes, which should have told me everything. When he came online he knew a lot more than he was prepared to let on.

'Trust me on this, Rob,' he said, 'I don't think you want to know. It will be out there soon enough.'

'At least tell me this: are any of my men under scrutiny?'

'No one from your multiple.'

At least that's something.

Twenty-four hours later the whole thing was in the media. The people arrested weren't named. But their charge was. I couldn't believe it. They'd all been picked up on suspicion of murder. *Murder?* What the hell had they been up to? From time to time you read about military men losing their shit with civilians and, because of the nature of their training, going too far in the ensuing fighting. But seven of them losing their tempers in a bar brawl? That didn't stack up. It had to be something else.

The truth proved to be even more unlikely. Over the next day or two I realised that the arrested parties had all served at Omar. For some reason the entire multiple was being shaken down. As the days passed, more information seeped out into the media. What I was reading blew my mind. The seven men hadn't strolled up to some bloke in a Devon pub and ended his life over a girlfriend dispute. The crime they were accused of committing had taken place in Afghanistan.

Afghanistan.

While they were on active service. While they were there to kill insurgents.

When they'd done their job.

Everyone I spoke to was as confused as I was. M'lord, H, Mac, Fergie, Si, Robbie, Matt, Pinky, Sibsy – all the boys were bewildered. How are marines who have been chosen for their almost superhuman abilities to end the lives of enemy forces suddenly being hunted down for doing exactly that? And why? You can't send an army to war and then punish it for being violent.

It was a mindfuck.

* * *

Over the course of the next few months, four of the seven were released. Thank God. That still left three facing serious charges. I assumed they would be let off in due course. It had to happen. We all believed it. The option was to arrest every soldier, sailor, marine and pilot who'd ever served.

Not so.

It transpired that, following a domestic quarrel and unfounded accusations, one of the marines was found to have files on his laptop that he had deleted but which were, unknown to any of us, recoverable – these were helmet-cam videos containing footage from 15 September 2011, when Al finished off the insurgent that the Apache helicopter had failed to kill. Everything that happened thereafter stemmed from that point. To be fair to them, the cops were just following procedure. And to their credit, they acknowledged that the file concerned matters beyond not only their jurisdiction, but their moral code. While they felt uneasy with its content they didn't know whether or not it was an issue legally. As a point of procedure they passed the file to the MOD. At that point I would have put money on someone high up in the food chain making the film disappear.

'Oh, thank you, officer. We'll take it from here.' Followed by the sound of the case file being stamped 'Closed'.

I'm sure that plenty of outsiders would assume that the military's own legal set-up would naturally tend to find in favour of its own men. Based on some of the decisions that had affected me in my career, I knew that wouldn't be the case. The wellbeing of their men seems hardly the armed forces' greatest concern. Having experienced in theatre the nonexistent levels of support that I had, I wouldn't have put a penny on anyone high up the military pole coming to the right decision. If anything, I wish I'd bet against it.

Not only was the file not lost, hidden or destroyed – any of the options I would still consider more practical in civilian life – a full-scale investigation was launched and the seven suspects taken into custody. When their number was whittled down to three no one celebrated. All seven were innocent. Maybe not in the civilian world, but totally within the framework of war. What the hell was going on?

The three Omar men still under suspicion were named simply as Marine A, Marine B and Marine C. At least in the media they were. Thanks to the jungle drums I knew exactly who those initials belonged to. Corporal Chris Watson and Marine Jack Hammond were as solid soldiers as you could hope for. Trust me, if your country needs defending, you want hundreds of Marines B and C.

As for Marine A, I don't care what the media called him. In my house he would only ever have one name. He was a marine, and my mate. He was a hero. He was Sergeant Al Blackman.

And no way was he guilty of murder. It made no sense to me. The order had been given: the insurgent must die. When the helicopter gunship assault had come up short, Al had done no more than administer the final blow. It wasn't as straightforward a kill as you'd hope but the net result was the same. HQ wanted the Taliban guy dead. By the end of the mission he was.

I've said it before and will say it again. On 15 September Al Blackman removed a terrorist from the playing board. A terrorist who had been trying to kill us and would have continued so to do for the duration of Herrick 14. I for one was grateful that Al had done what he did. Nothing since then has changed that opinion. There were so many other opportunities where similar action should have been taken.

In a strange way, my wife took Al's arrest almost harder than I did. One of her good friends was Claire, Al's wife. For the seven months that he and I had been away, the two Taunton women had become even closer. In the same way that no one understands a soldier's experiences like another soldier, the only person who truly appreciates what a military wife goes through is another military wife. When J Company returned from Afghan the four of us began socialising. Dinners, lunches, family afternoons, Claire's fortieth birthday party. It was great. Refreshing, and sometimes quite surreal. What other table in a restaurant would have diners discussing the kind of topics we were? We were lucky to have each other.

From the point of being charged with murder, despite the world remaining oblivious of his name, Al was not allowed to leave Bickleigh Barracks. He was virtually under house arrest. There were no visitors, at least not from the likes of me, no phone calls and no emails. Once the investigation had been completed, however, he was allowed a bit more freedom. In fact, one day I took the boys to our local driving range and there he was, in the flesh: Sergeant Al Blackman.

I say 'in the flesh'. There was nothing of him. He was skeleton thin.

He had sunken eyes, a dishevelled air. When he saw me he smiled with his mouth, but his eyes were dead.

'Mate,' I said, 'how's it going? How are you?'

'I'm good, Rob.' He paused. 'Good as can be expected.'

My kids were running around me. He was with a friend. We were both distracted. But I couldn't take my eyes off him. Al Blackman. My mate. Hero sergeant of Omar CP for seven months in 2011. Leader of men, scourge of enemy agents. Why did he seem so weak?

Our time together was limited. But I wouldn't be a mate if I didn't ask him if there was anything I could do. 'No,' he said. 'But if the worst comes to the worst, please look after Claire.'

As I have said, his wife was a close friend of Carly's. But even if she weren't, of course we would do everything we could.

'Al, you're going to be all right,' I said. I genuinely believed it. 'They've got nothing on you. No one would call you a murderer. No one who knows anything about what we went through.'

'I dunno, Rob,' he said. 'They look pretty confident.'

I'd spoken about Al's case with my dad. Neither of us was an expert on court-martial procedure but if anyone knew his way around a court room plea it was Detective Chief Inspector Clive Driscoll.

'He has to come clean,' Dad said. 'Bombard the court with stories of the environment, the hierarchy, the pressures, the lack of sleep. Give them more information than they can process. If his tour was half as bad as yours, they've got to let him off.'

Al didn't have access to my dad, but he did have a team of civilian counsel led by Anthony Berry, QC.

'I'm pleading ignorance,' Al said. 'I didn't know he [the insurgent] was still alive.'

'Shit,' I said. 'Really?'

I'd heard the original radio transmissions. More importantly I'd seen the helmet-camera video. I will defend the actions of Al Blackman until my dying day because he did nothing wrong. Why didn't he just say that? We both knew what had gone on that day of 15 September. *And he'd done nothing wrong.*

'I have to follow the advice,' he said, absently. 'They know what they're doing.'

'Let's hope so. But if you ever need to talk . . .'

'Yeah, cheers . . .'

* * *

Every month that passed I fully expected to read that the charges against Al and the others had been dropped. Not only dropped, but retracted with full apologies. That didn't happen. In October 2013, two years after we'd returned broken and disillusioned from an Afghan mission that was as poorly co-ordinated as it was supplied, the full court martial of Marines A, B and C commenced.

I wasn't sure whether I felt more angry or ill. The idea that three of my colleagues were being hung out to dry for doing their job terrified and sickened me in equal measure. If the murder charges stuck, these men would become the first serving members of the British military since the Second World War to have been found guilty of murder while on active service. It would be a black day for the marines in question. It would be a worse day for the UK and its armed forces.

What young person in his right mind is going to sign up for a career where you're given a gun and told to shoot strangers – knowing that, if you do, you could find yourself facing a lifetime in jail for murder? What naïve youngster is going to be swayed by pull-up tests and fancy promotional posters when that is the potential outcome?

Whoever had sanctioned the arrest order was not a patriot. They were not thinking of the bigger picture. Of the protection of the UK's borders. Of seventy million hearts and minds at home.

* * *

Once the whispers around the armed forces got going, however, I realised there was more to it. The full weight of the British military machine appeared, to me, to be working against my mates. Not only was Al giving – on the advice of his counsel – a defence plea which, to me and to many others, made no sense, the court martial panel – its version of a jury – comprised worthy people but some of whom were undeniably desk bunnies. I would have felt far more comfortable with a full panel of men who had seen active service sitting in judgement on my friends. Servicemen or women who'd faced bullets and the daily – and nightly – threat of death at enemy hands. Courts martial are not civilian courts. Twelve good men and true are not enough

Al's defence was ridiculous in my opinion. But it was the defence he'd been advised to mount. That wasn't the worst of it. Behind the scenes I heard that various high-profile Marine men had been denied the opportunity to speak on behalf of the accused.

Al and the others gave their evidence at the Military Court Centre in Bulford, Wiltshire, from behind screens. The principle of anonymity needed to be upheld for fear of terrorist reprisal. I have to believe that the process unfurled without influence or collusion. When the verdict came on 8 November 2013 I was more confident than hopeful. Not because Al was a friend, not because I was scared for my own integrity, not even because I believed he'd mounted a good defence (I didn't, and still don't).

The single reason that I believed Sergeant Al Blackman would be pronounced 'innocent' is because I wholeheartedly believed that to be true.

Unfortunately, that was not the conclusion of the seven-strong court-martial board. While Marines B and C were exonerated – and rightly so – for their part in the insurgent's execution, Marine A was declared 'guilty' of murder. What a joke! What a farce! What a stain on the character of a good man! He had been tried by a military court but in the public eye he was suddenly judged as no better than Fred West or the Yorkshire Ripper. And that is an abomination. I believe it now as I believed it then. On 6 December Al Blackman was handed a life sentence, ordered to serve a minimum of ten years.

The outrage among my family, my friends and all my old team from 42 Commando reverberated for weeks. Each day I had the same conversations with new people. Even my physio clients got their ears bent. I was furious and ashamed and I didn't care who knew it.

I managed to get an email address for Al in prison and fired off regular messages. He didn't reply, and I had to assume that was his choice. In the meantime I did the next best thing and offered the full weight of my help to his wife, Claire.

'I'm being deluged by the press,' she said. 'Will you help?'

'Whatever you want. Although I've not had any media training.'

'You don't need training,' she said. 'You just need to believe in Al.'

Well, that was easy. Over the next few months – years, in fact – I spoke to news outlets from all over the world. Whoever Claire passed my way I made time for. BBC News, the *Daily Mail*, the *Daily Telegraph*, you name it, I did it. I never asked for payment even though some of the work – for example, an excellent *Panorama* programme – took up a lot of my time. At stake was the integrity not only of my friend, but of everyone who has ever served his country.

I wasn't the only one fighting the good fight. Some very influential media people helped Claire wage a war against the decision. Most vocal among them was the thriller writer Frederick Forsyth. He is a man who had fought for Britain. He knows what is involved in maintaining national security. He was generous with his time and his money and his reputation. In part thanks to the media campaign, the courts-martial appeal court reconsidered Al's case. Although the verdict was upheld, the sentence was commuted to a minimum of eight years.

Behind the scenes we all did as much as we could. Claire worked tirelessly to throw sympathetic journalists in my direction and I told them whatever I could to get positive PR for our guy. I kept sending Al emails although I never received a reply. I was sad that he didn't think he could connect with me. In 2015, eighteen months after my friend's incarceration, I finally plucked up the courage to visit HMP Erlestoke, near Salisbury. I went with Steve McCulley who, after months of treatment, had made a remarkable recovery.

Al looked better physically than the previous time we had met. Mentally, I'd have to say, he was still more docile than I remembered. I think he was on medication. At best it took the edge off his normally upbeat personality. At worst he was neutered by it.

'Mate,' I said, 'I'm really sorry it's taken so long to get here.'

'Don't mention it,' he said. 'I know Claire's been working you hard.'

Then Al asked me: 'What are you up to?'

Weirdly, it was at that point I told him I was considering writing my own story. *This* story.

'Are you going to mention Afghan?' he said.

'Totally.'

'Are you going to mention me?'

'If you want me to.'

'Yeah. Tell everyone the truth. Clear my name. Let the world know that I am not a murderer.'

I like to think that I have done that, in interviews and now in this account. Happily, in March 2017 Claire's team succeeded in getting Al a second appeal judgement. This time medical reports not available in 2013 were drawn upon. Al was diagnosed with 'Adjustment Disorder' – a debilitating condition that affected a good many combatants in the field and thereafter. The fact that he had also been near suicidal following his service in Iraq and the death of his father on the eve of his departure for Afghanistan were all brought to bear. Any one of those could have driven a man to behave irrationally. While I still don't accept that he did, I appreciate the civilian need for 'a reason'. The enforced absence of people like Colonel Lee was also taken into account. It all helped. The result wasn't perfect, but it was substantial. Al's conviction was reduced from murder to manslaughter and his sentence to seven years. Under modern justice guidelines that meant a release within weeks, not months. By the time you read this book, Sergeant Al Blackman will be walking among us a free man.

And that is where this story ends. Not with my military career being cut short, my marriage failing after seven impossible months in Afghan, or with me rebuilding my marine contacts to become a trainer on the international market. It ends with a friend and hero able to walk proudly amongst us. Military service, and war in particular, changes us all. Most of us for the better. The ones who return with scars need help and care and love. Most of all, they need and deserve respect. For everything I've seen, everything I've experienced and everything I've done, I know I've escaped very, very lightly. Not all of my friends can say the same. To those men and women and our successors still serving, I can only offer my thanks, my hope and my encouragement.

Keep fighting the good fight. Know your enemy. And never – ever – hold back from taking a lethal shot. I did, and I regret it to this day. Be bold, be brave and make a difference.

And come back safely home.